D1306634

# Guide

## to Canadian Ministries since Confederation

(July 1, 1867
February 1, 1982)

Government of Canada
Privy Council Office

Gouvernement du Canada
Bureau du Conseil privé

Public Archives
Canada

Archives publiques
Canada

*Canadian Cataloguing in Publication Data*
Main entry under title:
Guide to Canadian Ministries since Confederation,
    July 1, 1867-February 1, 1982

    Issued also in French under title: Répertoire des
ministères canadiens depuis la Confédération, 1er
juillet 1867-1er février 1982.
    Co-published by Public Archives Canada.
    Update to: Guide to Canadian ministries since
Confederation, July 1, 1867-April 1, 1973 / Public
Archives of Canada; and, Guide to Canadian ministries
since Confederation, April 1, 1973-June 1, 1976 /
Jack L. Cross.
    Includes index.
    DSS cat. no. SA2-32/1982E
    ISBN 0-660-11156-X: $12.95
1. Cabinet officers — Canada. I. Cross, Jack L.
Guide to Canadian ministries since Confederation,
April 1, 1973-June 1, 1976. II. Canada. Privy
Council. III. Public Archives Canada. IV. Public
Archives of Canada. Guide to Canadian ministries
since Confederation, July 1, 1867, 1973.

JL97.G8 1982      354.7104      C82-097010-7

Catalogue No. SA2-32/1982E
ISBN 0-660-11156-X

Canada: $12.95
Other countries: $15.50

Price subject to change without notice

# Contents

Introduction _____ v

**First Ministry**
Hon. Sir John Alexander Macdonald (1867–1873) _____ 1

**Second Ministry**
Hon. Alexander Mackenzie (1873–1878) _____ 7

**Third Ministry**
Rt. Hon. Sir John Alexander Macdonald (1878–1891) _____ 13

**Fourth Ministry**
Hon. Sir John Joseph Caldwell Abbott (1891–1892) _____ 21

**Fifth Ministry**
Rt. Hon. Sir John Sparrow David Thompson (1892–1894) _____ 25

**Sixth Ministry**
Hon. Sir Mackenzie Bowell (1894–1896) _____ 29

**Seventh Ministry**
Hon. Sir Charles Tupper (1896) _____ 35

**Eighth Ministry**
Rt. Hon. Sir Wilfrid Laurier (1896–1911) _____ 39

**Ninth Ministry**
Rt. Hon. Sir Robert Laird Borden (1911–1917) _____ 47

**Tenth Ministry**
Rt. Hon. Sir Robert Laird Borden (1917–1920) _____ 55

**Eleventh Ministry**
Rt. Hon. Arthur Meighen (1920–1921) _____ 63

**Twelfth Ministry**
Rt. Hon. William Lyon Mackenzie King (1921–1926) _____ 69

**Thirteenth Ministry**
Rt. Hon. Arthur Meighen (1926) _____ 77

**Fourteenth Ministry**
Rt. Hon. William Lyon Mackenzie King (1926–1930) _____ 83

**Fifteenth Ministry**
Rt. Hon. Richard Bedford Bennett (1930–1935) _____ 89

**Sixteenth Ministry**
Rt. Hon. William Lyon Mackenzie King (1935–1948) _____ 95

**Seventeenth Ministry**
Rt. Hon. Louis Stephen St-Laurent (1948–1957) _____ 109

**Eighteenth Ministry**
Rt. Hon. John George Diefenbaker (1957–1963) _____ 121

**Nineteenth Ministry**
Rt. Hon. Lester Bowles Pearson (1963–1968) _____ 137

**Twentieth Ministry**
Rt. Hon. Pierre Elliott Trudeau (1968–1979) _____ 153

**Twenty-First Ministry**
Rt. Hon. Charles Joseph Clark (1979–1980) _____ 193

**Twenty-Second Ministry**
Rt. Hon. Pierre Elliott Trudeau (1980-    ) _____ 203

**Appendix** _____ 223

**Index** _____ 313

# Introduction

The *Guide to Canadian Ministries since Confederation, July 1, 1867 – January 1, 1957* appeared in 1957, followed by a supplement in 1966. A Guide combining the earlier publications was published in 1974. This new *Guide to Canadian Ministries* combines all these earlier publications with new information concerning the Twentieth, Twenty-First and Twenty-Second Ministries. Changes have been made in the format of the Guide, which should facilitate its use. The compiling of the information has been largely the work of Mr. Henri Chassé, Assistant Clerk of the Privy Council, with the assistance of Communication Services, Public Archives.

## Terms of Reference

The *Guide to Canadian Ministries* is divided into two parts. The first is a chronological list of the ministries since Confederation. For each ministry, there is an alphabetical list of departments followed by the names and dates of service of the incumbents. The accompanying footnotes record offices held concurrently as well as subsequent appointments. They also indicate offices held *ex officio* and provide information on the creation and abolition of ministerial offices.

The second section is the appendix. It is an alphabetical list of all those considered to be of the Ministry. The appendix gives a brief summary of each individual's ministerial career: appointments as Parliamentary Assistant or Parliamentary Secretary; appointment to the Privy Council and to the United Kingdom Privy Council; appointment to ministerial office, to the Senate and as Government Leader in the Senate. However, only the resignations or dissolutions of ministries are indicated.

In some cases, it has been found necessary to interpret dates regarding terms of office in a manner that may not always correspond to the strict constitutional position.

## Life of a Ministry
### The First Day

There have been twenty-two ministries since Confederation. The life of each is dependent on the tenure of its Prime Minister. The simplest way of determining the day on which a Ministry commenced is the date of the oath of office taken as Prime Minister. However, there is no legal requirement that a Prime Minister take such an oath. Only six have done so: Arthur Meighen in 1920, William Lyon Mackenzie King in 1921, John George Diefenbaker in 1957, Lester Bowles Pearson in 1963, Pierre Elliott Trudeau in 1968 and 1980, and Charles Joseph Clark in 1979. Until 1957 the Prime Minister held at least one portfolio. If no oath of office as Prime Minister was taken, the life of the Ministry began on the day he was sworn to that portfolio. If the Prime Minister retained the same portfolio from the previous ministry, the first day is that on which the ministers were sworn to office.[1]

*The Last Day*

The day the Prime Minister died[2] or the Governor General accepted his resignation is the last day of a Ministry. Before 1920 a Prime Minister's resignation was accepted immediately. The Ministry was dissolved *ipso facto*, but individual ministers continued to carry on the routine business of their departments until their own resignation was accepted by the new Prime Minister or a new appointment was made. This continuance in office is indicated in the appendix but not in the text. In 1920 Sir Robert Laird Borden indicated his intention to resign, but offered his formal resignation only when Arthur Meighen was ready to form a government. This practice continues today.

There are some apparent discrepancies between the text and the appendix respecting the final date of offices of ministries. The date in the text corresponds to the date of acceptance of the Prime Minister's resignation or the date of his death. In the appendix the final date in office of a Ministry corresponds to the Interpretation Act, 1967. Where an appointment is made effective or terminates on a specified day, that appointment is considered to be effective or to terminate after the end of the previous day.[3] Individual resignations conform to the Interpretation Act in both the text and the appendix.

## Appointment of Ministers

Ministers are usually appointed by commission under the Great Seal of Canada. During the thirteen years following Confederation the appointments of ministers were recommended orally by the Prime Minister. The dates of such appointments have been determined from the notices appearing in the *Canada Gazette*. In most cases since Confederation the date of appointment corresponds to the date the Minister took his oath of office. Between 1880 and 1953 a Minute of Council was approved recommending to the Governor General that a commission of appointment be issued. Since September 1953 a recommendation for ministerial appointment has been effected by an Instrument of Advice, a letter from the Prime Minister to the Governor General.[4]

Ministers are sworn in as members of the Privy Council before being sworn to their first portfolio. As a result they are accorded the title *honourable*. The date on which they are sworn in as members of the Privy Council is considered that day on which they assume office.[5] In the case of subsequent appointments, only a new oath of office is taken.

Most Prime Ministers and a number of other ministers have been sworn as members of the United Kingdom Privy Council. As a result they are accorded the title *right honourable*. The actual date of swearing in has been used rather than the date of appointment of office. In March 1968 the Table of Titles to be used in Canada was amended to accord the title *right honourable* for life to Prime Ministers on their assumption of office.

## Ministers without Portfolio

There have been a number of Ministers without Portfolio in all except the First Ministry.[6] Until 26 September 1926 the term Minister without Portfolio was used. Incumbents were sworn as Privy Councillors and attended Cabinet meetings on the invitation of the Prime Minister. However, after 1926 they were appointed as Members of the Administration and Ministers without Portfolio.[7] Until 1968 they took an oath of office as Members of the Administration. At that time the traditional title of Minister without Portfolio was reintroduced. The title has been used throughout the Guide until 11 June 1971 when the Government Organization Act, 1970-71, was proclaimed in force. The Act provided for the appointment of Ministers of State who may be assigned to assist any Minister having responsibility for a department or portion of the public service.

## Acting Ministers

Acting Ministers are shown when an office has been vacated during a Ministry and an acting minister has been appointed to fill the vacancy. On 3 December 1886 provision was made for the appointment of acting ministers by Order in Council when a Minister was absent or incapacitated. For most appointments prior to this date[8] it has been necessary to rely on the signatures on departmental submissions to the Governor in Council. Since 1886, the date of approval of the Order in Council appointing an acting minister is the date on which he began to serve. In 1965 provision was made for the appointment of acting ministers on a continuing basis to act when a Minister is absent or incapacitated or when the office is vacant. This is done by Order in Council and provision is usually made for an alternative acting minister.

## Offices of the Ministry but not of the Cabinet

There have been several offices that were considered of the Ministry but not of the Cabinet. The Solicitor General of Canada, Controller of Customs, and Controller of Inland Revenue have all, at various times, fallen into this category. They were not appointed to the Privy Council and did not attend cabinet meetings.[9] Parliamentary Secretaries and Parliamentary Under Secretaries during the Ninth and Tenth Ministries are also included in this group.

Parliamentary Secretaries and Parliamentary Under Secretaries were appointed from among Members of the House of Commons to assist various ministers or to act in their absence. Two, the Parliamentary Secretary of Militia and Defence and the Parliamentary Under Secretary for External Affairs, were appointed by Order in Council on 15 July 1916. A Parliamentary Secretary of Soldiers' Civil Re-establishment was appointed in February 1918. Since their duties were ministerial in nature, Parliamentary Secretaries and Parliamentary Under Secretaries were considered of the Ministry but not of the Cabinet.[10] An annual salary of $5000 was provided for in September 1917 by

Statute Geo. V, c. 35. It also provided for the abolition of the offices of Parliamentary Secretary of Militia and Defence and Parliamentary Under Secretary for External Affairs, at the end of the session of Parliament in which World War I ended. The office of Parliamentary Secretary of Soldiers' Civil Re-establishment was abolished in June 1928.

## Parliamentary Assistants and Parliamentary Secretaries not of the Ministry

Parliamentary Assistants were first appointed in the Sixteenth Ministry. Provision for their appointment and a salary of $4000 per annum was made by an annual vote in the House of Commons estimates. Formal appointments were made by Order in Council and they ceased to hold office on the dissolution of the House. Parliamentary Assistants were not considered to be of the Ministry. By the Parliamentary Secretaries Act, 1959, the office of Parliamentary Assistant was replaced by that of Parliamentary Secretary. The Act provided for the appointment of a maximum of 16 Parliamentary Secretaires. In 1970 it was amended to allow the appointment of a Parliamentary Secretary to assist each minister.

1    This was the case with the ministries of Sir John Sparrow David Thompson (Fifth), Sir Charles Tupper (Seventh) and Sir Robert Laird Borden (Tenth).

2    Only two ministries have been dissolved because of the death of the Prime Minister: the Third Ministry with Sir John A. Macdonald's death on 6 June 1891 and the Fifth Ministry with Sir John Sparrow David Thompson's death on 12 December 1894.

3    Interpretation Act, Statute 16 Eliz. II, c. 7, Section 22:5.

4    The Solicitor General was not appointed through the use of the Instrument of Advice until 1966.

5    The Hon. Hugh McDonald is the exception to this rule, having served as President of the Privy Council and Ministry of Militia and Defence before being sworn as a Privy Councillor.

6    During the First Ministry James Cox Aikins was appointed to the Privy Council on 16 November 1869 and at that time was invited by Macdonald to attend Cabinet meetings. He cannot be considered a Minister without Portfolio, however, as he was not sworn of the Privy Council until 8 December 1869, which coincided with his appointment as Secretary of State.

7    William Frederic Kay was appointed with the title Minister without Portfolio in 1930.

8    Appointments were occasionally recorded by Order in Council after 1879.

9    Hon. Sir Charles Hibbert Tupper had been sworn of the Privy Council on 1 June 1888. During the Seventh Ministry he was Solicitor General of Canada, 1 May 1896 to 8 July 1896, but he was not invited by the Prime Minister to be a member of the cabinet.

10   P.C. 1916-1970 describes the office of Parliamentary Secretary of Militia and Defence as follows: ". . . a Parliamentary Secretary who shall assist the Minister of Militia and Defence, and within certain limits shall act for him during his absence . . . . The Parliamentary Secretary shall *ex officio* be a member of the Militia Council and in the absence of the Minister shall act as chairman thereof . . . . In the absence of the Minister from Ottawa and the Parliamentary Secretary shall preside over and administer the Department of Militia and Defence."

# First Ministry

## LIBERAL-CONSERVATIVE  1

1 July 1867 to 5 November 1873

## PRIME MINISTER

The Honourable Sir John Alexander Macdonald  2

## THE MINISTRY

### Minister of Agriculture  3

| | |
|---|---|
| Hon. Jean-Charles Chapais  4  *Senator* | 1 July  1867  –  15 Nov.  1869 |
| Hon. Christopher Dunkin | 16 Nov.  1869  –  24 Oct.  1871 |
| Hon. John Henry Pope | 25 Oct.  1871  –   5 Nov.  1873 |

### Minister of Customs  5

| | |
|---|---|
| Hon. Samuel Leonard Tilley  6 | 1 July  1867  –  21 Feb.  1873 |
| Hon. Charles Tupper  7 | 22 Feb.  1873  –   5 Nov.  1873 |

### Minister of Finance  8

| | |
|---|---|
| Hon. Alexander Tilloch Galt | 1 July  1867  –   7 Nov.  1867 |
| Vacant | 8 Nov.  1867  –  17 Nov.  1867 |
| Hon. John Rose | 18 Nov.  1867  –  30 Sept. 1869 |
| Vacant | 1 Oct.  1869  –   8 Oct.  1869 |
| Hon. Sir Francis Hincks | 9 Oct.  1869  –  21 Feb.  1873 |
| Hon. Samuel Leonard Tilley | 22 Feb.  1873  –   5 Nov.  1873 |

### Superintendent-General of Indian Affairs

| | |
|---|---|
| Hon. Hector Louis Langevin  9 | 22 May  1868  –   7 Dec.  1869 |
| Hon. Joseph Howe | 8 Dec.  1869  –   6 May  1873 |
| Hon. James Cox Aikins  9  *Senator – Acting Minister* | 7 May  1873  –  13 June 1873 |
| Hon. Thomas Nicholson Gibbs | 14 June 1873  –  30 June 1873 |
| Hon. Alexander Campbell  *Senator* | 1 July  1873  –   5 Nov.  1873 |

1   Sir John A. Macdonald was formally commissioned by Lord Monck on 24 May 1867 to form the first Government under Confederation. On 1 July 1867 the First Ministry assumed office. By Order in Council dated 1 July 1867 the following ministerial offices were "constituted until Parliament otherwise provides": Justice and Attorney General, Militia Customs, Finance, Public Works, Inland Revenue, Secretary of State for the Provinces, President of the Privy Council, Marine and Fisheries, Postmaster General, Agriculture, Secretary of State of Canada, and Receiver General. During the following two years statutory provision was made for most of these offices.

2   Macdonald was also Minister of Justice and Attorney General.

3   The office of Minister of Agriculture was created by Statute 31 Vict., c. 53, and assented to on 22 May 1868.

4   Chapais was appointed Receiver General on 16 Nov. 1869.

5   The office of Minister of Customs was created by Statute 31 Vict., c. 43, and assented to on 22 May 1868.

6   Tilley was appointed Minister of Finance on 22 Feb. 1873.

7   Tupper was also Minister of Inland Revenue.

8   The office of Minister of Finance was created by Statute 32-33 Vict., c. 4, and assented to on 22 June 1869.

9   Langevin and Aikins both also held the portfolios of the Secretary of State of Canada.

## Minister of Inland Revenue 10

| | | |
|---|---|---|
| Hon. William Pearce Howland | 1 July 1867 – | 14 July 1868 |
| Hon. Alexander Campbell  *Senator – Acting Minister* | 15 July 1868 – | 15 Nov. 1869 |
| Hon. Alexander Morris | 16 Nov. 1869 – | 1 July 1872 |
| Hon. Charles Tupper  11 | 2 July 1872 – | 3 Mar. 1873 |
| Hon. John O'Connor  12 | 4 Mar. 1873 – | 30 June 1873 |
| Hon. Thomas Nicholson Gibbs | 1 July 1873 – | 5 Nov. 1873 |

## Minister of the Interior 13

| | | |
|---|---|---|
| Hon. Alexander Campbell  *Senator* | 1 July 1873 – | 5 Nov. 1873 |

## Minister of Justice and Attorney General 14

| | | |
|---|---|---|
| Hon. Sir John Alexander Macdonald | 1 July 1867 – | 5 Nov. 1873 |

## Minister of Marine and Fisheries 15

| | | |
|---|---|---|
| Hon. Peter Mitchell  *Senator* | 1 July 1867 – | 5 Nov. 1873 |

## Minister of Militia and Defence 16

| | | |
|---|---|---|
| Hon. Sir George Étienne Cartier | 1 July 1867 – | 20 May 1873 |
| Hon. Hector Louis Langevin  *Acting Minister* | 21 May 1873 – | 30 June 1873 |
| Hon. Hugh McDonald | 1 July 1873 – | 4 Nov. 1873 |
| Vacant | 5 Nov. 1873 | |

## Postmaster General 17

| | | |
|---|---|---|
| Hon. Alexander Campbell  18  *Senator* | 1 July 1867 – | 30 June 1873 |
| Hon. John O'Connor | 1 July 1873 – | 5 Nov. 1873 |

## President of the Privy Council 19

| | | |
|---|---|---|
| Hon. Adam Johnston Fergusson Blair  *Senator* | 1 July 1867 – | 29 Dec. 1867 |
| Vacant | 30 Dec. 1867 – | 29 Jan. 1869 |
| Hon. Joseph Howe  20 | 30 Jan. 1869 – | 15 Nov. 1869 |
| Hon. Edward Kenny  *Senator* | 16 Nov. 1869 – | 20 June 1870 |
| Hon. Charles Tupper  21 | 21 June 1870 – | 1 July 1872 |
| Hon. John O'Connor  22 | 2 July 1872 – | 3 Mar. 1873 |
| Vacant | 4 Mar. 1873 – | 13 June 1873 |
| Hon. Hugh McDonald  23 | 14 June 1873 – | 30 June 1873 |
| Vacant | 1 July 1873 – | 5 Nov. 1873 |

3

10  The office of Minister of Inland Revenue was created by Statute 31 Vict., c. 49, and assented to on 22 May 1868.

11  Tupper was also Minister of Customs.

12  O'Connor was appointed Postmaster General on 1 July 1873.

13  The office of Secretary of State for the Provinces was abolished and the office of Minister of the Interior created by Statute 36 Vict., c. 4, assented to on 3 May 1873, and proclaimed in force on 1 July 1873. By this Act the Minister was to be *ex officio* the Superintendent-General of Indian Affairs. See Secretary of State of Canada.

14  The offices of Minister of Justice and Attorney General were created by Statute 31 Vict., c. 39, and assented to on 22 May 1868. By this Act the Minister of Justice was to be *ex officio* the Attorney General of Canada.

15  The office of Minister of Marine and Fisheries was created by Statute 31 Vict., c. 57, and assented to on 22 May 1868.

16  The office of Minister of Militia and Defence was created by Statute 31 Vict., c. 40, assented to on 22 May 1868 and proclaimed in force on 1 Oct. 1868.

17  The office of Postmaster General was created by Statute 31 Vict., c. 10, assented to on 21 Dec. 1867 and proclaimed in force on 1 Apr. 1868.

18  Campbell was appointed Minister of the Interior on 1 July 1873.

19  The portfolio of President of the Privy Council was not specifically created by statute, but was recognized by the Salaries Act (Statute 31 Vict., c. 33), and first assented to on 22 May 1868.

20  Howe was appointed Secretary of State for the Provinces on 16 Nov. 1869.

21  Tupper was appointed Minister of Inland Revenue on 2 July 1872.

22  O'Connor was appointed Minister of Inland Revenue on 4 Mar. 1873.

23  McDonald was appointed Minister of Militia and Defence on 1 July 1873.

## Minister of Public Works  24

| | |
|---|---|
| Hon. William McDougall | 1 July 1867 – 27 Sept. 1869 |
| Vacant | 28 Sept. 1869 |
| Hon. Hector Louis Langevin  *Acting Minister* | 29 Sept. 1869 – 7 Dec. 1869 |
| Hon. Hector Louis Langevin | 8 Dec. 1869 – 5 Nov. 1873 |

## Receiver General  25

| | |
|---|---|
| Vacant | 1 July 1867 – 3 July 1867 |
| Hon. Edward Kenny  26  *Senator* | 4 July 1867 – 15 Nov. 1869 |
| Hon. Jean-Charles Chapais  *Senator* | 16 Nov. 1869 – 29 Jan. 1873 |
| Hon. Théodore Robitaille | 30 Jan. 1873 – 5 Nov. 1873 |

## Secretary of State of Canada  27

| | |
|---|---|
| Hon. Hector Louis Langevin  28 | 1 July 1867 – 7 Dec. 1869 |
| Hon. James Cox Aikins  *Senator* | 8 Dec. 1869 – 5 Nov. 1873 |

## Secretary of State for the Provinces  29

| | |
|---|---|
| Hon. Adams George Archibald | 1 July 1867 – 30 Apr. 1868 |
| Vacant | 1 May 1868 – 15 Nov. 1869 |
| Hon. Joseph Howe | 16 Nov. 1869 – 6 May 1873 |
| Hon. James Cox Aikins  *Senator – Acting Minister* | 7 May 1873 – 13 June 1873 |
| Hon. Thomas Nicholson Gibbs  30 | 14 June 1873 – 30 June 1873 |

24    The office of Minister of Public Works was created by Statute 31 Vict., c. 12, and assented to on 21 Dec. 1867.

25    The portfolio of Receiver General was not specifically created by statute, but was recognized by the Salaries Act (Statute 31 Vict., c. 33), and first assented to on 22 May 1868.

26    Kenny was appointed President of the Privy Council on 16 Nov. 1869.

27    The offices of Secretary of State of Canada, Registrar General of Canada and Superintendent-General of Indian Affairs were created by Statute 31 Vict., c. 42, and assented to on 22 May 1868. By this Act the Secretary of State of Canada was to hold these latter two offices *ex officio*. By Order in Council dated 8 Dec. 1869, pursuant to section 40 of the aforesaid Act, the duties and powers of the Superintendent-General of Indian Affairs were transferred to the Secretary of State for the Provinces and were exercised by him until 1 July 1873. See Minister of the Interior.

28    Langevin was appointed Minister of Public Works on 8 Dec. 1869.

29    The portfolio of Secretary of State for the Provinces was not specifically created by statute, but was recognized by the Salaries Act (Statute 31 Vict., c. 33), and first assented to on 22 May 1868. See Secretary of State of Canada and Minister of the Interior.

30    Gibbs was appointed Minister of Inland Revenue on 1 July 1873.

# Second Ministry

## LIBERAL  1

7 November 1873 to 8 October 1878

## PRIME MINISTER

The Honourable Alexander Mackenzie  2

## THE MINISTRY

### Minister of Agriculture

| | |
|---|---|
| Hon. Luc Letellier de St-Just  *Senator* | 7 Nov. 1873 – 14 Dec. 1876 |
| Hon. Isaac Burpee  *Acting Minister* | 15 Dec. 1876 – 25 Jan. 1877 |
| Hon. Charles Alphonse Pantaléon Pelletier  *Senator* | 26 Jan. 1877 –  8 Oct. 1878 |

### Minister of Customs

| | |
|---|---|
| Hon. Isaac Burpee | 7 Nov. 1873 –  8 Oct. 1878 |

### Minister of Finance

| | |
|---|---|
| Hon. Richard John Cartwright | 7 Nov. 1873 –  8 Oct. 1878 |

### Superintendent-General of Indian Affairs  3

| | |
|---|---|
| Hon. David Laird | 7 Nov. 1873 –  6 Oct. 1876 |
| Hon. Richard William Scott  *Senator – Acting Minister* | 7 Oct. 1876 – 23 Oct. 1876 |
| Hon. David Mills | 24 Oct. 1876 –  8 Oct. 1878 |

### Minister of Inland Revenue

| | |
|---|---|
| Hon. Télesphore Fournier  4 | 7 Nov. 1873 –  7 July 1874 |
| Hon. Félix Geoffrion | 8 July 1874 –  8 Nov. 1876 |
| Hon. Toussaint Antoine Rodolphe Laflamme  5 | 9 Nov. 1876 –  7 June 1877 |
| Hon. Joseph Édouard Cauchon | 8 June 1877 –  7 Oct. 1877 |
| Hon. Wilfrid Laurier | 8 Oct. 1877 –  8 Oct. 1878 |

### Minister of the Interior  6

| | |
|---|---|
| Hon. David Laird | 7 Nov. 1873 –  6 Oct. 1876 |
| Hon. Richard William Scott  *Senator – Acting Minister* | 7 Oct. 1876 – 23 Oct. 1876 |
| Hon. David Mills | 24 Oct. 1876 –  8 Oct. 1878 |

1     On 5 Nov. 1873 Macdonald resigned and the Governor General invited Mackenzie to form a Government. The Second Ministry assumed office on 7 Nov. 1873.

2     Mackenzie was also Minister of Public Works.

3     See Minister of the Interior.

4     Fournier was appointed Minister of Justice and Attorney General on 8 July 1874.

5     Laflamme was appointed Minister of Justice and Attorney General on 8 July 1877.

6     The Minister of the Interior was *ex officio* the Superintendent-General of Indian Affairs.

## Minister of Justice and Attorney General

| | | |
|---|---|---|
| Hon. Antoine-Aimé Dorion | 7 Nov. 1873 – | 31 May 1874 |
| Hon. Sir Albert James Smith   *Acting Minister* | 1 June 1874 – | 7 July 1874 |
| Hon. Télesphore Fournier   7 | 8 July 1874 – | 18 May 1875 |
| Hon. Dominick Edward Blake   8 | 19 May 1875 – | 7 June 1877 |
| Hon. Toussaint Antoine Rodolphe Laflamme | 8 June 1877 – | 8 Oct. 1878 |

## Minister of Marine and Fisheries

| | | |
|---|---|---|
| Hon. Sir Albert James Smith | 7 Nov. 1873 – | 8 Oct. 1878 |

## Minister of Militia and Defence

| | | |
|---|---|---|
| Hon. William Ross | 7 Nov. 1873 – | 29 Sept. 1874 |
| Hon. William Berrian Vail | 30 Sept. 1874 – | 20 Jan. 1878 |
| Hon. Alfred Gilpin Jones | 21 Jan. 1878 – | 8 Oct. 1878 |

## Postmaster General

| | | |
|---|---|---|
| Hon. Donald Alexander Macdonald | 7 Nov. 1873 – | 17 May 1875 |
| Vacant | 18 May 1875 | |
| Hon. Télesphore Fournier | 19 May 1875 – | 7 Oct. 1875 |
| Vacant | 8 Oct. 1875 | |
| Hon. Lucius Seth Huntington | 9 Oct. 1875 – | 8 Oct. 1878 |

## President of the Privy Council

| | | |
|---|---|---|
| Vacant | 7 Nov. 1873 – | 19 Jan. 1874 |
| Hon. Lucius Seth Huntington   9 | 20 Jan. 1874 – | 8 Oct. 1875 |
| Vacant | 9 Oct. 1875 – | 6 Dec. 1875 |
| Hon. Joseph Édouard Cauchon   10 | 7 Dec. 1875 – | 7 June 1877 |
| Hon. Dominick Edward Blake | 8 June 1877 – | 17 Jan. 1878 |
| Vacant | 18 Jan. 1878 – | 8 Oct. 1878 |

## Minister of Public Works

| | | |
|---|---|---|
| Hon. Alexander Mackenzie | 7 Nov. 1873 – | 8 Oct. 1878 |

## Receiver General

| | | |
|---|---|---|
| Hon. Thomas Coffin | 7 Nov. 1873 – | 8 Oct. 1878 |

## Secretary of State of Canada   11

| | | |
|---|---|---|
| Hon. David Christie   *Senator* | 7 Nov. 1873 – | 8 Jan. 1874 |
| Hon. Richard William Scott   *Senator* | 9 Jan. 1874 – | 8 Oct. 1878 |

7     Fournier was appointed Postmaster General on 19 May 1875.

8     Blake was appointed President of the Privy Council on 8 June 1877.

9     Huntington was appointed Postmaster General on 9 Oct. 1875.

10    Cauchon was appointed Minister of Inland Revenue on 8 June 1877.

11    The Secretary of State of Canada was *ex officio* the Registrar General of Canada.

**Minister without Portfolio**

| | |
|---|---|
| Hon. Dominick Edward Blake   12 | 7 Nov. 1873 —  13 Feb. 1874 |
| Hon. Richard William Scott   13 | 7 Nov. 1873 —   8 Jan. 1874 |

12  Blake resigned from the ministry on 13 Feb. 1874, but subsequently rejoined it as Minister of Justice and Attorney General on 19 May 1875.

13  Scott was appointed Secretary of State of Canada on 9 Jan. 1874.

# Third Ministry

**LIBERAL-CONSERVATIVE** 1

17 October 1878 to 6 June 1891

**PRIME MINISTER**

The Right Honourable Sir John Alexander Macdonald   2

**THE MINISTRY**

**Minister of Agriculture**

| | |
|---|---|
| Hon. John Henry Pope   3 | 17 Oct.  1878 – 24 Sept. 1885 |
| Hon. John Carling | 25 Sept. 1885 –   6 June 1891 |

**Minister of Customs**

| | |
|---|---|
| Vacant | 17 Oct.  1878 – 18 Oct.  1878 |
| Hon. Mackenzie Bowell | 19 Oct.  1878 –   6 June 1891 |

**Minister of Finance**   4

| | |
|---|---|
| Hon. Sir Samuel Leonard Tilley   5 | 17 Oct.  1878 – 19 May  1879 |

**Minister of Finance and Receiver General**

| | |
|---|---|
| Hon. Sir Samuel Leonard Tilley | 20 May  1879 – 10 Nov. 1885 |
| Vacant | 11 Nov. 1885 –   9 Dec. 1885 |
| Hon. Archibald Woodbury McLelan   6 | 10 Dec. 1885 – 26 Jan.  1887 |
| Hon. Sir Charles Tupper | 27 Jan.  1887 – 22 May  1888 |
| Vacant | 23 May  1888 – 28 May  1888 |
| Hon. George Eulas Foster | 29 May  1888 –   6 June 1891 |

**Superintendent-General of Indian Affairs**   7

| | |
|---|---|
| Rt. Hon. Sir John Alexander Macdonald | 17 Oct.  1878 –   2 Oct.  1887 |
| Hon. Thomas White | 3 Oct.  1887 – 21 Apr.  1888 |
| Vacant | 22 Apr.  1888 –   7 May  1888 |
| Rt. Hon. Sir John Alexander Macdonald   *Acting Minister* | 8 May  1888 – 24 Sept. 1888 |
| Hon. Edgar Dewdney | 25 Sept. 1888 –   6 June 1891 |

1    The Mackenzie Government was defeated in the general election of 17 Sept. 1878. On 8 Oct. Mackenzie resigned and the next day Macdonald was invited to form a Government. Eight days later, on 17 Oct., six members of the Third Ministry assumed office. Five more portfolios were filled on 19 Oct., one on 26 Oct., and two on 8 Nov.

2    During the Third Ministry Macdonald held successively the portfolios of the Interior, Privy Council, and Railways and Canals.

3    Pope was appointed Minister of Railways and Canals on 25 Sept. 1885.

4    Under the provisions of Statute 42 Vict., c. 7, assented to on 15 May 1879 and proclaimed in force on 20 May 1879, the Minister of Finance was to be *ex officio* the Receiver General of Canada.

5    Tilley was appointed Minister of Finance and Receiver General on 20 May 1879.

6    McLelan was appointed Postmaster General on 27 Jan. 1887.

7    See Minister of the Interior.

**Minister of Inland Revenue**

| | | |
|---|---|---|
| Vacant | 17 Oct. 1878 – | 25 Oct. 1878 |
| Hon. Louis François Georges Baby | 26 Oct. 1878 – | 28 Oct. 1880 |
| Vacant | 29 Oct. 1880 – | 7 Nov. 1880 |
| Hon. James Cox Aikins  *Senator* | 8 Nov. 1880 – | 22 May 1882 |
| Hon. John Costigan | 23 May 1882 – | 6 June 1891 |

**Minister of the Interior**  8

| | | |
|---|---|---|
| Rt. Hon. Sir John Alexander Macdonald | 17 Oct. 1878 – | 16 Oct. 1883 |
| Hon. Sir David Lewis Macpherson  *Senator* | 17 Oct. 1883 – | 4 Aug. 1885 |
| Hon. Thomas White | 5 Aug. 1885 – | 21 Apr. 1888 |
| Vacant | 22 Apr. 1888 – | 7 May 1888 |
| Rt. Hon. Sir John Alexander Macdonald  *Acting Minister* | 8 May 1888 – | 24 Sept. 1888 |
| Hon. Edgar Dewdney | 25 Sept. 1888 – | 6 June 1891 |

**Minister of Justice and Attorney General**

| | | |
|---|---|---|
| Hon. James McDonald | 17 Oct. 1878 – | 19 May 1881 |
| Hon. Sir Alexander Campbell  9  *Senator* | 20 May 1881 – | 24 Sept. 1885 |
| Vacant | 25 Sept. 1885 | |
| Hon. Sir John Sparrow David Thompson | 26 Sept. 1885 – | 6 June 1891 |

**Minister of Marine and Fisheries**

| | | |
|---|---|---|
| Vacant | 17 Oct. 1878 – | 18 Oct. 1878 |
| Hon. James Colledge Pope | 19 Oct. 1878 – | 9 July 1882 |
| Hon. Archibald Woodbury McLelan  10 | 10 July 1882 – | 9 Dec. 1885 |
| Hon. George Eulas Foster  11 | 10 Dec. 1885 – | 28 May 1888 |
| Vacant | 29 May 1888 – | 31 May 1888 |
| Hon. Charles Hibbert Tupper | 1 June 1888 – | 6 June 1891 |

**Minister of Militia and Defence**

| | | |
|---|---|---|
| Vacant | 17 Oct. 1878 – | 18 Oct. 1878 |
| Hon. Louis François Rodrigue Masson  12 | 19 Oct. 1878 – | 15 Jan. 1880 |
| Hon. Sir Alexander Campbell  13  *Senator* | 16 Jan. 1880 – | 7 Nov. 1880 |
| Hon. Sir Joseph Philippe René Adolphe Caron | 8 Nov. 1880 – | 6 June 1891 |

8    Until 1883 the Minister of the Interior was *ex officio* the Superintendent-General of Indian Affairs. In that year Statute 46 Vict., c. 6, assented to on 25 May 1883, provided for the Minister of the Interior, or the head of any other department appointed for that purpose by the Governor in Council, to hold the office *ex officio*. By Order in Council dated 17 Oct. 1883 the President of the Privy Council was designated to be Superintendent-General of Indian Affairs. On 3 Oct. 1887 the office was transferred back to the Minister of the Interior, who then, except for a brief period in 1930, continued to hold the office *ex officio* until its abolition in 1936. The Department of Indian Affairs was created by Statute 43 Vict., c. 28, assented to on 7 May 1880.

9    Campbell was appointed Postmaster General on 25 Sept. 1885.

10   McLelan was appointed Minister of Finance and Receiver General on 10 Dec. 1885.

11   Foster was appointed Minister of Finance and Receiver General on 29 May 1885.

12   Masson was appointed President of the Privy Council on 16 Jan. 1880.

13   Campbell was appointed Postmaster General on 8 Nov. 1880.

## Postmaster General

| | | |
|---|---|---|
| Vacant | 17 Oct. 1878 – | 18 Oct. 1878 |
| Hon. Hector Louis Langevin  14 | 19 Oct. 1878 – | 19 May 1879 |
| Hon. Sir Alexander Campbell  15  *Senator* | 20 May 1879 – | 15 Jan. 1880 |
| Hon. John O'Connor  16 | 16 Jan. 1880 – | 7 Nov. 1880 |
| Hon. Sir Alexander Campbell  17  *Senator* | 8 Nov. 1880 – | 19 May 1881 |
| Hon. John O'Connor | 20 May 1881 – | 22 May 1882 |
| Hon. John Carling  18 | 23 May 1882 – | 24 Sept. 1885 |
| Hon. Sir Alexander Campbell  *Senator* | 25 Sept. 1885 – | 26 Jan. 1887 |
| Hon. Archibald Woodbury McLelan | 27 Jan. 1887 – | 9 July 1888 |
| Vacant | 10 July 1888 | |
| Hon. John Carling  *Acting Minister* | 11 July 1888 – | 5 Aug. 1888 |
| Hon. John Graham Haggart | 6 Aug. 1888 – | 6 June 1891 |

## President of the Privy Council  19

| | | |
|---|---|---|
| Hon. John O'Connor  20 | 17 Oct. 1878 – | 15 Jan. 1880 |
| Hon. Louis François Rodrigue Masson | 16 Jan. 1880 – | 31 July 1880 |
| Vacant | 1 Aug. 1880 – | 7 Nov. 1880 |
| Hon. Joseph-Alfred Mousseau  21 | 8 Nov. 1880 – | 19 May 1881 |
| Hon. Archibald Woodbury McLelan  22 | 20 May 1881 – | 9 July 1882 |
| Vacant | 10 July 1882 – | 16 Oct. 1883 |
| Rt. Hon. Sir John Alexander Macdonald | 17 Oct. 1883 – | 27 Nov. 1889 |
| Hon. Charles Carrol Colby | 28 Nov. 1889 – | 30 Apr. 1891 |
| Vacant | 1 May 1891 – | 6 June 1891 |

## Minister of Public Works

| | | |
|---|---|---|
| Hon. Sir Charles Tupper  23 | 17 Oct. 1878 – | 19 May 1879 |
| Hon. Sir Hector Louis Langevin | 20 May 1879 – | 6 June 1891 |

## Minister of Railways and Canals  24

| | | |
|---|---|---|
| Hon. Sir Charles Tupper  25 | 20 May 1879 – | 28 May 1884 |
| Hon. John Henry Pope  *Acting Minister* | 29 May 1884 – | 24 Sept. 1885 |
| Hon. John Henry Pope | 25 Sept. 1885 – | 1 Apr. 1889 |
| Vacant | 2 Apr. 1889 – | 9 Apr. 1889 |
| Rt. Hon. Sir John Alexander Macdonald  *Acting Minister* | 10 Apr. 1889 – | 27 Nov. 1889 |
| Rt. Hon. Sir John Alexander Macdonald | 28 Nov. 1889 – | 6 June 1891 |

14   Langevin was appointed Minister of Public Works on 20 May 1879.

15   Campbell was appointed Minister of Militia and Defence on 16 Jan. 1880.

16   O'Connor was appointed Secretary of State of Canada on 8 Nov. 1880.

17   Campbell was appointed Minister of Justice and Attorney General on 20 May 1881.

18   Carling was appointed Minister of Agriculture on 25 Sept. 1885.

19   See Note 8.

20   O'Connor was appointed Postmaster General on 16 Jan. 1880.

21   Mousseau was appointed Secretary of State of Canada on 20 May 1881.

22   McLelan was appointed Minister of Marine and Fisheries on 10 July 1882.

23   Tupper was appointed Minister of Railways and Canals on 20 May 1879.

24   The Office of Minister of Railways and Canals was created by Statute 42 Vict., c. 7, assented to on 15 May 1879, and proclaimed in force on 20 May 1879.

25   On 30 May 1883 Sir Charles Tupper was appointed High Commissioner for Canada in the United Kingdom, but an arrangement was made whereby he would serve in this capacity without salary. He continued to hold the portfolio of Minister of Railways and Canals until 28 May 1884 when a new commission was issued to him granting a salary as High Commissioner. This effected his resignation from the ministry. On 27 Jan. 1887 Tupper resigned as High Commissioner and re-entered the ministry as Minister of Finance.

## Receiver General

| | | |
|---|---|---|
| Vacant | 17 Oct. 1878 – | 7 Nov. 1878 |
| Hon. Alexander Campbell  26  *Senator* | 8 Nov. 1878 – | 19 May 1879 |

## Secretary of State of Canada  27

| | | |
|---|---|---|
| Vacant | 17 Oct. 1878 – | 18 Oct. 1878 |
| Hon. James Cox Aikins  28  *Senator* | 19 Oct. 1878 – | 7 Nov. 1880 |
| Hon. John O'Connor  29 | 8 Nov. 1880 – | 19 May 1881 |
| Hon. Joseph-Alfred Mousseau | 20 May 1881 – | 28 July 1882 |
| Hon. Joseph Adolphe Chapleau | 29 July 1882 – | 6 June 1891 |

## Minister without Portfolio

| | | |
|---|---|---|
| Hon. Robert Duncan Wilmot  *Senator* | 8 Nov. 1878 – | 10 Feb. 1880 |
| Hon. David Lewis Macpherson  30  *Senator* | 11 Feb. 1880 – | 16 Oct. 1883 |
| Hon. Frank Smith  *Senator* | 2 Aug. 1882 – | 6 June 1891 |
| Hon. John Joseph Caldwell Abbott  *Senator* | 13 May 1887 – | 6 June 1891 |

26   Campbell was appointed Postmaster General on 20 May 1879.

27   The Secretary of State of Canada was *ex officio* the Registrar General of Canada.

28   Aikins was appointed Minister of Inland Revenue on 8 Nov. 1880.

29   O'Connor was appointed Postmaster General on 20 May 1881.

30   Macpherson was appointed Minister of the Interior on 17 Oct. 1883.

# Fourth Ministry

**LIBERAL-CONSERVATIVE** 1

16 June 1891 to 24 November 1892

**PRIME MINISTER**

The Honourable Sir John Joseph Caldwell Abbott  2  *Senator*

**THE MINISTRY**

**Minister of Agriculture**

Hon. John Carling  *Senator*                16 June 1891 – 24 Nov. 1892

**Minister of Customs**

Hon. Mackenzie Bowell  3                    16 June 1891 – 24 Jan. 1892
Hon. Joseph Adolphe Chapleau               25 Jan. 1892 – 24 Nov. 1892

**Minister of Finance and Receiver General**

Hon. George Eulas Foster                   16 June 1891 – 24 Nov. 1892

**Superintendent-General of Indian Affairs**  4

Hon. Edgar Dewdney                         16 June 1891 – 16 Oct. 1892
Hon. Thomas Mayne Daly                     17 Oct. 1892 – 24 Nov. 1892

**Minister of Inland Revenue**

Hon. John Costigan                         16 June 1891 – 24 Nov. 1892

**Minister of the Interior**  5

Hon. Edgar Dewdney                         16 June 1891 – 16 Oct. 1892
Hon. Thomas Mayne Daly                     17 Oct. 1892 – 24 Nov. 1892

**Minister of Justice and Attorney General**

Hon. Sir John Sparrow David Thompson       16 June 1891 – 24 Nov. 1892

**Minister of Marine and Fisheries**

Hon. Charles Hibbert Tupper                16 June 1891 – 24 Nov. 1892

**Minister of Militia and Defence**

Hon. Sir Joseph Philippe René Adolphe Caron  6   16 June 1891 – 24 Jan. 1892
Hon. Mackenzie Bowell                      25 Jan. 1892 – 24 Nov. 1892

1    The death of Macdonald on 6 June 1891 dissolved the Third Ministry *ipso facto*. On 15 June 1891 Abbott accepted the Governor General's invitation to form a Government and on 16 June the Fourth Ministry assumed office. The new Cabinet was composed entirely of ministers from the Third Ministry and with the exception of Abbott, they all retained their previous portfolios.

2    Abbott was also President of the Privy Council.

3    Bowell was appointed Minister of Militia and Defence on 25 Jan. 1892.

4,5   The Minister of the Interior was *ex officio* the Superintendent-General of Indian Affairs.

6    Caron was appointed Postmaster General on 25 Jan. 1892.

## Postmaster General

| | |
|---|---|
| Hon. John Graham Haggart   7 | 16 June 1891  –  10 Jan.  1892 |
| Vacant | 11 Jan.  1892  –  24 Jan.  1892 |
| Hon. Sir Joseph Philippe René Adolphe Caron | 25 Jan.  1892  –  24 Nov.  1892 |

## President of the Privy Council

| | |
|---|---|
| Hon. Sir John Joseph Caldwell Abbott   *Senator* | 16 June 1891  –  24 Nov.  1892 |

## Minister of Public Works

| | |
|---|---|
| Hon. Sir Hector Louis Langevin | 16 June 1891  –  11 Aug.  1891 |
| Vacant | 12 Aug.  1891  –  13 Aug.  1891 |
| Hon. Frank Smith   8   *Senator* | 14 Aug.  1891  –  10 Jan.  1892 |
| Hon. Joseph Aldéric Ouimet | 11 Jan.  1892  –  24 Nov.  1892 |

## Minister of Railways and Canals

| | |
|---|---|
| Vacant | 16 June 1891 |
| Hon. Mackenzie Bowell   *Acting Minister* | 17 June 1891  –  10 Jan.  1892 |
| Hon. John Graham Haggart | 11 Jan.  1892  –  24 Nov.  1892 |

## Secretary of State of Canada   9

| | |
|---|---|
| Hon. Joseph Adolphe Chapleau   10 | 16 June 1891  –  24 Jan.  1892 |
| Hon. James Colebrooke Patterson | 25 Jan.  1892  –  24 Nov.  1892 |

## Minister without Portfolio

| | |
|---|---|
| Hon. Frank Smith   11   *Senator* | 16 June 1891  –  13 Aug.  1891 |
| Hon. Frank Smith   *Senator* | 11 Jan.  1892  –  24 Nov.  1892 |

7    Haggart was appointed Minister of Railways and Canals on 11 Jan. 1892.

8    Smith was appointed Minister without Portfolio on 11 Jan. 1892.

9    The Secretary of State of Canada was *ex officio* the Registrar General of Canada.

10   Chapleau was appointed Minister of Customs on 25 Jan. 1892.

11   Smith was appointed Minister of Public Works on 14 Aug. 1891.

# Fifth
# Ministry

**LIBERAL-CONSERVATIVE**   1

5 December 1892 to 12 December 1894

**PRIME MINISTER**

The Right Honourable Sir John Sparrow David Thompson   2

**THE MINISTRY**

**Minister of Agriculture**
| | | |
|---|---|---|
| Vacant | 5 Dec. 1892 – | 6 Dec. 1892 |
| Hon. Auguste Réal Angers   *Senator* | 7 Dec. 1892 – | 12 Dec. 1894 |

**Minister of Finance and Receiver General**
| | |
|---|---|
| Hon. George Eulas Foster | 5 Dec. 1892 – 12 Dec. 1894 |

**Superintendent-General of Indian Affairs**   3
| | |
|---|---|
| Hon. Thomas Mayne Daly | 5 Dec. 1892 – 12 Dec. 1894 |

**Minister of the Interior**   4
| | |
|---|---|
| Hon. Thomas Mayne Daly | 5 Dec. 1892 – 12 Dec. 1894 |

**Minister of Justice and Attorney General**
| | |
|---|---|
| Rt. Hon. Sir John Sparrow David Thompson | 5 Dec. 1892 – 12 Dec. 1894 |

**Minister of Marine and Fisheries**
| | |
|---|---|
| Hon. Sir Charles Hibbert Tupper | 5 Dec. 1892 – 12 Dec. 1894 |

**Minister of Militia and Defence**
| | |
|---|---|
| Hon. James Colebrooke Patterson | 5 Dec. 1892 – 12 Dec. 1894 |

**Postmaster General**
| | |
|---|---|
| Hon. Sir Joseph Philippe René Adolphe Caron | 5 Dec. 1892 – 12 Dec. 1894 |

**President of the Privy Council**
| | | |
|---|---|---|
| Vacant | 5 Dec. 1892 – | 6 Dec. 1892 |
| Hon. William Bullock Ives | 7 Dec. 1892 – | 12 Dec. 1894 |

**Minister of Public Works**
| | |
|---|---|
| Hon. Joseph Aldéric Ouimet | 5 Dec. 1892 – 12 Dec. 1894 |

1    On 25 Nov. 1892, the day after the resignation of Abbott, the Governor General invited Thompson to form a Government. The Fifth Ministry assumed office on 5 Dec. 1892. Eleven ministers from the Fourth Ministry continued during the Fifth, with Thompson and eight of the ministers retaining the same portfolios.

2    Thompson was also Minister of Justice and Attorney General.

3,4    The Minister of the Interior was *ex officio* the Superintendent-General of Indian Affairs.

**Minister of Railways and Canals**

Hon. John Graham Haggart                 5 Dec. 1892 – 12 Dec. 1894

**Secretary of State of Canada**   5

Hon. John Costigan                       5 Dec. 1892 – 12 Dec. 1894

**Minister of Trade and Commerce**   6

Hon. Mackenzie Bowell   *Senator*        5 Dec. 1892 – 12 Dec. 1894

**Minister without Portfolio**

Hon. Sir John Carling                    5 Dec. 1892 – 12 Dec. 1894
Hon. Sir Frank Smith   *Senator*         5 Dec. 1892 – 12 Dec. 1894


**NOT OF THE CABINET**

**Controller of Customs**   7

Hon. Nathaniel Clarke Wallace            5 Dec. 1892 – 12 Dec. 1894

**Controller of Inland Revenue**

Hon. John Fisher Wood                    5 Dec. 1892 – 12 Dec. 1894

**Solicitor General of Canada**   8

Hon. John Joseph Curran                  5 Dec. 1892 – 12 Dec. 1894

5       The Secretary of State of Canada was *ex officio* the Registrar General of Canada.

6       The office of Minister of Trade and Commerce was created by Statute 50-51 Vict., c. 10, assented to on 23 June 1887, and proclaimed in force on 3 Dec. 1892.

7       Statute 50-51 Vict., c. 11, assented to on 23 June 1887 and proclaimed in force on 3 Dec. 1892, abolished the offices of Minister of Customs and Minister of Inland Revenue and created the positions of Controller of Customs and Controller of Inland Revenue. These latter offices were not Cabinet portfolios *per se*, though considered of the ministry.

8       The office of Solicitor General of Canada was created by Statute 50-51 Vict., c. 14, assented to on 23 June 1887 and proclaimed in force on 3 Dec. 1892. By this Act the Solicitor General was designated an officer to assist the Minister of Justice. The office was not a Cabinet portfolio *per se*, though considered of the ministry.

# Sixth
# Ministry

**LIBERAL-CONSERVATIVE**  1

21 December 1894 to 27 April 1896

**PRIME MINISTER**

The Honourable Sir Mackenzie Bowell   2   *Senator*

**THE MINISTRY**

**Minister of Agriculture**

| | | |
|---|---|---|
| Hon. Auguste Réal Angers   *Senator* | 21 Dec. 1894 – | 12 July 1895 |
| Hon. Joseph Aldéric Ouimet   *Acting Minister* | 13 July 1895 – | 20 Dec. 1895 |
| Hon. Walter Humphries Montague | 21 Dec. 1895 – | 5 Jan. 1896 |
| Hon. Donald Ferguson   *Senator – Acting Minister* | 6 Jan. 1896 – | 14 Jan. 1896 |
| Hon. Walter Humphries Montague | 15 Jan. 1896 – | 27 Apr. 1896 |

**Controller of Customs**   3

| | | |
|---|---|---|
| Hon. John Fisher Wood | 24 Dec. 1895 – | 5 Jan. 1896 |
| Hon. Sir Frank Smith   *Senator – Acting Minister* | 6 Jan. 1896 – | 14 Jan. 1896 |
| Hon. John Fisher Wood | 15 Jan. 1896 – | 27 Apr. 1896 |

**Minister of Finance and Receiver General**

| | | |
|---|---|---|
| Hon. George Eulas Foster | 21 Dec. 1894 – | 5 Jan. 1896 |
| Hon. Sir Mackenzie Bowell   *Senator – Acting Minister* | 6 Jan. 1896 – | 14 Jan. 1896 |
| Hon. George Eulas Foster | 15 Jan. 1896 – | 27 Apr. 1896 |

**Superintendent-General of Indian Affairs**   5

| | | |
|---|---|---|
| Hon. Thomas Mayne Daly | 21 Dec. 1894 – | 27 Apr. 1896 |

**Controller of Inland Revenue**   4

| | | |
|---|---|---|
| Hon. Edward Gawler Prior | 17 Dec. 1895 – | 27 Apr. 1896 |

**Minister of the Interior**   5

| | | |
|---|---|---|
| Hon. Thomas Mayne Daly | 21 Dec. 1894 – | 27 Apr. 1896 |

**Minister of Justice and Attorney General**

| | | |
|---|---|---|
| Hon. Sir Charles Hibbert Tupper | 21 Dec. 1894 – | 5 Jan. 1896 |
| Hon. Thomas Mayne Daly   *Acting Minister* | 6 Jan. 1896 – | 14 Jan. 1896 |
| Hon. Arthur Rupert Dickey | 15 Jan. 1896 – | 27 Apr. 1896 |

1    On 13 Dec. 1894, the day after the death of Thompson, Bowell was invited by the Governor General to form a Government. The Sixth Ministry assumed office on 21 Dec. 1894 and included fifteen ministers from the Fifth Ministry, eleven of whom retained their previous portfolios.

2    Bowell was also President of the Privy Council.

3    See also NOT OF THE CABINET, Controller of Customs.

4    See also NOT OF THE CABINET, Controller of Inland Revenue.

5    The Minister of the Interior was *ex officio* the Superintendent-General of Indian Affairs.

## Minister of Marine and Fisheries

Hon. John Costigan                                         21 Dec. 1894 – 27 Apr. 1896

## Minister of Militia and Defence

Hon. James Colebrooke Patterson   6         21 Dec. 1894 – 25 Mar. 1895
Hon. Arthur Rupert Dickey   7                 26 Mar. 1895 – 5 Jan. 1896
Hon. Sir Mackenzie Bowell   *Senator – Acting Minister*    6 Jan. 1896 – 14 Jan. 1896
Hon. Alphonse Desjardins   *Senator*           15 Jan. 1896 – 27 Apr. 1896

## Postmaster General

Hon. Sir Joseph Philippe René Adolphe Caron       21 Dec. 1894 – 27 Apr. 1896

## President of the Privy Council

Hon. Sir. Mackenzie Bowell   *Senator*         21 Dec. 1894 – 27 Apr. 1896

## Minister of Public Works

Hon. Joseph Aldéric Ouimet                    21 Dec. 1894 – 27 Apr. 1896

## Minister of Railways and Canals

Hon. John Graham Haggart                   21 Dec. 1894 – 5 Jan. 1896
Hon. Joseph Aldéric Ouimet   *Acting Minister*     6 Jan. 1896 – 14 Jan. 1896
Hon. John Graham Haggart                   15 Jan. 1896 – 27 Apr. 1896

## Secretary of State of Canada   8

Hon. Arthur Rupert Dickey   9              21 Dec. 1894 – 25 Mar. 1895
Hon. Walter Humphries Montague   10      26 Mar. 1895 – 20 Dec. 1895
Vacant                                      21 Dec. 1895 – 26 Dec. 1895
Hon. Joseph Aldéric Ouimet   *Acting Minister*    27 Dec. 1895 – 5 Jan. 1896
Hon. Thomas Mayne Daly   *Acting Minister*      6 Jan. 1896 – 14 Jan. 1896
Hon. Sir Charles Tupper                     15 Jan. 1896 – 27 Apr. 1896

## Minister of Trade and Commerce

Hon. William Bullock Ives                    21 Dec. 1894 – 5 Jan. 1896
Hon. John Costigan   *Acting Minister*          6 Jan. 1896 – 14 Jan. 1896
Hon. William Bullock Ives                    15 Jan. 1896 – 27 Apr. 1896

6   Patterson was appointed Minister without Portfolio on 26 Mar. 1895.

7   Dickey was appointed Minister of Justice and Attorney General on 15 Jan. 1896.

8   The Secretary of State of Canada was *ex officio* the Registrar General of Canada.

9   Dickey was appointed Minister of Militia and Defence on 26 Mar. 1895.

10  Montague was appointed Minister of Agriculture on 21 Dec. 1895.

## Minister without Portfolio

| | |
|---|---|
| Hon. Walter Humphries Montague   11 | 21 Dec. 1894  –  25 Mar. 1895 |
| Hon. Sir Frank Smith   *Senator* | 21 Dec. 1894  –  27 Apr. 1896 |
| Hon. Donald Ferguson   *Senator* | 2 Jan. 1895  –  27 Apr. 1896 |
| Hon. James Colebrooke Patterson | 26 Mar. 1895  –  1 Sept. 1895 |

## NOT OF THE CABINET

### Controller of Customs   12

| | |
|---|---|
| Hon. Nathaniel Clarke Wallace | 21 Dec. 1894  –  13 Dec. 1895 |
| Hon. John Fisher Wood   *Acting Minister* | 14 Dec. 1895  –  16 Dec. 1895 |
| Hon. John Fisher Wood   13 | 17 Dec. 1895  –  23 Dec. 1895 |

### Controller of Inland Revenue   14

| | |
|---|---|
| Hon. John Fisher Wood   15 | 21 Dec. 1894  –  16 Dec. 1895 |

### Solicitor General of Canada

| | |
|---|---|
| Hon. John Joseph Curran | 21 Dec. 1894  –  17 Oct.  1895 |
| Vacant | 18 Oct.  1895  –  27 Apr. 1896 |

11    Montague was appointed Secretary of State of Canada on 26 Mar. 1895.

12    See also THE MINISTRY, Controller of Customs.

13    Wood was sworn of the Privy Council and considered of the Cabinet on 24 Dec. 1895.

14    See also THE MINISTRY, Controller of Inland Revenue.

15    Wood was appointed Controller of Customs on 17 Dec. 1895.

# Seventh Ministry

**LIBERAL-CONSERVATIVE** 1

1 May 1896 to 8 July 1896

**PRIME MINISTER**

The Honourable Sir Charles Tupper  2

**THE MINISTRY**

**Minister of Agriculture**
Hon. Walter Humphries Montague                  1 May  1896 –   8 July  1896

**Controller of Customs**
Hon. John Fisher Wood                            1 May  1896 –   8 July  1896

**Minister of Finance and Receiver General**
Hon. George Eulas Foster                         1 May  1896 –   8 July  1896

**Superintendent-General of Indian Affairs**  3
Hon. Hugh John Macdonald                         1 May  1896 –   8 July  1896

**Controller of Inland Revenue**
Hon. Edward Gawler Prior                         1 May  1896 –   8 July  1896

**Minister of the Interior**  3
Hon. Hugh John Macdonald                         1 May  1896 –   8 July  1896

**Minister of Justice and Attorney General**
Hon. Arthur Rupert Dickey                        1 May  1896 –   8 July  1896

**Minister of Marine and Fisheries**
Hon. John Costigan                               1 May  1896 –   8 July  1896

**Minister of Militia and Defence**
Hon. David Tisdale                               1 May  1896 –   8 July  1896

**Postmaster General**
Hon. Louis-Olivier Taillon                       1 May  1896 –   8 July  1896

**President of the Privy Council**
Hon. Auguste Réal Angers  *Senator*              1 May  1896 –   8 July  1896

1    On 27 April 1896 with the resignation of Bowell, the Governor General invited Tupper to form a Government. The Seventh Ministry, which included twelve ministers from the Sixth Ministry, eleven of whom retained their previous portfolios, assumed office on 1 May 1896.

2    Tupper was also Secretary of State of Canada.

3    The Minister of the Interior was *ex officio* the Superintendent-General of Indian Affairs.

**Minister of Public Works**

Hon. Alphonse Desjardins   *Senator*                      1 May  1896  –   8 July  1896

**Minister of Railways and Canals**

Hon. John Graham Haggart                                  1 May  1896  –   8 July  1896

**Secretary of State of Canada   4**

Hon. Sir Charles Tupper                                   1 May  1896  –   8 July  1896

**Minister of Trade and Commerce**

Hon. William Bullock Ives                                 1 May  1896  –   8 July  1896

**Minister without Portfolio**

Hon. Donald Ferguson   *Senator*                          1 May  1896  –   8 July  1896
Hon. John Jones Ross   *Senator*                          1 May  1896  –   8 July  1896
Hon. Sir Frank Smith   *Senator*                          1 May  1896  –   8 July  1896


**NOT OF THE CABINET**

**Solicitor General of Canada**

Hon. Sir Charles Hibbert Tupper                           1 May  1896  –   8 July  1896

4    The Secretary of State was *ex officio* the Registrar General of Canada.

# Eighth Ministry

**LIBERAL** 1

11 July 1896 to 6 October 1911

**PRIME MINISTER**

The Right Honourable Sir Wilfrid Laurier  2

**THE MINISTRY**

**Minister of Agriculture**

| | | |
|---|---|---|
| Hon. Sydney Arthur Fisher | 13 July  1896 – | 6 Oct.  1911 |

**Minister of Customs**  3

| | | |
|---|---|---|
| Hon. William Paterson | 30 June 1897 – | 6 Oct.  1911 |

**Minister of Finance and Receiver General**

| | | |
|---|---|---|
| Vacant | 13 July  1896 – | 19 July  1896 |
| Hon. William Stevens Fielding | 20 July  1896 – | 6 Oct.  1911 |

**Superintendent-General of Indian Affairs**  4

| | | |
|---|---|---|
| Vacant | 13 July  1896 – | 16 July  1896 |
| Hon. Richard William Scott  *Senator – Acting Minister* | 17 July  1896 – | 16 Nov.  1896 |
| Hon. Clifford Sifton | 17 Nov.  1896 – | 28 Feb.  1905 |
| Vacant | 29 Feb.  1905 – | 12 Mar.  1905 |
| Rt. Hon. Sir Wilfrid Laurier  *Acting Minister* | 13 Mar.  1905 – | 7 Apr.  1905 |
| Hon. Frank Oliver | 8 Apr.  1905 – | 6 Oct.  1911 |

**Minister of Inland Revenue**

| | | |
|---|---|---|
| Hon. Sir Henri Gustave Joly de Lotbinière | 30 June 1897 – | 21 June 1900 |
| Hon. Michel Esdras Bernier | 22 June 1900 – | 18 Jan.  1904 |
| Hon. Louis-Philippe Brodeur  5 | 19 Jan.  1904 – | 5 Feb.  1906 |
| Hon. William Templeman | 6 Feb.  1906 – | 6 Oct.  1911 |

1    With the defeat of the Government in the general election of 23 June 1896, Tupper resigned from office on 8 July 1896. The next day the Governor General invited Laurier to reform a Government. On 11 July Laurier, acting alone as the Committee of the Privy Council, advised his own appointment as President of the Privy Council and on 13 July the remainder of the Cabinet was appointed to office.

2    Laurier was also President of the Privy Council.

3    Statute 60-61 Vict., c. 18, assented to on 29 June 1897, revived the offices of Minister of Customs and Minister of Inland Revenue, See Controller of Customs and Controller of Inland Revenue.

4    See Note 6.

5    Brodeur was appointed Minister of Marine and Fisheries on 6 Feb. 1906.

## Minister of the Interior  6

| | | |
|---|---|---|
| Vacant | 13 July 1896 – | 16 July 1896 |
| Hon. Richard William Scott  *Senator – Acting Minister* | 17 July 1896 – | 16 Nov. 1896 |
| Hon. Clifford Sifton | 17 Nov. 1896 – | 28 Feb. 1905 |
| Vacant | 29 Feb. 1905 – | 12 Mar. 1905 |
| Rt. Hon. Sir Wilfrid Laurier  *Acting Minister* | 13 Mar. 1905 – | 7 Apr. 1905 |
| Hon. Frank Oliver | 8 Apr. 1905 – | 6 Oct. 1911 |

## Minister of Justice and Attorney General

| | | |
|---|---|---|
| Hon. Sir Oliver Mowat  *Senator* | 13 July 1896 – | 17 Nov. 1897 |
| Hon. David Mills  *Senator* | 18 Nov. 1897 – | 7 Feb. 1902 |
| Vacant | 8 Feb. 1902 – | 10 Feb. 1902 |
| Hon. Charles Fitzpatrick | 11 Feb. 1902 – | 3 June 1906 |
| Hon. Sir Allen Bristol Aylesworth | 4 June 1906 – | 6 Oct. 1911 |

## Minister of Labour  7

| | | |
|---|---|---|
| Vacant | 19 May 1909 – | 1 June 1909 |
| Hon. William Lyon Mackenzie King | 2 June 1909 – | 6 Oct. 1911 |

## Minister of Marine and Fisheries

| | | |
|---|---|---|
| Hon. Sir Louis Henry Davies | 13 July 1896 – | 24 Sept. 1901 |
| Vacant | 25 Sept. 1901 – | 14 Jan. 1902 |
| Hon. James Sutherland  8 | 15 Jan. 1902 – | 10 Nov. 1902 |
| Hon. Joseph Raymond Fournier Préfontaine | 11 Nov. 1902 – | 25 Dec. 1905 |
| Vacant | 26 Dec. 1905 – | 5 Jan. 1906 |
| Rt. Hon. Sir Wilfrid Laurier  *Acting Minister* | 6 Jan. 1906 – | 5 Feb. 1906 |
| Hon. Louis-Philippe Brodeur | 6 Feb. 1906 – | 10 Aug. 1911 |
| Hon. Rodolphe Lemieux | 11 Aug. 1911 – | 6 Oct. 1911 |

## Minister of Militia and Defence

| | | |
|---|---|---|
| Hon. Sir Frederick William Borden | 13 July 1896 – | 6 Oct. 1911 |

## Minister of Mines  9

| | | |
|---|---|---|
| Vacant | 27 Apr. 1907 – | 2 May 1907 |
| Hon. William Templeman | 3 May 1907 – | 6 Oct. 1911 |

## Minister of the Naval Service  10

| | | |
|---|---|---|
| Hon. Louis-Philippe Brodeur | 4 May 1910 – | 10 Aug. 1911 |
| Hon. Rodolphe Lemieux | 11 Aug. 1911 – | 6 Oct. 1911 |

6    The Minister of the Interior was *ex officio* the Superintendent-General of Indian Affairs.

7    The Department of Labour was established pursuant to the Conciliation Act, 1900 (Statute 63-64 Vict., c. 24, assented to on 18 July 1900). The department was under the control of the minister designated by the Governor in Council to administer the aforesaid Act. Mulock, Aylesworth and Lemieux, who were successively Postmasters General, were so designated during their terms in that portfolio. The office of Minister of Labour was created by Statute 8-9 Edw. VII, c. 22, and assented to on 19 May 1909.

8    Sutherland was appointed Minister of Public Works on 11 Nov. 1902.

9    The Department of Mines was created by Statute 6-7 Edw. VII, c. 29, and assented to on 27 Apr. 1907. The department was to be presided over by the minister of another department who was to be named by the Governor in Council and who was to be called "The Minister of Mines". The Minister of Inland Revenue was the first to be named Minister of Mines.

10   The Department of the Naval Service was created by Statute 9-10 Edw. VII, c. 43, was assented to on 4 May 1910, and was to be presided over by the Minister of Marine and Fisheries, who was to be the Minister of the Naval Service.

## Postmaster General

| | |
|---|---|
| Hon. Sir William Mulock | 13 July 1896 – 15 Oct. 1905 |
| Hon. Allen Bristol Aylesworth  11 | 16 Oct. 1905 – 3 June 1906 |
| Hon. Rodolphe Lemieux  12 | 4 June 1906 – 10 Aug. 1911 |
| Vacant | 11 Aug. 1911 – 18 Aug. 1911 |
| Hon. Henri Sévérin Béland | 19 Aug. 1911 – 6 Oct. 1911 |

## President of the Privy Council

| | |
|---|---|
| Rt. Hon. Sir Wilfrid Laurier | 11 July 1896 – 6 Oct. 1911 |

## Minister of Public Works

| | |
|---|---|
| Hon. Joseph Israël Tarte | 13 July 1896 – 21 Oct. 1902 |
| Vacant | 22 Oct. 1902 – 10 Nov. 1902 |
| Hon. James Sutherland | 11 Nov. 1902 – 3 May 1905 |
| Vacant | 4 May 1905 – 21 May 1905 |
| Hon. Charles Smith Hyman | 22 May 1905 – 29 Aug. 1907 |
| Hon. William Pugsley | 30 Aug. 1907 – 6 Oct. 1911 |

## Minister of Railways and Canals

| | |
|---|---|
| Vacant | 13 July 1896 – 19 July 1896 |
| Hon. Andrew George Blair | 20 July 1896 – 20 July 1903 |
| Hon. William Stevens Fielding  *Acting Minister* | 21 July 1903 – 14 Jan. 1904 |
| Hon. Henry Robert Emmerson | 15 Jan. 1904 – 2 Apr. 1907 |
| Vacant | 3 Apr. 1907 – 8 Apr. 1907 |
| Hon. William Stevens Fielding  *Acting Minister* | 9 Apr. 1907 – 29 Aug. 1907 |
| Hon. George Perry Graham | 30 Aug. 1907 – 6 Oct. 1911 |

## Secretary of State of Canada  13

| | |
|---|---|
| Hon. Richard William Scott  14  *Senator* | 13 July 1896 – 8 Oct. 1908 |
| Hon. Charles Murphy | 9 Oct. 1908 – 6 Oct. 1911 |

## Minister of Trade and Commerce

| | |
|---|---|
| Rt. Hon. Sir Richard John Cartwright  *Senator* | 13 July 1896 – 6 Oct. 1911 |

11 Aylesworth was appointed Minister of Justice and Attorney General on 4 June 1906.

12 Lemieux was appointed Minister of Marine and Fisheries on 11 Aug. 1911.

13 The Department of External Affairs was created by Statute 8-9 Edw. VII, c. 13, assented to on 19 May 1909, proclaimed in force on 1 June 1909, and was to be presided over by the Secretary of State of Canada, who was also *ex officio* the Registrar General of Canada.

14 Scott resigned on 16 Sept. 1908, but on the Prime Minister's request continued to administer the department until his successor took charge.

**Minister without Portfolio**

| | |
|---|---|
| Hon. Richard Reid Dobell | 13 July 1896 – 11 Jan. 1902 |
| Hon. Christophe Alphonse Geoffrion | 21 Aug. 1896 – 18 July 1899 |
| Hon. James Sutherland  15 | 30 Sept. 1899 – 14 Jan. 1902 |
| Hon. William Templeman  16  *Senator* | 25 Feb. 1902 – 5 Feb. 1906 |
| Hon. Charles Smith Hyman  17 | 5 Feb. 1904 – 21 May 1905 |

**NOT OF THE CABINET**

**Controller of Customs**

| | |
|---|---|
| Hon. William Paterson  18 | 13 July 1896 – 29 June 1897 |

**Controller of Inland Revenue**

| | |
|---|---|
| Hon. Sir Henri Gustave Joly de Lotbinière  19 | 13 July 1896 – 29 June 1897 |

**Solicitor General of Canada**

| | |
|---|---|
| Hon. Charles Fitzpatrick  20 | 13 July 1896 – 9 Feb. 1902 |
| Hon. Henry George Carroll | 10 Feb. 1902 – 28 Jan. 1904 |
| Hon. Rodolphe Lemieux  21 | 29 Jan. 1904 – 3 June 1906 |
| Vacant | 4 June 1906 – 13 Feb. 1907 |
| Hon. Jacques Bureau | 14 Feb. 1907 – 6 Oct. 1911 |

15    Sutherland was appointed Minister of Marine and Fisheries on 15 Jan. 1902.

16    Templeman was appointed Minister of Inland Revenue on 6 Feb. 1906.

17    Hyman was appointed Minister of Public Works on 22 May 1905.

18    Paterson was appointed Minister of Customs on 30 June 1897.

19    Joly de Lotbinière was appointed Minister of Inland Revenue on 29 June 1897.

20    Fitzpatrick was appointed Minister of Justice and Attorney General on 11 Feb. 1902.

21    Lemieux was appointed Postmaster General on 4 June 1906.

# Ninth Ministry

**CONSERVATIVE** 1

10 October 1911 to 12 October 1917

**PRIME MINISTER**

The Right Honourable Sir Robert Laird Borden   2

**THE MINISTRY**

**Minister of Agriculture**

| | | |
|---|---|---|
| Vacant | 10 Oct. 1911 – | 15 Oct. 1911 |
| Hon. Martin Burrell | 16 Oct. 1911 – | 12 Oct. 1917 |

**Minister of Customs**

| | | |
|---|---|---|
| Hon. John Dowsley Reid | 10 Oct. 1911 – | 12 Oct. 1917 |

**Secretary of State for External Affairs**   3

| | | |
|---|---|---|
| Rt. Hon. Sir Robert Laird Borden | 1 Apr. 1912 – | 12 Oct. 1917 |

**Minister of Finance and Receiver General**

| | | |
|---|---|---|
| Hon. Sir William Thomas White | 10 Oct. 1911 – | 12 Oct. 1917 |

**Superintendent-General of Indian Affairs**   4

| | | |
|---|---|---|
| Hon. Robert Rogers | 10 Oct. 1911 – | 28 Oct. 1912 |
| Hon. William James Roche | 29 Oct. 1912 – | 12 Oct. 1917 |

**Minister of Inland Revenue**

| | | |
|---|---|---|
| Hon. Wilfrid Bruno Nantel | 10 Oct. 1911 – | 19 Oct. 1914 |
| Hon. Pierre-Édouard Blondin   5 | 20 Oct. 1914 – | 5 Oct. 1915 |
| Hon. Esioff-Léon Patenaude   6 | 6 Oct. 1915 – | 7 Jan. 1917 |
| Hon. Albert Sévigny | 8 Jan. 1917 – | 12 Oct. 1917 |

**Minister of the Interior**   7

| | | |
|---|---|---|
| Hon. Robert Rogers   8 | 10 Oct. 1911 – | 28 Oct. 1912 |
| Hon. William James Roche   9 | 9 Oct. 1912 – | 12 Oct. 1917 |

**Minister of Justice and Attorney General**

| | | |
|---|---|---|
| Hon. Charles Joseph Doherty | 10 Oct. 1911 – | 12 Oct. 1917 |

1    Defeated in the general election of 21 Sept. 1911, Laurier resigned on 6 Oct. 1911. The following day the Governor General requested Borden to form a Government and three days later, on 10 Oct., the Ninth Ministry assumed office.

2    Borden was also President of the Privy Council.

3    Prior to 1 April 1912, the Secretary of State of Canada presided over the Department of External Affairs. The office of Secretary of State for External Affairs was created by Statute 2 Geo. V, c. 22, and assented to on 1 April 1912. By this Act the Prime Minister was to hold the office *ex officio*.

4    See Minister of the Interior.

5    Blondin was appointed Secretary of State of Canada on 6 Oct. 1915.

6    Patenaude was appointed Secretary of State of Canada on 8 Jan. 1917.

7    The Minister of the Interior was *ex officio* the Superintendent-General of Indian Affairs. See Minister of Mines.

8    Rogers was appointed Minister of Public Works on 29 Oct. 1912.

9    Roche was also Minister of Mines and Secretary of State.

## Minister of Labour

| | | |
|---|---|---|
| Hon. Thomas Wilson Crothers | 10 Oct. 1911 | 12 Oct. 1917 |

## Minister of Marine and Fisheries   10

| | | |
|---|---|---|
| Hon. John Douglas Hazen | 10 Oct. 1911 | 12 Oct. 1917 |

## Minister of Militia and Defence

| | | |
|---|---|---|
| Hon. Sir Samuel Hughes | 10 Oct. 1911 | 12 Oct. 1916 |
| Vacant | 13 Oct. 1916 | 22 Nov. 1916 |
| Hon. Sir Albert Edward Kemp | 23 Nov. 1916 | 12 Oct. 1917 |

## Minister of Mines   11

| | | |
|---|---|---|
| Hon. Wilfrid Bruno Nantel | 10 Oct. 1911 | 29 Mar. 1912 |
| Hon. Robert Rogers | 30 Mar. 1912 | 28 Oct. 1912 |
| Hon. William James Roche | 29 Oct. 1912 | 9 Feb. 1913 |
| Hon. Louis Coderre | 10 Feb. 1913 | 5 Oct. 1915 |
| Hon. Pierre-Édouard Blondin | 6 Oct. 1915 | 7 Jan. 1917 |
| Hon. Esioff-Léon Patenaude | 8 Jan. 1917 | 12 June 1917 |
| Hon. Albert Sévigny   *Acting Minister* | 13 June 1917 | 24 Aug. 1917 |
| Hon. Arthur Meighen | 25 Aug. 1917 | 12 Oct. 1917 |

## Minister of the Naval Service   12

| | | |
|---|---|---|
| Hon. John Douglas Hazen | 10 Oct. 1911 | 12 Oct. 1917 |

## Minister of the Overseas Military Forces   13

| | | |
|---|---|---|
| Hon. Sir George Halsey Perley | 31 Oct. 1916 | 12 Oct. 1917 |

## Postmaster General

| | | |
|---|---|---|
| Hon. Louis-Philippe Pelletier | 10 Oct. 1911 | 19 Oct. 1914 |
| Hon. Thomas Chase Casgrain | 20 Oct. 1914 | 29 Dec. 1916 |
| Vacant | 30 Dec. 1916 | 7 Jan. 1917 |
| Hon. Pierre-Édouard Blondin | 8 Jan. 1917 | 12 Oct. 1917 |

## President of the Privy Council

| | | |
|---|---|---|
| Rt. Hon. Sir Robert Laird Borden | 10 Oct. 1911 | 12 Oct. 1917 |

10    The Minister of Marine and Fisheries was *ex officio* the Minister of the Naval Service.

11    The Department of Mines was presided over by the minister of another department who was to be named by the Governor in Council and who was to be called "The Minister of Mines". The Minister of Inland Revenue, the Minister of the Interior and the Secretary of State of Canada were designated to be *ex officio* the Minister of Mines on 10 Oct. 1911, 30 Mar. 1912 and 10 Feb. 1913 respectively.

12    See Minister of Marine and Fisheries.

13    The office of Minister of the Overseas Military Forces was created by Order in Council dated 31 Oct. 1916, pursuant to the War Measures Act. The minister was to reside in London, administer the affairs of Canadian military forces in the United Kingdom and Europe, and submit recommendations to the Governor in Council through the President of the Privy Council. Statutory provision for this office and those of Parliamentary Under Secretary of State for External Affairs and Parliamentary Secretary of Militia and Defence was made by Statute 7-8 Geo. V, c. 35, and assented to on 20 Sept. 1917. This Statute also provided for its own termination at the end of the parliamentary session in which the war, which had been declared on 4 Aug. 1914, ended.

## Minister of Public Works

| | |
|---|---|
| Hon. Frederick Debartzch Monk | 10 Oct. 1911 — 28 Oct. 1912 |
| Hon. Robert Rogers | 29 Oct. 1912 — 22 Aug. 1917 |
| Vacant | 23 Aug. 1917 — 2 Oct. 1917 |
| Hon. Charles Colquhoun Ballantyne | 3 Oct. 1917 — 12 Oct. 1917 |

## Minister of Railways and Canals

| | |
|---|---|
| Hon. Francis Cochrane | 10 Oct. 1911 — 12 Oct. 1917 |

## Secretary of State of Canada  14

| | |
|---|---|
| Hon. William James Roche  15 | 10 Oct. 1911 — 28 Oct. 1912 |
| Hon. Louis Coderre | 29 Oct. 1912 — 5 Oct. 1915 |
| Hon. Pierre Édouard Blondin  16 | 6 Oct. 1915 — 7 Jan. 1917 |
| Hon. Esioff Léon Patenaude | 8 Jan. 1917 — 12 June 1917 |
| Hon. Albert Sévigny  *Acting Minister* | 13 June 1917 — 24 Aug. 1917 |
| Hon. Arthur Meighen | 25 Aug. 1917 — 12 Oct. 1917 |

## Solicitor General of Canada  17

| | |
|---|---|
| Hon. Arthur Meighen  18 | 2 Oct. 1915 — 24 Aug. 1917 |
| Vacant | 25 Aug. 1917 — 30 Aug. 1917 |
| Hon. Arthur Meighen  *Acting Minister* | 31 Aug. 1917 — 3 Oct. 1917 |

## Minister of Trade and Commerce

| | |
|---|---|
| Rt. Hon. Sir George Eulas Foster | 10 Oct. 1911 — 12 Oct. 1917 |

## Minister without Portfolio

| | |
|---|---|
| Hon. Sir George Halsey Perley  19 | 10 Oct. 1911 — 30 Oct. 1916 |
| Hon. Albert Edward Kemp  20 | 10 Oct. 1911 — 22 Nov. 1916 |
| Hon. Sir James Alexander Lougheed  *Senator* | 10 Oct. 1911 — 12 Oct. 1917 |

## NOT OF THE CABINET

## Parliamentary Under Secretary of State for External Affairs  21

| | |
|---|---|
| Vacant | 15 July 1916 — 20 Oct. 1916 |
| Hugh Clark | 21 Oct. 1916 — 12 Oct. 1917 |

14    The Secretary of State of Canada was *ex officio* the Registrar General of Canada and until 1 April 1912 also presided *ex officio* over the Department of External Affairs. See Minister of Mines.

15    Roche was appointed Minister of the Interior on 29 Oct. 1912.

16    Blondin was appointed Postmaster General on 8 Jan. 1917.

17    See also NOT OF THE CABINET, Solicitor General of Canada.

18    Meighen was appointed Secretary of State of Canada on 25 Aug. 1917.

19    From 4 Aug. 1914 to 12 Oct. 1917 Perley exercised the functions of High Commissioner in London although he was not officially appointed to that office. He was appointed Minister of the Overseas Military Forces on 31 Oct. 1916.

20    Kemp was appointed Minister of Militia and Defence on 23 Nov. 1916.

21    The offices of Parliamentary Under Secretary of State for External Affairs and Parliamentary Secretary of Militia and Defence were created by Orders in Council dated 15 July 1916.

**Parliamentary Secretary of Militia and Defence**

| | |
|---|---|
| Vacant | 15 July 1916 – 18 July 1916 |
| Fleming Blanchard McCurdy | 19 July 1916 – 12 Oct. 1917 |

**Solicitor General of Canada**  22

| | |
|---|---|
| Vacant | 10 Oct. 1911 – 25 June 1913 |
| Hon. Arthur Meighen | 26 June 1913 – 1 Oct. 1915 |
| Hon. Hugh Guthrie | 4 Oct. 1917 – 12 Oct. 1917 |

22   See also THE MINISTRY, Solicitor General of Canada.

# Tenth Ministry

## UNIONIST  1

12 October 1917 to 10 July 1920

## PRIME MINISTER

The Right Honourable Sir Robert Laird Borden

## THE MINISTRY

### Minister of Agriculture

| | |
|---|---|
| Hon. Thomas Alexander Crerar  *L* | 12 Oct.  1917 — 11 June 1919 |
| Vacant | 12 June 1919 — 17 June 1919 |
| Hon. James Alexander Calder  *L  Acting Minister* | 18 June 1919 — 11 Aug.  1919 |
| Hon. Simon Fraser Tolmie  *C* | 12 Aug.  1919 — 10 July  1920 |

### Minister of Customs  2

| | |
|---|---|
| Hon. Arthur Lewis Sifton  3  *L* | 12 Oct.  1917 — 17 May  1918 |

### Minister of Customs and Inland Revenue  4

| | |
|---|---|
| Hon. Arthur Lewis Sifton  5  *L* | 18 May  1918 —  1 Sept. 1919 |
| Hon. John Dowsley Reid  *C  Acting Minister* | 2 Sept. 1919 — 30 Dec.  1919 |
| Hon. Martin Burrell  *C* | 31 Dec.  1919 —  7 July  1920 |
| Vacant | 8 July  1920 — 10 July  1920 |

### Secretary of State for External Affairs  6

| | |
|---|---|
| Rt. Hon. Sir Robert Laird Borden  *C* | 12 Oct.  1917 — 10 July  1920 |

### Minister of Finance and Receiver General

| | |
|---|---|
| Hon. Sir William Thomas White  *C* | 12 Oct.  1917 —  1 Aug.  1919 |
| Hon. Sir Henry Lumley Drayton  *C* | 2 Aug.  1919 — 10 July  1920 |

### Minister of Immigration and Colonization  7

| | |
|---|---|
| Hon. James Alexander Calder  *L* | 12 Oct.  1917 — 10 July  1920 |

### Superintendent-General of Indian Affairs  8

| | |
|---|---|
| Hon. Arthur Meighen  *C* | 12 Oct.  1917 — 10 July  1920 |

1   The Tenth Ministry was in effect a re-organization of the Ninth with the addition of a number of Liberal and Labour Ministers. In addition to Borden, it was composed of 15 Conservatives, 9 Liberals and 1 Labour.

2   See Minister of Customs and Inland Revenue.

3   Sifton was also Minister of Inland Revenue. He was appointed Minister of Customs and Inland Revenue on 18 May 1918.

4   The Department of Customs and the Department of Inland Revenue amalgamated and combined under the name of the Department of Customs and Inland Revenue and the office of Minister of Customs and Inland Revenue was created by Order in Council dated 18 May 1918, pursuant to the Public Service Rearrangement and Transfer of Duties Act. Statutory provision was not made for the office.

5   Sifton was appointed Minister of Public Works on 3 Sept. 1919.

6   The Prime Minister was *ex officio* the Secretary of State for External Affairs.

7   The office of Minister of Immigration and Colonization was created effective 12 Oct. 1917 by Order in Council dated 29 Oct. 1917, pursuant to the War Measures Act. Statutory provision for the office was made by Statute 8-9 Geo. V, c. 3, and assented to on 12 Apr. 1918.

8   See Note 11.

**Minister of Inland Revenue** 9

| | | |
|---|---|---|
| Hon. Albert Sévigny *C* | 12 Oct. 1917 – | 1 Apr. 1918 |
| Vacant | 2 Apr. 1918 – | 13 May 1918 |
| Hon. Arthur Lewis Sifton 10 *L* | 14 May 1918 – | 17 May 1918 |

**Minister of the Interior** 11

Hon. Arthur Meighen *C*    12 Oct. 1917 – 10 July 1920

**Minister of Justice and Attorney General**

Hon. Charles Joseph Doherty *C*    12 Oct. 1917 – 10 July 1920

**Minister of Labour**

| | | |
|---|---|---|
| Hon. Thomas Wilson Crothers *C* | 12 Oct. 1917 – | 6 Nov. 1918 |
| Vacant | 7 Nov. 1918 | |
| Hon. Gideon Decker Robertson *Lab. Senator* | 8 Nov. 1918 – | 10 July 1920 |

**Minister of Marine and Fisheries** 12

| | | |
|---|---|---|
| Vacant 13 | 12 Oct. 1917 | |
| Hon. Charles Colquhoun Ballantyne *L* | 13 Oct. 1917 – | 10 July 1920 |

**Minister of Militia and Defence**

| | | |
|---|---|---|
| Hon. Sydney Chilton Mewburn *L* | 12 Oct. 1917 – | 15 Jan. 1920 |
| Hon. James Alexander Calder *L  Acting Minister* | 16 Jan. 1920 – | 23 Jan. 1920 |
| Hon. Hugh Guthrie *L* | 24 Jan. 1920 – | 10 July 1920 |

**Minister of Mines** 14

| | | |
|---|---|---|
| Hon. Martin Burrell *C* | 12 Oct. 1917 – | 30 Dec. 1919 |
| Hon. Arthur Meighen *C* | 31 Dec. 1919 – | 10 July 1920 |

**Minister of the Naval Service** 15

| | | |
|---|---|---|
| Vacant | 12 Oct. 1917 | |
| Hon. Charles Colquhoun Ballantyne *L* | 13 Oct. 1917 – | 10 July 1920 |

**Minister of the Overseas Military Forces** 16

Hon. Sir Albert Edward Kemp *C*    12 Oct. 1917 – 1 July 1920

**Postmaster General**

Hon. Pierre-Édouard Blondin *C  Senator*    12 Oct. 1917 – 10 July 1920

9       See Minister of Customs and Inland Revenue.

10      Sifton was also Minister of Customs. He was appointed Minister of Customs and Inland Revenue on 18 May 1918.

11      The Minister of the Interior was *ex officio* the Superintendent-General of Indian Affairs.

12      The Minister of Marine and Fisheries was *ex officio* the Minister of the Naval Service.

13      Hazen, Minister of Marine and Fisheries in the Ninth Ministry, resigned from office on 13 Oct. 1917. Since he could not be considered a member of the Tenth Ministry, the office is shown vacant for 12 Oct.

14      The Department of Mines was presided over by the minister of another department who was to be named by the Governor in Council and who was to be called "The Minister of Mines". Until 31 Dec. 1919 the Secretary of State of Canada was *ex officio* the Minister of Mines, at which time the Minister of the Interior was named Minister of Mines.

15      The Minister of the Naval Service was also the Minister of Marine and Fisheries.

16      Statute 7-8 Geo. V, c. 35, assented to on 20 Sept. 1917, provided for the termination of the offices of Minister of the Overseas Military Forces, Parliamentary Under Secretary of State for External Affairs and Parliamentary Secretary of Militia and Defence at the end of the session of Parliament in which the war, which had been declared on 4 Aug. 1914, ended. An Imperial Order in Council declared the war terminated as of 31 August 1921. However, on 20 Dec. 1919 the Governor in Council had approved an Order in Council which recognized that the war had in effect ceased to exist and provided for the repeal of all Orders in Council passed pursuant to the War Measures Act by the end of the next session of Parliament. That session of Parliament terminated on 1 July 1920, and as of that date the Government considered the Act creating these offices to be spent.

**President of the Privy Council** 17

| | |
|---|---|
| Hon. Newton Wesley Rowell  *L* | 12 Oct.  1917  –  10 July  1920 |

**Minister of Public Works**

| | |
|---|---|
| Hon. Charles Colquhoun Ballantyne  18  *L* | 12 Oct.  1917 |
| Hon. Frank Broadstreet Carvell · *L* | 13 Oct.  1917  –   1 Aug.  1919 |
| Vacant | 2 Aug.  1919  –   5 Aug.  1919 |
| Hon. John Dowsley Reid  *C  Acting Minister* | 6 Aug.  1919  –   2 Sept. 1919 |
| Hon. Arthur Lewis Sifton  19  *L* | 3 Sept. 1919  –  30 Dec.  1919 |
| Hon. John Dowsley Reid  *C  Acting Minister* | 31 Dec.  1919  –  10 July  1920 |

**Minister of Railways and Canals**

| | |
|---|---|
| Hon. John Dowsley Reid  *C* | 12 Oct.  1917  –  10 July  1920 |

**Secretary of State of Canada**  20

| | |
|---|---|
| Hon. Martin Burrell  21  *C* | 12 Oct.  1917  –  30 Dec.  1919 |
| Rt. Hon. Arthur Lewis Sifton  *L* | 31 Dec.  1919  –  10 July  1920 |

**Minister of Soldiers' Civil Re-establishment**  22

| | |
|---|---|
| Hon. Sir James Alexander Lougheed  *C  Senator* | 21 Feb.  1918  –  10 July  1920 |

**Solicitor General of Canada**  23

| | |
|---|---|
| Hon. Hugh Guthrie  24  *L* | 5 July  1919  –  23 Jan.  1920 |
| Hon. Hugh Guthrie  *L* | 24 Jan.  1920  –  10 July  1920 |

**Minister of Trade and Commerce**

| | |
|---|---|
| Rt. Hon. Sir George Eulas Foster  *C* | 12 Oct.  1917  –  10 July  1920 |

**Minister without Portfolio**

| | |
|---|---|
| Hon. Francis Cochrane  *C* | 12 Oct.  1917  –  22 Sept. 1919 |
| Hon. Sir James Alexander Lougheed  25  *C  Senator* | 12 Oct.  1917  –  20 Feb.  1918 |
| Hon. Alexander Kenneth Maclean  *L* | 23 Oct.  1917  –  24 Feb.  1920 |
| Hon. Gideon Decker Robertson  26  *Lab.* | 23 Oct.  1917  –   7 Nov.  1918 |

## NOT OF THE CABINET

**Parliamentary Under Secretary of State for External Affairs**

| | |
|---|---|
| Hugh Clark  27 | 12 Oct.  1917  –   6 Nov.  1918 |
| Francis Henry Keefer | 7 Nov.  1918  –   1 July  1920 |

17     The Department of Health was created by Statute 9-10 Geo. V, c. 24, assented to on 6 June 1919, and was to be presided over by the minister of another department who was to be named by the Governor in Council. During the Tenth Ministry the President of the Privy Council was designated to be *ex officio* the minister to preside over the department.

18     Ballantyne was appointed Minister of Marine and Fisheries on 13 Oct. 1917.

19     Sifton was appointed Secretary of State of Canada on 31 Dec. 1919.

20     The Secretary of State of Canada was *ex officio* the Registrar General of Canada. See Note 14.

21     Burrell was appointed Minister of Customs and Inland Revenue on 31 Dec. 1919.

22     The office of Minister of Soldiers' Civil Re-establishment was created by Order in Council dated 21 Feb. 1918, pursuant to the War Measures Act. Statutory provision for the office was made by Statute 8-9 Geo. V, c. 42, and assented to on 24 May 1918.

23     See also NOT OF THE CABINET, Solicitor General of Canada.

24     Guthrie was appointed Minister of Militia and Defence on 24 Jan. 1920.

25     Lougheed was appointed Minister of Soldiers' Civil Re-establishment on 21 Feb. 1918.

26     Robertson was appointed Minister of Labour on 8 Nov. 1918.

27     Clark was appointed Parliamentary Secretary for Militia and Defence on 7 Nov. 1918.

**Parliamentary Secretary of Militia and Defence**

| | |
|---|---|
| Fleming Blanchard McCurdy   28 | 12 Oct.  1917  –  22 Feb.  1918 |
| Vacant | 23 Feb.  1918  –   6 Nov.  1918 |
| Hugh Clark | 7 Nov.  1918  –   1 July  1920 |

**Parliamentary Secretary of Soldiers'**
**Civil Re-establishment**   29

| | |
|---|---|
| Vacant | 21 Feb.  1918  –  22 Feb.  1918 |
| Fleming Blanchard McCurdy | 23 Feb.  1918  –   6 Nov.  1918 |
| Vacant | 7 Nov.  1918  –   1 July  1920 |

**Solicitor General of Canada**   30

| | |
|---|---|
| Hon. Hugh Guthrie   *L* | 12 Oct.  1917  –   4 July  1919 |

28    McCurdy was appointed Parliamentary Secretary of Soldiers' Civil Re-establishment on 23
      Feb. 1918.

29    The office of Parliamentary Secretary of Soldiers' Civil Re-establishment was created by
      Order in Council dated 21 Feb. 1918. The terms of appointment were similar to those for the
      two parliamentary secretary offices established during the Ninth Ministry. Statute 8-9 Geo. V,
      c. 42, assented to on 24 May 1918, made statutory provision for the office, which was
      abolished by Statute 18-19 Geo. V, c. 39, assented to on 11 June 1928.

30    See also THE MINISTRY, Solicitor General of Canada.

# Eleventh Ministry

**UNIONIST – "NATIONAL LIBERAL AND CONSERVATIVE PARTY"** 1

10 July 1920 to 29 December 1921

**PRIME MINISTER**

The Right Honourable Arthur Meighen

**THE MINISTRY**

**Minister of Agriculture**

| | |
|---|---|
| Hon. Simon Fraser Tolmie | 10 July 1920 – 29 Dec. 1921 |

**Minister of Customs and Excise** 2

| | |
|---|---|
| Hon. Rupert Wilson Wigmore | 4 June 1921 – 20 Sept. 1921 |
| Hon. John Babington Macaulay Baxter | 21 Sept. 1921 – 29 Dec. 1921 |

**Minister of Customs and Inland Revenue** 2

| | |
|---|---|
| Vacant | 10 July 1920 – 12 July 1920 |
| Hon. Rupert Wilson Wigmore 3 | 13 July 1920 – 3 June 1921 |

**Secretary of State for External Affairs** 4

| | |
|---|---|
| Rt. Hon. Arthur Meighen | 10 July 1920 – 29 Dec. 1921 |

**Minister of Finance and Receiver General**

| | |
|---|---|
| Hon. Sir Henry Lumley Drayton | 10 July 1920 – 29 Dec. 1921 |

**Minister of Immigration and Colonization** 5

| | |
|---|---|
| Hon. James Alexander Calder 6 | 10 July 1920 – 20 Sept. 1921 |
| Hon. John Wesley Edwards | 21 Sept. 1921 – 29 Dec. 1921 |

**Superintendent-General of Indian Affairs** 7

| | |
|---|---|
| Hon. Sir James Alexander Lougheed *Senator* | 10 July 1920 – 29 Dec. 1921 |

**Minister of the Interior** 7

| | |
|---|---|
| Hon. Sir James Alexander Lougheed *Senator* | 10 July 1920 – 29 Dec. 1921 |

1     On 10 July 1920 Borden resigned as Prime Minister and Meighen and most of the Eleventh Ministry were sworn to office. Initially twelve of the ministers were from the Tenth Ministry, and ten retained their previous portfolios.

2     The office of Minister of Customs and Inland Revenue was abolished and the office of Minister of Customs and Excise was created by Statute 11-12 Geo. V, c. 26, and assented to on 4 June 1921.

3     Wigmore was appointed Minister of Customs and Excise on 4 June 1921.

4     The Prime Minister was *ex officio* the Secretary of State for External Affairs.

5     The Department of Health was presided over by the minister of another department who was to be named by the Governor in Council. Until 21 Sept. 1921 the President of the Privy Council was designated to be *ex officio* the minister to preside over the department. On that date the Minister of Immigration and Colonization was designated to administer the department.

6     Calder was also President of the Privy Council.

7     The Minister of the Interior was *ex officio* the Superintendent-General of Indian Affairs.

## Minister of Justice and Attorney General

| | |
|---|---|
| Hon. Charles Joseph Doherty | 10 July 1920 – 20 Sept. 1921 |
| Vacant | 21 Sept. 1921 – 3 Oct. 1921 |
| Hon. Richard Bedford Bennett | 4 Oct. 1921 – 29 Dec. 1921 |

## Minister of Labour

| | |
|---|---|
| Hon. Gideon Decker Robertson  *Senator* | 10 July 1920 – 29 Dec. 1921 |

## Minister of Marine and Fisheries  8

| | |
|---|---|
| Hon. Charles Colquhoun Ballantyne | 10 July 1920 – 29 Dec. 1921 |

## Minister of Militia and Defence

| | |
|---|---|
| Hon. Hugh Guthrie | 10 July 1920 – 29 Dec. 1921 |

## Minister of Mines  9

| | |
|---|---|
| Hon. Sir James Alexander Lougheed  *Senator* | 10 July 1920 – 29 Dec. 1921 |

## Minister of the Naval Service  8

| | |
|---|---|
| Hon. Charles Colquhoun Ballantyne | 10 July 1920 – 29 Dec. 1921 |

## Postmaster General

| | |
|---|---|
| Hon. Pierre-Édouard Blondin  *Senator* | 10 July 1920 – 20 Sept. 1921 |
| Hon. Louis-de-Gonzague Belley | 21 Sept. 1921 – 29 Dec. 1921 |

## President of the Privy Council

| | |
|---|---|
| Hon. James Alexander Calder  10 | 10 July 1920 – 20 Sept. 1921 |
| Hon. Louis-Philippe Normand | 21 Sept. 1921 – 29 Dec. 1921 |

## Minister of Public Works

| | |
|---|---|
| Hon. John Dowsley Reid  *Acting Minister* | 10 July 1920 – 12 July 1920 |
| Hon. Fleming Blanchard McCurdy | 13 July 1920 – 29 Dec. 1921 |

## Minister of Railways and Canals

| | |
|---|---|
| Hon. John Dowsley Reid | 10 July 1920 – 20 Sept. 1921 |
| Hon. John Alexander Stewart | 21 Sept. 1921 – 29 Dec. 1921 |

8       The Minister of Marine and Fisheries was *ex officio* the Minister of the Naval Service.

9       The Department of Mines was presided over by the minister of another department, who was to be named by the Governor in Council and who was to be called "The Minister of Mines". During the Eleventh Ministry the Minister of the Interior was named Minister of Mines.

10      Calder was also Minister of Immigration and Colonization.

### Secretary of State of Canada   11

| | |
|---|---|
| Rt. Hon. Arthur Lewis Sifton | 10 July  1920  –  21 Jan.  1921 |
| Vacant | 22 Jan.  1921  –  23 Jan.  1921 |
| Hon. Sir Henry Lumley Drayton   *Acting Minister* | 24 Jan.  1921  –  20 Sept. 1921 |
| Hon. Rodolphe Monty | 21 Sept. 1921  –  29 Dec.  1921 |

### Minister of Soldiers' Civil Re-establishment

| | |
|---|---|
| Vacant | 10 July  1920  –  18 July  1920 |
| Hon. Sir James Alexander Lougheed<br>*Senator – Acting Minister* | 19 July  1920  –  21 Sept. 1921 |
| Hon. Robert James Manion | 22 Sept. 1921  –  29 Dec.  1921 |

### Solicitor General of Canada   12

| | |
|---|---|
| Hon. Hugh Guthrie   *Acting Minister* | 10 July  1920  –  30 Sept. 1921 |

### Minister of Trade and Commerce

| | |
|---|---|
| Rt. Hon. Sir George Eulas Foster | 10 July  1920  –  20 Sept. 1921 |
| Hon. Henry Herbert Stevens | 21 Sept. 1921  –  29 Dec.  1921 |

### Minister without Portfolio

| | |
|---|---|
| Hon. Sir Albert Edward Kemp   *Senator* | 13 July  1920  –  29 Dec.  1921 |
| Hon. Edgar Keith Spinney | 13 July  1920  –  29 Dec.  1921 |
| Hon. Edmund James Bristol | 21 Sept. 1921  –  29 Dec.  1921 |
| Hon. James Robert Wilson | 26 Sept. 1921  –  29 Dec.  1921 |

## NOT OF THE CABINET

### Parliamentary Secretary of Soldiers' Civil Re-establishment

| | |
|---|---|
| Vacant | 10 July  1920  –  29 Dec.  1921 |

### Solicitor General of Canada   13

| | |
|---|---|
| Hon. Guillaume André Fauteux | 1 Oct.  1921  –  29 Dec.  1921 |

11    The Secretary of State of Canada was *ex officio* the Registrar General of Canada.

12    See also NOT OF THE CABINET, Solicitor General of Canada.

13    See also THE MINISTRY, Solicitor General of Canada.

# Twelfth Ministry

**LIBERAL** 1

29 December 1921 to 28 June 1926

**PRIME MINISTER**

The Right Honourable William Lyon Mackenzie King   2

**THE MINISTRY**

**Minister of Agriculture**

| | | |
|---|---|---|
| Hon. William Richard Motherwell | 29 Dec. 1921 – | 28 June 1926 |

**Minister of Customs and Excise**

| | | |
|---|---|---|
| Hon. Jacques Bureau | 29 Dec. 1921 – | 4 Sept. 1925 |
| Hon. Georges-Henri Boivin | 5 Sept. 1925 – | 28 June 1926 |

**Secretary of State for External Affairs**   3

| | | |
|---|---|---|
| Rt. Hon. William Lyon Mackenzie King | 29 Dec. 1921 – | 28 June 1926 |

**Minister of Finance and Receiver General**

| | | |
|---|---|---|
| Rt. Hon. William Stevens Fielding | 29 Dec. 1921 – | 4 Sept. 1925 |
| Hon. James Alexander Robb | 5 Sept. 1925 – | 28 June 1926 |

**Minister of Immigration and Colonization**

| | | |
|---|---|---|
| Vacant | 29 Dec. 1921 – | 2 Jan. 1922 |
| Hon. Hewitt Bostock   *Senator – Acting Minister* | 3 Jan. 1922 – | 2 Feb. 1922 |
| Vacant | 3 Feb. 1922 – | 19 Feb. 1922 |
| Hon. Charles Stewart   *Acting Minister* | 20 Feb. 1922 – | 16 Aug. 1923 |
| Hon. James Alexander Robb   4 | 17 Aug. 1923 – | 4 Sept. 1925 |
| Vacant | 5 Sept. 1925 – | 6 Sept. 1925 |
| Hon. George Newcombe Gordon | 7 Sept. 1925 – | 12 Nov. 1925 |
| Hon. Charles Stewart   *Acting Minister* | 13 Nov. 1925 – | 28 June 1926 |

**Superintendent-General of Indian Affairs**   5

| | | |
|---|---|---|
| Hon. Charles Stewart | 29 Dec. 1921 – | 28 June 1926 |

**Minister of the Interior**   5

| | | |
|---|---|---|
| Hon. Charles Stewart | 29 Dec. 1921 – | 28 June 1926 |

1    With the defeat of the Government in the general election of 6 Dec. 1921, Meighen resigned
     from office. His resignation was accepted and the Twelfth Ministry was sworn to office on 29
     Dec. 1921. In the general election of 29 Oct. 1925 the ministry was returned to office, but King
     himself was defeated. He was re-elected to the House of Commons in a by-election on 15
     Feb. 1926.

2    King was also President of the Privy Council.

3    The Prime Minister was *ex officio* the Secretary of State for External Affairs.

4    Robb was appointed Minister of Finance and Receiver General on 5 Sept. 1925.

5    The Minister of the Interior was *ex officio* the Superintendent-General of Indian Affairs.

## Minister of Justice and Attorney General

| | |
|---|---|
| Hon. Sir Jean Lomer Gouin | 29 Dec. 1921 — 3 Jan. 1924 |
| Hon. Ernest Lapointe   *Acting Minister* | 4 Jan. 1924 — 29 Jan. 1924 |
| Hon. Ernest Lapointe   6 | 30 Jan. 1924 — 28 June 1926 |

## Minister of Labour

| | |
|---|---|
| Hon. James Murdock | 29 Dec. 1921 — 12 Nov. 1925 |
| Hon. James Horace King   *Acting Minister* | 13 Nov. 1925 — 7 Mar. 1926 |
| Hon. John Campbell Elliott   7 | 8 Mar. 1926 — 28 June 1926 |

## Minister of Marine and Fisheries

| | |
|---|---|
| Hon. Ernest Lapointe   8 | 29 Dec. 1921 — 29 Jan. 1924 |
| Hon. Pierre Joseph Arthur Cardin | 30 Jan. 1924 — 28 June 1926 |

## Minister of Militia and Defence   9

| | |
|---|---|
| Hon. George Perry Graham   10 | 29 Dec. 1921 — 31 Dec. 1922 |

## Minister of Mines   11

| | |
|---|---|
| Hon. Charles Stewart | 29 Dec. 1921 — 28 June 1926 |

## Minister of National Defence   12

| | |
|---|---|
| Hon. George Perry Graham   13 | 1 Jan. 1923 — 27 Apr. 1923 |
| Hon. Edward Mortimer Macdonald   *Acting Minister* | 28 Apr. 1923 — 16 Aug. 1923 |
| Hon. Edward Mortimer Macdonald | 17 Aug. 1923 — 28 June 1926 |

## Minister of the Naval Service   9

| | |
|---|---|
| Hon. George Perry Graham | 29 Dec. 1921 — 31 Dec. 1922 |

## Postmaster General

| | |
|---|---|
| Hon. Charles Murphy   *Senator* | 29 Dec. 1921 — 28 June 1926 |

## President of the Privy Council

| | |
|---|---|
| Rt. Hon. William Lyon Mackenzie King | 29 Dec. 1921 — 28 June 1926 |

## Minister of Public Works

| | |
|---|---|
| Hon. Hewitt Bostock   *Senator* | 29 Dec. 1921 — 2 Feb. 1922 |
| Hon. James Horace King | 3 Feb. 1922 — 28 June 1926 |

6    Lapointe was also Secretary of State of Canada.

7    Elliott was also Minister of Soldiers' Civil Re-establishment.

8    Lapointe was appointed Minister of Justice and Attorney General on 30 Jan. 1924.

9    On the formation of the Twelfth Ministry, Graham was appointed both Minister of Militia and Defence and Minister of the Naval Service. On 10 Feb. 1922, by Order in Council pursuant to the Public Service Rearrangement and Transfer of Duties Act, the powers, duties and functions of the Minister of the Naval Service were transferred from the Minister of Marine and Fisheries to the Minister of Militia and Defence. See Minister of National Defence.

10   Graham was appointed Minister of National Defence on 1 Jan. 1923.

11   The Department of Mines was presided over by the minister of another department who was to be named by the Governor in Council and who was to be called "The Minister of Mines". During the Twelfth Ministry the Minister of the Interior was named Minister of Mines.

12   The offices of Minister of Militia and Defence and Minister of the Naval Service were abolished and the office of Minister of National Defence was created by Statute 12-13 Geo. V, c. 34, assented to on 28 June 1922 and proclaimed in force on 1 Jan. 1923.

13   Graham was appointed Minister of Railways and Canals on 28 April 1923.

## Minister of Railways and Canals

| | |
|---|---|
| Hon. William Costello Kennedy | 29 Dec. 1921 – 18 Jan. 1923 |
| Vacant | 19 Jan. 1923 – 27 Apr. 1923 |
| Hon. George Perry Graham   14 | 28 Apr. 1923 – 19 Feb. 1926 |
| Vacant | 20 Feb. 1926 – 28 Feb. 1926 |
| Hon. Charles Avery Dunning | 1 Mar. 1926 – 28 June 1926 |

## Minister of Soldiers' Civil Re-establishment   15

| | |
|---|---|
| Hon. Henri Sévérin Béland   *Senator* | 29 Dec. 1921 – 14 Apr. 1926 |
| Hon. John Campbell Elliott   16 | 15 Apr. 1926 – 28 June 1926 |

## Secretary of State of Canada   17

| | |
|---|---|
| Hon. Arthur Bliss Copp | 29 Dec. 1921 – 24 Sept. 1925 |
| Vacant | 25 Sept. 1925 |
| Hon. Walter Edward Foster | 26 Sept. 1925 – 12 Nov. 1925 |
| Hon. Charles Murphy   *Senator – Acting Minister* | 13 Nov. 1925 – 23 Mar. 1926 |
| Hon. Ernest Lapointe   18 | 24 Mar. 1926 – 28 June 1926 |

## Solicitor General of Canada   19

| | |
|---|---|
| Hon. Daniel Duncan McKenzie | 29 Dec. 1921 – 10 Apr. 1923 |
| Vacant | 11 Apr. 1923 – 13 Nov. 1923 |
| Hon. Edward James McMurray | 14 Nov. 1923 – 22 May 1925 |
| Vacant | 23 May 1925 – 4 Sept. 1925 |

## Minister of Trade and Commerce

| | |
|---|---|
| Hon. James Alexander Robb   20 | 29 Dec. 1921 – 16 Aug. 1923 |
| Hon. Thomas Andrew Low | 17 Aug. 1923 – 12 Nov. 1925 |
| Hon. James Alexander Robb   *Acting Minister* | 13 Nov. 1925 – 28 June 1926 |

## Minister without Portfolio

| | |
|---|---|
| Hon. Raoul Dandurand   *Senator* | 29 Dec. 1921 – 28 June 1926 |
| Hon. Thomas Andrew Low   21 | 29 Dec. 1921 – 16 Aug. 1923 |
| Hon. John Ewen Sinclair | 30 Dec. 1921 – 29 Oct. 1925 |
| Hon. Edward Mortimer Macdonald   22 | 12 Apr. 1923 – 16 Aug. 1923 |
| Hon. Harold Buchanan McGiverin | 20 Sept. 1924 – 29 Oct. 1925 |
| Hon. Herbert Meredith Marler | 9 Sept. 1925 – 6 Jan. 1926 |
| Hon. Charles Vincent Massey | 16 Sept. 1925 – 12 Nov. 1925 |
| Hon. George Perry Graham | 20 Feb. 1926 – 6 Apr. 1926 |

14    Graham was appointed Minister without Porfolio on 20 Feb. 1926.

15    The Department of Health was presided over by the minister of another department who was to be named by the Governor in Council. During the Twelfth Ministry each successive Minister of Soldiers' Civil Re-establishment was designated to preside over the department.

16    Elliott was also Minister of Labour.

17    The Secretary of State of Canada was *ex officio* the Registrar General of Canada.

18    Lapointe was also Minister of Justice and Attorney General.

19    See also NOT OF THE CABINET, Solicitor General of Canada.

20    Robb was appointed Minister of Immigration and Colonization on 17 Aug. 1923.

21    Low was appointed Minister of Trade and Commerce on 17 Aug. 1923.

22    Macdonald was appointed Minister of National Defence on 17 Aug. 1923.

## NOT OF THE CABINET

**Parliamentary Secretary of Soldiers' Civil Re-establishment**

Vacant                                              29 Dec. 1921 — 28 June 1926

**Solicitor General of Canada** 23

Hon. Lucien Cannon                                  5 Sept. 1925 — 28 June 1926

## NOT OF THE MINISTRY

**Parliamentary Under Secretary of State
for External Affairs** 24

Lucien-Turcotte Pacaud                              29 Dec. 1921 — 26 Oct. 1922

23    See also THE MINISTRY, Solicitor General of Canada.

24    In an effort to develop a system whereby ministers would adopt the practice of having parliamentary secretaries, King appointed Lucien-Turcotte Pacaud, M.P., Parliamentary Under Secretary of State for External Affairs. The appointment was an informal one and no provision was made in Parliament for payment for services.

# Thirteenth Ministry

**CONSERVATIVE**  1

29 June 1926 to 25 September 1926

**PRIME MINISTER**

The Right Honourable Arthur Meighen  2

**THE MINISTRY**

**Minister of Agriculture**

| | |
|---|---|
| Hon. Henry Herbert Stevens  *Acting Minister* | 29 June 1926  –  12 July  1926 |
| Hon. Simon Fraser Tolmie | 13 July  1926  –  25 Sept. 1926 |

**Minister of Customs and Excise**

| | |
|---|---|
| Hon. Henry Herbert Stevens  *Acting Minister* | 29 June 1926  –  12 July  1926 |
| Hon. Henry Herbert Stevens | 13 July  1926  –  25 Sept. 1926 |

**Secretary of State for External Affairs**  3

| | |
|---|---|
| Rt. Hon. Arthur Meighen | 29 June 1926  –  25 Sept. 1926 |

**Minister of Finance and Receiver General**

| | |
|---|---|
| Hon. Sir Henry Lumley Drayton  *Acting Minister* | 29 June 1926  –  12 July  1926 |
| Hon. Richard Bedford Bennett | 13 July  1926  –  25 Sept. 1926 |

**Minister of Immigration and Colonization**

| | |
|---|---|
| Hon. Robert James Manion  *Acting Minister* | 29 June 1926  –  12 July  1926 |
| Hon. Sir Henry Lumley Drayton  *Acting Minister* | 13 July  1926  –  25 Sept. 1926 |

**Superintendent-General of Indian Affairs**  4

| | |
|---|---|
| Hon. Henry Herbert Stevens  *Acting Minister* | 29 June 1926  –  12 July  1926 |
| Hon. Richard Bedford Bennett  *Acting Minister* | 13 July  1926  –  25 Sept. 1926 |

**Minister of the Interior**  4

| | |
|---|---|
| Hon. Henry Herbert Stevens  *Acting Minister* | 29 June 1926  –  12 July  1926 |
| Hon. Richard Bedford Bennett  *Acting Minister* | 13 July  1926  –  25 Sept. 1926 |

**Minister of Justice and Attorney General**

| | |
|---|---|
| Hon. Hugh Guthrie  *Acting Minister* | 29 June 1926  –  12 July  1926 |
| Hon. Esioff-Léon Patenaude | 13 July  1926  –  25 Sept. 1926 |

1    On 28 June 1926, with the refusal of the Governor General to accept the Prime Minister's recommendation for the dissolution of Parliament, King informed the House of Commons that the Government had resigned. The Governor General invited Meighen, the Leader of the Opposition, to form a Government, and on 29 June a statement was made in the House of Commons announcing the appointment of a "temporary ministry composed of seven ministers" of which all but Meighen were Acting Ministers of departments. In accordance with Canadian customs and precedent the six Acting Ministers of departments were not sworn to office, but for all intents and purposes they could exercise the full powers of ministers. The Government was defeated in the House on 1 July and the next day Meighen asked for and was granted a dissolution. On 13 July the composition of the re-organized ministry was announced, the ministers having been appointed and sworn that day in the usual manner.

2    Meighen was also President of the Privy Council.

3    The Prime Minister was *ex officio* the Secretary of State for External Affairs.

4    The Minister of the Interior was *ex officio* the Superintendent-General of Indian Affairs.

## Minister of Labour

| | |
|---|---|
| Hon. Robert James Manion   *Acting Minister* | 29 June 1926  –  12 July  1926 |
| Hon. George Burpee Jones | 13 July  1926  –  25 Sept. 1926 |

## Minister of Marine and Fisheries

| | |
|---|---|
| Hon. William Anderson Black   *Acting Minister* | 29 June 1926  –  12 July  1926 |
| Hon. Esioff-Léon Patenaude   *Acting Minister* | 13 July  1926  –  25 Sept. 1926 |

## Minister of Mines   5

| | |
|---|---|
| Hon. Henry Herbert Stevens   *Acting Minister* | 29 June 1926  –  12 July  1926 |
| Hon. Richard Bedford Bennett   *Acting Minister* | 13 July  1926  –  25 Sept. 1926 |

## Minister of National Defence

| | |
|---|---|
| Hon. Hugh Guthrie   *Acting Minister* | 29 June 1926  –  12 July  1926 |
| Hon. Hugh Guthrie | 13 July  1926  –  25 Sept. 1926 |

## Postmaster General

| | |
|---|---|
| Hon. Robert James Manion   *Acting Minister* | 29 June 1926  –  12 July  1926 |
| Hon. Robert James Manion | 13 July  1926  –  25 Sept. 1926 |

## President of the Privy Council

| | |
|---|---|
| Rt. Hon. Arthur Meighen | 29 June 1926  –  25 Sept. 1926 |

## Minister of Public Works

| | |
|---|---|
| Hon. Sir George Halsey Perley   *Acting Minister* | 29 June 1926  –  12 July  1926 |
| Hon. Edmond Baird Ryckman | 13 July  1926  –  25 Sept. 1926 |

## Minister of Railways and Canals

| | |
|---|---|
| Hon. Sir Henry Lumley Drayton   *Acting Minister* | 29 June 1926  –  12 July  1926 |
| Hon. William Anderson Black | 13 July  1926  –  25 Sept. 1926 |

## Secretary of State of Canada   6

| | |
|---|---|
| Hon. Sir George Halsey Perley   *Acting Minister* | 29 June 1926  –  12 July  1926 |
| Hon. Sir George Halsey Perley | 13 July  1926  –  25 Sept. 1926 |

## Minister of Soldiers' Civil Re-establishment   7

| | |
|---|---|
| Hon. Robert James Manion   *Acting Minister* | 29 June 1926  –  12 July  1926 |
| Hon. Raymond Ducharme Morand   *Acting Minister* | 13 July  1926  –  22 Aug.  1926 |
| Hon. Eugène Paquet | 23 Aug.  1926  –  25 Sept. 1926 |

5 The Department of Mines was presided over by the minister of another department who was to be named by the Governor in Council and who was to be called "The Minister of Mines". During the Thirteenth Ministry each successive Minister of the Interior was named Acting Minister of Mines.

6 The Secretary of State of Canada was *ex officio* the Registrar General of Canada.

7 The Department of Health was presided over by the minister of another department who was to be named by the Governor in Council. During the Thirteenth Ministry each successive Minister of Soldiers' Civil Re-establishment was designated to preside over the department.

**Minister without Portfolio**

| | |
|---|---|
| Hon. Richard Bedford Bennett  8 | 7 July  1926  –  12 July  1926 |
| Hon. Sir Henry Lumley Drayton | 13 July  1926  –  25 Sept. 1926 |
| Hon. Raymond Ducharme Morand | 13 July  1926  –  25 Sept. 1926 |
| Hon. John Alexander Macdonald | 13 July  1926  –  25 Sept. 1926 |
| Hon. Donald Sutherland | 13 July  1926  –  25 Sept. 1926 |

**Solicitor General of Canada**

| | |
|---|---|
| Vacant | 29 June 1926  –  22 Aug.  1926 |
| Hon. Guillaume André Fauteux | 23 Aug.  1926  –  25 Sept. 1926 |

**Minister of Trade and Commerce**

| | |
|---|---|
| Hon. Henry Herbert Stevens  *Acting Minister* | 29 June 1926  –  12 July  1926 |
| Hon. James Dew Chaplin | 13 July  1926  –  25 Sept. 1926 |

**NOT OF THE CABINET**

**Parliamentary Secretary of Soldiers' Civil Re-establishment**

| | |
|---|---|
| Vacant | 29 June 1926  –  12 July  1926 |

8    Bennett was appointed Minister of Finance and Receiver General on 13 July 1926.

# Fourteenth Ministry

**LIBERAL** 1

25 September 1926 to 7 August 1930

**PRIME MINISTER**

The Right Honourable William Lyon Mackenzie King   2

**THE MINISTRY**

**Minister of Agriculture**
Hon. William Richard Motherwell

25 Sept. 1926 –   7 Aug. 1930

**Minister of Customs and Excise**
Hon. William Daum Euler   3

25 Sept. 1926 – 30 Mar. 1927

**Secretary of State for External Affairs**   4
Rt. Hon. William Lyon Mackenzie King

25 Sept. 1926 –   7 Aug. 1930

**Minister of Finance and Receiver General**
Hon. James Alexander Robb

25 Sept. 1926 – 11 Nov. 1929

Vacant

12 Nov. 1929 – 25 Nov. 1929

Hon. Charles Avery Dunning

26 Nov. 1929 –   7 Aug. 1930

**Minister of Fisheries**   5
Vacant

14 June 1930 – 16 June 1930

Hon. Cyrus Macmillan

17 June 1930 –   7 Aug. 1930

**Minister of Immigration and Colonization**
Hon. Robert Forke

25 Sept. 1926 – 29 Dec. 1929

Hon. Charles Stewart   6   *Acting Minister*

30 Dec. 1929 – 26 June 1930

Hon. Ian Alistair Mackenzie

27 June 1930 –   7 Aug. 1930

**Superintendent-General of Indian Affairs**   7
Hon. Charles Stewart

25 Sept. 1926 – 18 June 1930

Hon. Charles Stewart   *Acting Minister*

19 June 1930 – 26 June 1930

Hon. Ian Alistair MacKenzie

27 June 1930 –   7 Aug. 1930

**Minister of the Interior**   7
Hon. Charles Stewart

25 Sept. 1926 –   7 Aug. 1930

1 Following the defeat of the Government in the general election of 14 Sept. 1926, Meighen formally resigned on 25 Sept. and the Fourteenth Ministry took office the same day.

2 King was also President of the Privy Council.

3 Euler was appointed Minister of National Revenue on 31 Mar. 1927.

4 The Prime Minister was *ex officio* the Secretary of State for External Affairs.

5 See Minister of Marine and Fisheries.

6 Stewart was also Superintendent-General of Indian Affairs and Minister of the Interior.

7 The Minister of the Interior was *ex officio* the Superintendent-General of Indian Affairs until 19 June 1930, when the Minister of Immigration and Colonization was designated by Order in Council to hold the office *ex officio*.

**Minister of Justice and Attorney General**

Hon. Ernest Lapointe — 25 Sept. 1926 – 7 Aug. 1930

**Minister of Labour**

Hon. Peter Heenan — 25 Sept. 1926 – 7 Aug. 1930

**Minister of Marine** 8

Hon. Pierre Joseph Arthur Cardin — 14 June 1930 – 7 Aug. 1930

**Minister of Marine and Fisheries** 9

Hon. Pierre Joseph Arthur Cardin  10 — 25 Sept. 1926 – 13 June 1930

**Minister of Mines** 11

Hon. Charles Stewart — 25 Sept. 1926 – 7 Aug. 1930

**Minister of National Defence**

| | | |
|---|---|---|
| Vacant | 25 Sept. 1926 – | 30 Sept. 1926 |
| Hon. James Alexander Robb  *Acting Minister* | 1 Oct.  1926 – | 7 Oct.  1926 |
| Hon. James Layton Ralston | 8 Oct.  1926 – | 7 Aug. 1930 |

**Minister of National Revenue** 12

Hon. William Daum Euler — 31 Mar.  1927 – 7 Aug. 1930

**Minister of Pensions and National Health** 13

| | | |
|---|---|---|
| Hon. James Horace King  *Senator* | 11 June 1928 – | 18 June 1930 |
| Hon. James Layton Ralston | 19 June 1930 – | 7 Aug. 1930 |

**Postmaster General**

Hon. Peter John Veniot — 25 Sept. 1926 – 7 Aug. 1930

**President of the Privy Council**

Rt. Hon. William Lyon Mackenzie King — 25 Sept. 1926 – 7 Aug. 1930

**Minister of Public Works**

Hon. John Campbell Elliott — 25 Sept. 1926 – 7 Aug. 1930

**Minister of Railways and Canals**

| | | |
|---|---|---|
| Hon. Charles Avery Dunning  14 | 25 Sept. 1926 – | 25 Nov. 1929 |
| Hon. Charles Avery Dunning  *Acting Minister* | 26 Nov. 1929 – | 29 Dec. 1929 |
| Hon. Thomas Alexander Crerar | 30 Dec. 1929 – | 7 Aug. 1930 |

8      See Minister of Marine and Fisheries.

9      The office of Minister of Marine and Fisheries was abolished and the offices of Minister of Fisheries and Minister of Marine created by Statute 20-21 Geo. V, c. 21 and c. 31 respectively. Both were assented to on 30 May 1930 and proclaimed in force on 14 June 1930.

10     Cardin was appointed Minister of Marine on 14 June 1930.

11     The Department of Mines was presided over by the minister of another department who was to be named by the Governor in Council and who was to be called "The Minister of Mines". During the Fourteenth Ministry the Minister of the Interior was named Minister of Mines.

12     The office of Minister of Customs and Excise was abolished and the office of Minister of National Revenue created by Statute 17 Geo. V, c. 34, and assented to on 31 Mar. 1927.

13     The Department of Health Act and the offices of Minister of Soldiers' Civil Re-establishment and Parliamentary Secretary of Soldiers' Civil Re-establishment were abolished and the office of Minister of Pensions and National Health created by Statute 18-19 Geo. V, c. 39, and assented to on 11 June 1928.

14     Dunning was appointed Minister of Finance and Receiver General on 26 Nov. 1929.

**Secretary of State of Canada**  15

Hon. Fernand Rinfret                                25 Sept. 1926  –   7 Aug.  1930

**Minister of Soldiers' Civil Re-establishment**

Hon. James Horace King  16                          25 Sept. 1926  –  10 June 1928

**Solicitor General of Canada**

Hon. Lucien Cannon                                  25 Sept. 1926  –   7 Aug.  1930

**Minister of Trade and Commerce**

Hon. James Malcolm                                  25 Sept. 1926  –   7 Aug.  1930

**Minister without Portfolio**

Hon. Raoul Dandurand  *Senator*                     25 Sept. 1926  –   7 Aug.  1930
Hon. William Frederic Kay                           17 June 1930  –   7 Aug.  1930


**NOT OF THE CABINET**

**Parliamentary Secretary of Soldiers' Civil Re-establishment**

Vacant                                              25 Sept. 1926  –  11 June 1928

15    The Secretary of State of Canada was *ex officio* the Registrar General of Canada.

16    King presided over the Department of Health until its abolition. He was appointed Minister of Pensions and National Health on 11 June 1928.

# Fifteenth Ministry

**CONSERVATIVE**  1

7 August 1930 to 23 October 1935

**PRIME MINISTER**

The Right Honourable Richard Bedford Bennett   2

**THE MINISTRY**

**Minister of Agriculture**

| | |
|---|---|
| Vacant | 7 Aug. 1930 |
| Hon. Robert Weir | 8 Aug. 1930 – 23 Oct. 1935 |

**Secretary of State for External Affairs   3**

| | |
|---|---|
| Rt. Hon. Richard Bedford Bennett | 7 Aug. 1930 – 23 Oct. 1935 |

**Minister of Finance and Receiver General**

| | |
|---|---|
| Rt. Hon. Richard Bedford Bennett | 7 Aug. 1930 –  2 Feb. 1932 |
| Hon. Edgar Nelson Rhodes   *Senator* | 3 Feb. 1932 – 23 Oct. 1935 |

**Minister of Fisheries**

| | |
|---|---|
| Hon. Edgar Nelson Rhodes   4 | 7 Aug. 1930 –  2 Feb. 1932 |
| Hon. Alfred Duranleau   *Acting Minister* | 3 Feb. 1932 – 16 Nov. 1934 |
| Hon. Grote Stirling   *Acting Minister* | 17 Nov. 1934 – 13 Aug. 1935 |
| Hon. William Gordon Ernst | 14 Aug. 1935 – 23 Oct. 1935 |

**Minister of Immigration and Colonization**

| | |
|---|---|
| Hon. Wesley Ashton Gordon   5 | 7 Aug. 1930 –  2 Feb. 1932 |
| Hon. Wesley Ashton Gordon   *Acting Minister* | 3 Feb. 1932 – 23 Oct. 1935 |

**Superintendent-General of Indian Affairs   6**

| | |
|---|---|
| Hon. Thomas Gerow Murphy | 7 Aug. 1930 – 23 Oct. 1935 |

**Minister of the Interior   6**

| | |
|---|---|
| Hon. Thomas Gerow Murphy | 7 Aug. 1930 – 23 Oct. 1935 |

**Minister of Justice and Attorney General**

| | |
|---|---|
| Hon. Hugh Guthrie | 7 Aug. 1930 – 11 Aug. 1935 |
| Vacant | 12 Aug. 1935 – 13 Aug. 1935 |
| Hon. George Reginald Geary | 14 Aug. 1935 – 23 Oct. 1935 |

1    On 7 Aug. 1930, after the defeat of the Government in the general election of 28 July, King formally tendered his resignation. On the same day the Fifteenth Ministry took office. In relation to the election of ministers, it is of interest to note that, pursuant to Statute 21-22 Geo. V, c. 52, assented to on 3 Aug. 1931, an amendment to the Senate and House of Commons Act, members of the House of Commons were no longer required to seek re-election when appointed to an office in the ministry.

2    Bennett was also President of the Privy Council, Minister of Finance, and Receiver General.

3    The Prime Minister was *ex officio* the Secretary of State for External Affairs.

4    Rhodes was appointed Minister of Finance and Receiver General on 3 Feb. 1932.

5    Gordon was also Minister of Mines. He was appointed Minister of Labour on 3 Feb. 1932.

6    On 19 June 1930 the office of Superintendent-General of Indian Affairs was transferred from the Minister of the Interior to the Minister of Immigration and Colonization. On 7 Aug. 1930 the Governor in Council cancelled the Order in Council and thus the Minister of the Interior once again held the office *ex officio*.

## Minister of Labour

| | |
|---|---|
| Hon. Gideon Decker Robertson  *Senator* | 7 Aug. 1930 – 2 Feb. 1932 |
| Hon. Wesley Ashton Gordon  .7 | 3 Feb. 1932 – 23 Oct. 1935 |

## Minister of Marine

| | |
|---|---|
| Hon. Alfred Duranleau | 7 Aug. 1930 – 19 July 1935 |
| Vacant | 20 July 1935 – 29 Aug. 1935 |
| Hon. Lucien Henri Gendron | 30 Aug. 1935 – 23 Oct. 1935 |

## Minister of Mines  8

| | |
|---|---|
| Hon. Wesley Ashton Gordon | 7 Aug. 1930 – 23 Oct. 1935 |

## Minister of National Defence

| | |
|---|---|
| Hon. Donald Matheson Sutherland  9 | 7 Aug. 1930 – 16 Nov. 1934 |
| Hon. Grote Stirling | 17 Nov. 1934 – 23 Oct. 1935 |

## Minister of National Revenue

| | |
|---|---|
| Hon. Edmond Baird Ryckman | 7 Aug. 1930 – 1 Dec. 1933 |
| Vacant | 2 Dec. 1933 – 5 Dec. 1933 |
| Hon. Robert Charles Matthews | 6 Dec. 1933 – 13 Aug. 1935 |
| Hon. James Earl Lawson | 14 Aug. 1935 – 23 Oct. 1935 |

## Minister of Pensions and National Health

| | |
|---|---|
| Hon. Murray MacLaren | 7 Aug. 1930 – 16 Nov. 1934 |
| Hon. Donald Matheson Sutherland | 17 Nov. 1934 – 23 Oct. 1935 |

## Postmaster General

| | |
|---|---|
| Hon. Arthur Sauvé | 7 Aug. 1930 – 13 Aug. 1935 |
| Vacant | 14 Aug. 1935 – 15 Aug. 1935 |
| Hon. Samuel Gobeil | 16 Aug. 1935 – 23 Oct. 1935 |

## President of the Privy Council

| | |
|---|---|
| Rt. Hon. Richard Bedford Bennett | 7 Aug. 1930 – 23 Oct. 1935 |

## Minister of Public Works

| | |
|---|---|
| Hon. Hugh Alexander Stewart | 7 Aug. 1930 – 23 Oct. 1935 |

## Minister of Railways and Canals

| | |
|---|---|
| Hon. Robert James Manion | 7 Aug. 1930 – 23 Oct. 1935 |

7 Gordon was also Minister of Mines.

8 The Department of Mines was presided over by the minister of another department, who was to be named by the Governor in Council and who was to be called "The Minister of Mines". The Minister of Immigration and Colonization and the Minister of Labour were designated to be *ex officio* the Minister of Mines on 7 Aug. 1930 and 3 Feb. 1932, respectively.

9 Sutherland was appointed Minister of Pensions and National Health on 17 Nov. 1934.

## Secretary of State of Canada 10

| | |
|---|---|
| Hon. Charles Hazlitt Cahan | 7 Aug. 1930 – 23 Oct. 1935 |

## Solicitor General of Canada

| | |
|---|---|
| Hon. Maurice Dupré | 7 Aug. 1930 – 23 Oct. 1935 |

## Minister of Trade and Commerce

| | |
|---|---|
| Hon. Henry Herbert Stevens | 7 Aug. 1930 – 26 Oct. 1934 |
| Vacant | 27 Oct. 1934 – 16 Nov. 1934 |
| Hon. Richard Burpee Hanson | 17 Nov. 1934 – 23 Oct. 1935 |

## Minister without Portfolio

| | |
|---|---|
| Hon. John Alexander Macdonald  *Senator* | 7 Aug. 1930 – 13 Aug. 1935 |
| Rt. Hon. Sir George Halsey Perley | 7 Aug. 1930 – 23 Oct. 1935 |
| Rt. Hon. Arthur Meighen  *Senator* | 3 Feb. 1932 – 23 Oct. 1935 |
| Hon. Onésime Gagnon | 30 Aug. 1935 – 23 Oct. 1935 |
| Hon. William Earl Rowe | 30 Aug. 1935 – 23 Oct. 1935 |

10    The Secretary of State of Canada was *ex officio* the Registrar General of Canada.

# Sixteenth Ministry

**LIBERAL** 1

23 October 1935 to 15 November 1948

**PRIME MINISTER**

The Right Honourable William Lyon Mackenzie King   2

**THE MINISTRY**

### Minister of Agriculture

| | | |
|---|---|---|
| Vacant | 23 Oct. 1935 – | 24 Oct. 1935 |
| Hon. Thomas Alexander Crerar   *Acting Minister* | 25 Oct. 1935 – | 3 Nov. 1935 |
| Rt. Hon. James Garfield Gardiner   3 | 4 Nov. 1935 – | 15 Nov. 1948 |

### Secretary of State for External Affairs   4

| | | |
|---|---|---|
| Rt. Hon. William Lyon Mackenzie King | 23 Oct. 1935 – | 3 Sept. 1946 |
| Rt. Hon. Louis Stephen St-Laurent   5 | 4 Sept. 1946 – | 9 Sept. 1948 |
| Hon. Lester Bowles Pearson | 10 Sept. 1948 – | 15 Nov. 1948 |

### Minister of Finance and Receiver General

| | | |
|---|---|---|
| Hon. Charles Avery Dunning | 23 Oct. 1935 – | 5 Sept. 1939 |
| Hon. James Layton Ralston   6 | 6 Sept. 1939 – | 4 July 1940 |
| Vacant | 5 July 1940 – | 7 July 1940 |
| Rt. Hon. James Lorimer Ilsley   7 | 8 July 1940 – | 9 Dec. 1946 |
| Hon. Douglas Charles Abbott | 10 Dec. 1946 – | 15 Nov. 1948 |

### Minister of Fisheries

| | | |
|---|---|---|
| Hon. Joseph-Enoil Michaud   8 | 23 Oct. 1935 – | 5 Oct. 1942 |
| Vacant | 6 Oct. 1942 | |
| Hon. Ernest Bertrand   9 | 7 Oct. 1942 – | 28 Aug. 1945 |
| Vacant | 29 Aug. 1945 | |
| Hon. Hedley Francis Gregory Bridges | 30 Aug. 1945 – | 10 Aug. 1947 |
| Vacant | 11 Aug. 1947 – | 13 Aug. 1947 |
| Hon. Ernest Bertrand   *Acting Minister* | 14 Aug. 1947 – | 1 Sept. 1947 |
| Hon. Milton Fowler Gregg   10 | 2 Sept. 1947 – | 18 Jan. 1948 |
| Hon. James Angus MacKinnon   11 | 19 Jan. 1948 – | 10 June 1948 |
| Hon. Robert Wellington Mayhew | 11 June 1948 – | 15 Nov. 1948 |

### Minister of Immigration and Colonization

| | | |
|---|---|---|
| Hon. Thomas Alexander Crerar   12 | 23 Oct. 1935 – | 30 Nov. 1936 |

1    The Government having been defeated in the general election of 14 Oct. 1935, Bennett formally tendered his resignation to the Governor General on 23 Oct. 1935. The Sixteenth Ministry assumed office the same day. It was returned to office in the general elections of both 1940 and 1945 but on the latter the Prime Minister failed to be re-elected. He was subsequently elected in a by-election on 6 Aug. 1945.

2    King was also Secretary of State for External Affairs and President of the Privy Council.

3    Gardiner was also Minister of National War Services.

4    The Prime Minister was *ex officio* the Secretary of State for External Affairs until 28 May 1946. Statute 10 Geo. VI, c. 6, assented to on 28 May 1946, terminated this *ex officio* relationship.

5    St-Laurent was also Minister of Justice and Attorney General to 9 Dec. 1946. He was reappointed Minister of Justice and Attorney General on 10 Sept. 1948.

6    Ralston was appointed Minister of National Defence on 5 July 1940.

7    Ilsley was appointed Minister of Justice and Attorney General on 10 Dec. 1946.

8    Michaud was appointed Minister of Transport on 6 Oct. 1942.

9    Bertrand was appointed Postmaster General on 29 Aug. 1945.

10   Gregg was appointed Minister of Veterans Affairs on 19 Jan. 1948.

11   MacKinnon was appointed Minister of Mines and Resources on 11 June 1948.

12   Crerar was also Minister of the Interior. He was appointed Minister of Mines and Resources on 1 Dec. 1936.

**Superintendent-General of Indian Affairs** 13

| | |
|---|---|
| Hon. Thomas Alexander Crerar | 23 Oct. 1935 — 30 Nov. 1936 |

**Minister of the Interior** 14

| | |
|---|---|
| Hon. Thomas Alexander Crerar 15 | 23 Oct. 1935 — 30 Nov. 1936 |

**Minister of Justice and Attorney General**

| | |
|---|---|
| Rt. Hon. Ernest Lapointe | 23 Oct. 1935 — 26 Nov. 1941 |
| Hon. Joseph-Enoil Michaud  *Acting Minister* | 27 Nov. 1941 — 9 Dec. 1941 |
| Rt. Hon. Louis Stephen St-Laurent  16 | 10 Dec. 1941 — 9 Dec. 1946 |
| Rt. Hon. James Lorimer Ilsley | 10 Dec. 1946 — 30 June 1948 |
| Rt. Hon. Louis Stephen St-Laurent  *Acting Minister* | 1 July 1948 — 9 Sept. 1948 |
| Rt. Hon. Louis Stephen St-Laurent | 10 Sept. 1948 — 15 Nov. 1948 |

**Minister of Labour**

| | |
|---|---|
| Hon. Norman McLeod Rogers  17 | 23 Oct. 1935 — 18 Sept. 1939 |
| Hon. Norman Alexander McLarty  18 | 19 Sept. 1939 — 14 Dec. 1941 |
| Hon. Humphrey Mitchell | 15 Dec. 1941 — 15 Nov. 1948 |

**Minister of Marine**

| | |
|---|---|
| Hon. Clarence Decatur Howe  19 | 23 Oct. 1935 — 1 Nov. 1936 |

**Minister of Mines** 20

| | |
|---|---|
| Hon. Thomas Alexander Crerar | 23 Oct. 1935 — 30 Nov. 1936 |

**Minister of Mines and Resources** 21

| | |
|---|---|
| Hon. Thomas Alexander Crerar | 1 Dec. 1936 — 17 Apr. 1945 |
| Hon. James Allison Glen | 18 Apr. 1945 — 10 June 1948 |
| Hon. James Angus MacKinnon | 11 June 1948 — 15 Nov. 1948 |

**Minister of Munitions and Supply** 22

| | |
|---|---|
| Hon. Clarence Decatur Howe  23 | 9 Apr. 1940 — 31 Dec. 1945 |

13    See Minister of the Interior and Minister of Mines and Resources.

14    The Minister of the Interior was *ex officio* the Superintendent-General of Indian Affairs. See Minister of Mines and Resources.

15    Crerar was also Minister of Immigration and Colonization. He was appointed Minister of Mines and Resources on 1 Dec. 1936.

16    St-Laurent was also Secretary of State for External Affairs.

17    Rogers was appointed Minister of National Defence on 19 Sept. 1939.

18    McLarty was appointed Secretary of State of Canada on 15 Dec. 1941.

19    Howe was also Minister of Railways and Canals. He was appointed Minister of Transport on 2 Nov. 1936.

20    The Department of Mines was to be presided over by the minister of another department who was to be named by the Governor in Council and who was to be called "The Minister of Mines". During the Sixteenth Ministry Crerar, who was both Minister of Immigration and Colonization and Minister of the Interior, was named Minister of Mines. See Minister of Mines and Resources.

21    The offices of Minister of Immigration and Colonization, Minister of the Interior, Minister of Mines and Superintendent-General of Indian Affairs were abolished and the office of Minister of Mines and Resources was created by Statute 1 Edw. VIII, c. 33, assented to on 23 June 1936 and proclaimed in force on 1 Dec. 1936.

22    The office of Minister of Munitions and Supply was created by Statute 3 Geo. VI, c. 3, assented to on 13 Sept. 1939 and proclaimed in force on 9 Apr. 1940. See Minister of Reconstruction and Supply.

23    Howe was also Minister of Transport and Minister of Reconstruction. He was appointed Minister of Reconstruction and Supply on 1 Jan. 1946.

## Minister of National Defence

| | |
|---|---|
| Hon. Ian Alistair Mackenzie  24 | 23 Oct. 1935 – 18 Sept. 1939 |
| Hon. Norman McLeod Rogers | 19 Sept. 1939 – 10 June 1940 |
| Hon. Charles Gavan Power  *Acting Minister* | 11 June 1940 –  4 July 1940 |
| Hon. James Layton Ralston | 5 July 1940 –  1 Nov. 1944 |
| Hon. Andrew George Latta McNaughton | 2 Nov. 1944 – 20 Aug. 1945 |
| Hon. Douglas Charles Abbott  25 | 21 Aug. 1945 – 11 Dec. 1946 |
| Hon. Brooke Claxton | 12 Dec. 1946 – 15 Nov. 1948 |

## Associate Minister of National Defence  26

| | |
|---|---|
| Hon. Charles Gavan Power  27 | 12 July 1940 – 26 Nov. 1944 |

## Minister of National Defence for Air  28

| | |
|---|---|
| Vacant | 22 May 1940 |
| Hon. Charles Gavan Power  29 | 23 May 1940 – 26 Nov. 1944 |
| Vacant | 27 Nov. 1944 – 29 Nov. 1944 |
| Hon. Angus Lewis Macdonald  *Acting Minister* | 30 Nov. 1944 – 10 Jan. 1945 |
| Hon. Colin William George Gibson  *Acting Minister* | 11 Jan. 1945 –  7 Mar. 1945 |
| Hon. Colin William George Gibson  30 | 8 Mar. 1945 – 11 Dec. 1946 |

24   Mackenzie was appointed Minister of Pensions and National Health on 19 Sept. 1939.

25   Abbott was also Minister of National Defence for Naval Service. He was appointed Minister of Finance and Receiver General on 10 Dec. 1946.

26   The office of Associate Minister of National Defence was created by Statute 4 Geo. VI, c. 21, and assented to on 12 July 1940. By this Act an Associate Minister of National Defence, a Minister of National Defence for Naval Services and a Minister of National Defence for Air could be appointed on the issuance by the Sovereign or the Governor in Council, pursuant to the War Measures Act, of a proclamation declaring the existence of war, invasion or insurrection, real or apprehended. Appointments to these three offices could be made until six months after the issuance of a further proclamation declaring that the war, invasion or insurrection no longer existed.

Proclamations declaring the existence of wars were issued on both 1 Sept. and 10 Sept. 1939. Active hostilities generally ceased in 1945. However, unlike after World War I, no proclamation was issued declaring an end to the state of war, though in 1947 the remaining Orders in Council approved pursuant to the War Measures Act were rescinded, thus in effect recognizing the termination of the state of war. Moreover, on 10 July 1951 a proclamation was issued proclaiming an end to the formal state of war between Canada and Germany, and in 1952 a Treaty of Peace with Japan was proclaimed in force. Consequently, it is difficult to determine when appointments to these offices could not have any longer been made. Nevertheless, on 15 Feb. 1952, pursuant to the National Defence Act of 1950 (14 Geo. VI, c. 43), a proclamation was issued repealing the relevant sections of the Act creating these offices and, indeed, they had in effect been superseded by sections of the National Defence Act of 1950 which had been proclaimed in force on 1 Aug. 1950.

27   Power was also Minister of National Defence for Air.

28   The office of Minister of National Defence for Air was created by Statute 4 Geo. VI, c. 1, assented to on 22 May 1940, abolished and re-created by Statute 4 Geo. VI, c. 21, and assented to on 12 July 1940. See Associate Minister of National Defence.

29   Power was also Associate Minister of National Defence.

30   Gibson was appointed Secretary of State of Canada on 12 Dec. 1946.

## Minister of National Defence for Naval Services   31

| | |
|---|---|
| Hon. Angus Lewis Macdonald | 12 July  1940  –  17 Apr.  1945 |
| Hon. Douglas Charles Abbott   32 | 18 Apr.  1945  –  11 Dec.  1946 |

## Minister of National Health and Welfare

| | |
|---|---|
| Hon. Brooke Claxton   33 | 18 Oct.  1944  –  11 Dec.  1946 |
| Hon. Paul Joseph James Martin | 12 Dec.  1946  –  15 Nov.  1948 |

## Minister of National Revenue

| | |
|---|---|
| Hon. James Lorimer Ilsley   34 | 23 Oct.  1935  –   7 July  1940 |
| Hon. Colin William George Gibson   35 | 8 July  1940  –   7 Mar.  1945 |
| Hon. James Angus MacKinnon   *Acting Minister* | 8 Mar.  1945  –  18 Apr.  1945 |
| Hon. David Laurence MacLaren | 19 Apr.  1945  –  29 July  1945 |
| Hon. James Angus MacKinnon   *Acting Minister* | 30 July  1945  –  28 Aug.  1945 |
| Hon. James Joseph McCann   36 | 29 Aug.  1945  –  15 Nov.  1948 |

## Minister of National War Services   37

| | |
|---|---|
| Hon. James Garfield Gardiner   38 | 12 July  1940  –  10 June 1941 |
| Hon. Joseph Thorarinn Thorson | 11 June 1941  –   5 Oct.  1942 |
| Vacant | 6 Oct.  1942 |
| Hon. Léo Richer Laflèche | 7 Oct.  1942  –  17 Apr.  1945 |
| Hon. James Joseph McCann   39 | 18 Apr.  1945  –  18 Jan.  1948 |
| Vacant | 19 Jan.  1948  –  15 Nov.  1948 |

## Minister of Pensions and National Health   40

| | |
|---|---|
| Hon. Charles Gavan Power   41 | 23 Oct.  1935  –  18 Sept. 1939 |
| Hon. Ian Alistair Mackenzie   42 | 19 Sept. 1939  –  17 Oct.  1944 |

## Postmaster General

| | |
|---|---|
| Hon. John Campbell Elliott | 23 Oct.  1935  –  22 Jan.  1939 |
| Hon. Norman Alexander McLarty   43 | 23 Jan.  1939  –  18 Sept. 1939 |
| Hon. Charles Gavan Power   44 | 19 Sept. 1939  –  22 May  1940 |
| Hon. James Lorimer Ilsley   *Acting Minister* | 23 May  1940  –   7 July  1940 |
| Hon. William Pate Mulock | 8 July  1940  –   8 June 1945 |
| Vacant | 9 June 1945  –  28 Aug.  1945 |
| Hon. Ernest Bertrand | 29 Aug.  1945  –  15 Nov.  1948 |

## President of the Privy Council

| | |
|---|---|
| Rt. Hon. William Lyon Mackenzie King | 23 Oct.  1935  –  15 Nov.  1948 |

31    The office of Minister of National Defence for Naval Services was created by Statute 4 Geo. VI, c. 21, and assented to on 12 July 1940. See Associate Minister of National Defence.

32    Abbott was also Minister of National Defence, and was appointed Minister of Finance and Receiver General on 10 Dec. 1946.

33    Claxton was appointed Minister of National Defence on 12 Dec. 1946.

34    Ilsley was appointed Minister of Finance and Receiver General on 8 July 1940.

35    Gibson was appointed Minister of National Defence for Air on 8 Mar. 1945.

36    McCann was also Minister of National War Services.

37    The office of Minister of National War Services was created by Statute 4 Geo. VI, c. 22, and assented to on 12 July 1940. The Act was not included in the 1952 Revised Statutes of Canada, as it was considered spent.

38    Gardiner was also Minister of Agriculture.

39    McCann was also Minister of National Revenue.

40    The office of Minister of Pensions and National Health was abolished and the offices of Minister of Veterans Affairs and Minister of National Health and Welfare created by Statute 8 Geo. VI, c. 19, assented to on 30 June 1944, and Statute 8 Geo. VI, c. 22, assented to on 24 July 1944, respectively. Both Acts were proclaimed in force on 18 Oct. 1944.

41    Power was appointed Postmaster General on 19 Sept. 1939.

42    Mackenzie was appointed Minister of Veterans Affairs on 18 Oct. 1944.

43    McLarty was appointed Minister of Labour on 19 Sept. 1939.

44    Power was appointed Minister of National Defence for Air on 23 May 1940.

## Minister of Public Works

| | | |
|---|---|---|
| Hon. Pierre Joseph Arthur Cardin  45 | 23 Oct.  1935 – | 12 May  1942 |
| Hon. Joseph-Enoil Michaud  *Acting Minister* | 13 May  1942 – | 6 Oct.  1942 |
| Hon. Alphonse Fournier | 7 Oct.  1942 – | 15 Nov.  1948 |

## Minister of Railways and Canals  46

| | | |
|---|---|---|
| Hon. Clarence Decatur Howe  47 | 23 Oct.  1935 – | 1 Nov.  1936 |

## Minister of Reconstruction  48

| | | |
|---|---|---|
| Vacant | 30 June 1944 – | 12 Oct.  1944 |
| Hon. Clarence Decatur Howe  49 | 13 Oct.  1944 – | 31 Dec.  1945 |

## Minister of Reconstruction and Supply  50

Hon. Clarence Decatur Howe  51

## Secretary of State of Canada  52

| | | |
|---|---|---|
| Hon. Fernand Rinfret | 23 Oct.  1935 – | 12 July  1939 |
| Vacant | 13 July  1939 – | 25 July  1939 |
| Rt. Hon. Ernest Lapointe  *Acting Minister* | 26 July  1939 – | 8 May  1940 |
| Hon. Pierre-François Casgrain | 9 May  1940 – | 14 Dec.  1941 |
| Hon. Norman Alexander McLarty | 15 Dec.  1941 – | 17 Apr.  1945 |
| Hon. Paul Joseph James Martin  53 | 18 Apr.  1945 – | 11 Dec.  1946 |
| Hon. Colin William George Gibson | 12 Dec.  1946 – | 15 Nov.  1948 |

## Solicitor General of Canada

| | | |
|---|---|---|
| Vacant | 23 Oct.  1935 – | 17 Apr.  1945 |
| Hon. Joseph Jean | 18 Apr.  1945 – | 15 Nov.  1948 |

## Minister of Trade and Commerce

| | | |
|---|---|---|
| Hon. William Daum Euler | 23 Oct.  1935 – | 8 May  1940 |
| Hon. James Angus MacKinnon  54 | 9 May  1940 – | 18 Jan.  1948 |
| Rt. Hon. Clarence Decatur Howe  55 | 19 Jan.  1948 – | 15 Nov.  1948 |

## Minister of Transport  46

| | | |
|---|---|---|
| Hon. Clarence Decatur Howe  56 | 2 Nov.  1936 – | 7 July  1940 |
| Hon. Pierre Joseph Arthur Cardin  57 | 8 July  1940 – | 12 May  1942 |
| Hon. Clarence Decatur Howe  *Acting Minister* | 13 May  1942 – | 5 Oct.  1942 |
| Hon. Joseph-Enoil Michaud | 6 Oct.  1942 – | 17 Apr.  1945 |
| Hon. Lionel Chevrier | 18 Apr.  1945 – | 15 Nov.  1948 |

45   Cardin was also Minister of Transport.

46   The offices of Minister of Marine and Minister of Railways and Canals were abolished and the office of Minister of Transport created by Statute 1 Edw. VIII, c. 34, assented to on 23 June 1936 and proclaimed in force on 2 Nov. 1936.

47   Howe was also Minister of Marine. He was appointed Minister of Transport on 2 Nov. 1936.

48   The office of Minister of Reconstruction was created by Statute 8 Geo. VI, c. 18, and assented to on 30 June 1944. See Minister of Reconstruction and Supply.

49   Howe was also Minister of Munitions and Supply. He was appointed Minister of Reconstruction and Supply on 1 Jan. 1946.

50   The offices of Minister of Munitions and Supply and Minister of Reconstruction were abolished and the office of Minister of Reconstruction and Supply created by Statute 9-10 Geo. VI, c. 16, and assented to on 18 Dec. 1945. The section of the Act creating the office was proclaimed in force on 1 Jan. 1946.

51   Howe was also Minister of Trade and Commerce.

52   The Secretary of State of Canada was *ex officio* the Registrar General of Canada.

53   Martin was appointed Minister of National Health and Welfare on 12 Dec. 1946.

54   MacKinnon was appointed Minister of Fisheries on 19 Jan. 1948.

55   Howe was also Minister of Reconstruction and Supply.

56   Howe was also Minister of Munitions and Supply.

57   Cardin was also Minister of Public Works.

### Minister of Veterans Affairs 58

| | |
|---|---|
| Rt. Hon. Ian Alistair Mackenzie | 18 Oct. 1944 – 18 Jan. 1948 |
| Hon. Milton Fowler Gregg | 19 Jan. 1948 – 15 Nov. 1948 |

### Minister without Portfolio

| | |
|---|---|
| Rt. Hon. Raoul Dandurand *Senator* | 23 Oct. 1935 – 11 Mar. 1942 |
| Hon. James Angus MacKinnon 59 | 23 Jan. 1939 – 8 May 1940 |
| Hon. James Horace King *Senator* | 26 May 1942 – 23 Aug. 1945 |
| Hon. Wishart McLea Robertson *Senator* | 4 Sept. 1945 – 15 Nov. 1948 |

## PARLIAMENTARY ASSISTANTS 60
## NOT OF THE MINISTRY

### Agriculture

| | |
|---|---|
| Robert McCubbin | 30 Oct. 1947 – 15 Nov. 1948 |

### External Affairs

| | |
|---|---|
| Walter Edward Harris | 30 Oct. 1947 – 15 Nov. 1948 |

### Finance

| | |
|---|---|
| Douglas Charles Abbott | 1 Apr. 1943 – 7 Mar. 1945 |
| Robert Wellington Mayhew | 25 Sept. 1945 – 10 June 1948 |
| Gleason Belzile | 30 Oct. 1947 – 15 Nov. 1948 |

### Fisheries

| | |
|---|---|
| Thomas Reid | 22 Apr. 1948 – 10 June 1948 |
| John Watson MacNaught | 11 June 1948 – 15 Nov. 1948 |

### Justice

| | |
|---|---|
| Joseph Jean | 6 May 1943 – 30 Nov. 1944 |

### Labour

| | |
|---|---|
| Paul Joseph James Martin | 7 May 1943 – 16 Apr. 1945 |
| Paul-Émile Côté | 30 Oct. 1947 – 15 Nov. 1948 |

### Munitions and Supply

| | |
|---|---|
| Lionel Chevrier | 1 Apr. 1943 – 16 Apr. 1945 |

58    See Note 40.

59    MacKinnon was appointed Minister of Trade and Commerce on 9 May 1940.

60    Statutory provision was not made for the office of Parliamentary Assistant. Appointment was
      by Order in Council and salaries were provided by an annual vote in the House of Commons
      Estimates.

## National Defence

| | |
|---|---|
| William Chisholm Macdonald | 1 Apr. 1943 – 14 Nov. 1944 |
| Douglas Charles Abbott | 8 Mar. 1945 – 16 Apr. 1945 |
| Hugues Lapointe | 25 Sept. 1945 – 15 Nov. 1948 |
| William Chisholm Macdonald | 25 Sept. 1945 – 19 Nov. 1946 |

## National Defence for Air

| | |
|---|---|
| Hon. Cyrus Macmillan | 1 Apr. 1943 – 6 June 1946 |

## National Health and Welfare

| | |
|---|---|
| Ralph Maybank | 30 Oct. 1947 – 15 Nov. 1948 |

## National Revenue

| | |
|---|---|
| Robert Henry Winters | 30 Oct. 1947 – 10 June 1948 |
| Thomas Reid | 11 June 1948 – 15 Nov. 1948 |

## Privy Council

| | |
|---|---|
| Brooke Claxton | 6 May 1943 – 12 Oct. 1944 |

## Reconstruction

| | |
|---|---|
| George James McIlraith | 28 Sept. 1945 – 31 Dec. 1945 |

## Reconstruction and Supply

| | |
|---|---|
| George James McIlraith | 1 Jan. 1946 – 15 Nov. 1948 |

## Trade and Commerce

| | |
|---|---|
| George James McIlraith | 3 Feb. 1948 – 15 Nov. 1948 |

## Transport

| | |
|---|---|
| Robert Henry Winters | 11 June 1948 – 15 Nov. 1948 |

## Veterans Affairs

| | |
|---|---|
| Walter Adam Tucker | 27 Sept. 1945 – 21 Apr. 1948 |
| Leslie Alexander Mutch | 11 June 1948 – 15 Nov. 1948 |

# Seventeenth Ministry

**LIBERAL** 1

15 November 1948 to 21 June 1957

**PRIME MINISTER**

The Right Honourable Louis Stephen St-Laurent  2

**THE MINISTRY**

**Minister of Agriculture**

| | | |
|---|---|---|
| Rt. Hon. James Garfield Gardiner | 15 Nov. 1948 – | 21 June 1957 |

**Minister of Citizenship and Immigration**

| | | |
|---|---|---|
| Hon. Walter Edward Harris  3 | 18 Jan. 1950 – | 30 June 1954 |
| Hon. John Whitney Pickersgill | 1 July 1954 – | 21 June 1957 |

**Minister of Defence Production**  4

| | | |
|---|---|---|
| Rt. Hon. Clarence Decatur Howe  5 | 1 Apr. 1951 – | 21 June 1957 |

**Secretary of State for External Affairs**

| | | |
|---|---|---|
| Hon. Lester Bowles Pearson | 15 Nov. 1948 – | 21 June 1957 |

**Minister of Finance and Receiver General**

| | | |
|---|---|---|
| Hon. Douglas Charles Abbott | 15 Nov. 1948 – | 30 June 1954 |
| Hon. Walter Edward Harris | 1 July 1954 – | 21 June 1957 |

**Minister of Fisheries**

| | | |
|---|---|---|
| Hon. Robert Wellington Mayhew | 15 Nov. 1948 – | 14 Oct. 1952 |
| Hon. James Sinclair | 15 Oct. 1952 – | 21 June 1957 |

**Minister of Justice and Attorney General**  6

| | | |
|---|---|---|
| Hon. Stuart Sinclair Garson | 15 Nov. 1948 – | 21 June 1957 |

**Minister of Labour**

| | | |
|---|---|---|
| Hon. Humphrey Mitchell | 15 Nov. 1948 – | 2 Aug. 1950 |
| Hon. Paul Joseph James Martin  *Acting Minister* | 3 Aug. 1950 – | 6 Aug. 1950 |
| Hon. Milton Fowler Gregg | 7 Aug. 1950 – | 21 June 1957 |

**Minister of Mines and Resources**  7

| | | |
|---|---|---|
| Hon. James Angus MacKinnon  8 | 15 Nov. 1948 – | 31 Mar. 1949 |
| Hon. Colin William George Gibson | 1 Apr. 1949 – | 17 Jan. 1950 |

1	On 15 Nov. 1948 King resigned as Prime Minister and President of the Privy Council. On the same day the Seventeenth Ministry assumed office. It included eighteen ministers from the Sixteenth Ministry, seventeen of whom retained their previous portfolios. Howe dropped one of his: Reconstruction and Supply.

2	St-Laurent was also President of the Privy Council.

3	Harris was appointed Minister of Finance and Receiver General on 1 July 1954.

4	The office of Minister of Defence Production was created by Statute 15 Geo. VI, c. 4, assented to on 21 Mar. 1951 and proclaimed in force on 1 Apr. 1951.

5	Howe was also Minister of Trade and Commerce.

6	By Order in Council dated 7 Aug. 1950, pursuant to the Public Service Rearrangement and Transfer of Duties Act, the powers, duties and functions of the Solicitor General of Canada were transferred to the Minister of Justice and Attorney General, and were exercised by him until 14 Oct. 1952.

7	The offices of Minister of Mines and Resources and Minister of Reconstruction and Supply were abolished by Statute 13 Geo. VI. c. 18, and the offices of the Minister of Citizenship and Immigration, Minister of Mines and Technical Surveys and Minister of Resources and Development created by Statues 13 Geo. VI, c. 16, 17 and 18 respectively, each assented to on 10 Dec. 1949 and proclaimed in force on 18 Jan. 1950.

8	MacKinnon was appointed Minister without Portfolio on 1 Apr. 1949.

### Minister of Mines and Technical Surveys   9

| | |
|---|---|
| Hon. James Joseph McCann   10 | 18 Jan.  1950 −  12 Dec.  1950 |
| Hon. George Prudham | 13 Dec.  1950 −  21 June 1957 |

### Minister of National Defence

| | |
|---|---|
| Hon. Brooke Claxton | 15 Nov.  1948 −  30 June 1954 |
| Hon. Ralph Osborne Campney | 1 July  1954 −  21 June 1957 |

### Associate Minister of National Defence   11

| | |
|---|---|
| Vacant | 11 Feb.  1953 |
| Hon. Ralph Osborne Campney   12 | 12 Feb.  1953 −  30 June 1954 |
| Vacant | 1 July  1954 −  25 Apr.  1957 |
| Hon. Paul Theodore Hellyer | 26 Apr.  1957 −  21 June 1957 |

### Minister of National Health and Welfare

| | |
|---|---|
| Hon. Paul Joseph James Martin | 15 Nov.  1948 −  21 June 1957 |

### Minister of National Revenue

| | |
|---|---|
| Hon. James Joseph McCann   13 | 15 Nov.  1948 −  21 June 1957 |

### Minister of Northern Affairs and National Resources   14

| | |
|---|---|
| Hon. Jean Lesage | 16 Dec.  1953 −  21 June 1957 |

### Postmaster General

| | |
|---|---|
| Hon. Ernest Bertrand | 15 Nov.  1948 −  23 Aug.  1949 |
| Vacant | 24 Aug.  1949 |
| Hon. Gabriel Édouard Rinfret | 25 Aug.  1949 −  12 Feb.  1952 |
| Hon. Alcide Côté | 13 Feb.  1952 −   7 Aug.  1955 |
| Vacant | 8 Aug.  1955 −  15 Aug.  1955 |
| Hon. Roch Pinard   *Acting Minister* | 16 Aug.  1955 −   2 Nov.  1955 |
| Hon. Hugues Lapointe   15 | 3 Nov.  1955 −  21 June 1957 |

### President of the Privy Council

| | |
|---|---|
| Rt. Hon. Louis Stephen St-Laurent | 15 Nov.  1948 −  24 Apr.  1957 |
| Hon. Lionel Chevrier | 25 Apr.  1957 −  21 June 1957 |

### Minister of Public Works

| | |
|---|---|
| Hon. Alphonse Fournier | 15 Nov.  1948 −  11 June 1953 |
| Hon. Walter Edward Harris   *Acting Minister* | 12 June 1953 −  16 Sept. 1953 |
| Hon. Robert Henry Winters | 17 Sept. 1953 −  21 June 1957 |

9       See Note 7.

10      McCann was also Minister of National Revenue.

11      Statute 1-2 Eliz. II, c. 6, assented to on 11 Feb. 1953, amended the National Defence Act to provide for the appointment at any time of an Associate Minister of National Defence. Previously the Act had provided for the appointment of three additional Ministers of National Defence and three Associate Ministers of National Defence only during an emergency.

12      Campney was also Solicitor General of Canada. He was appointed Minister of National Defence on 1 July 1954.

13      McCann was also Minister of Mines and Technical Surveys.

14      The office of Minister of Resources and Development was abolished and the office of Minister of Northern Affairs and National Resources created by Statute 2-3 Eliz. II, c. 4, and assented to on 16 Dec. 1953.

15      Lapointe was also Minister of Veterans Affairs.

**Minister of Reconstruction and Supply**  16

Hon. Robert Henry Winters  17        15 Nov. 1948  –  17 Jan.  1950

**Minister of Resources and Development**  18

Hon. Robert Henry Winters  19        18 Jan.  1950  –  16 Sept. 1953
Hon. Jean Lesage  20        17 Sept. 1953  –  15 Dec.  1953

**Secretary of State of Canada**  21

Hon. Colin William George Gibson  22        15 Nov. 1948  –  31 Mar.  1949
Hon. Frederick Gordon Bradley         1 Apr.  1949  –  11 June 1953
Hon. John Whitney Pickersgill  23        12 June 1953  –  30 June 1954
Hon. Roch Pinard         1 July  1954  –  21 June 1957

**Solicitor General of Canada**  24

Hon. Joseph Jean        15 Nov. 1948  –  23 Aug. 1949
Vacant        24 Aug. 1949
Hon. Hugues Lapointe  25        25 Aug. 1949  –   6 Aug.  1950
Hon. Stuart Sinclair Garson         7 Aug.  1950  –  14 Oct.  1952
Hon. Ralph Osborne Campney  26        15 Oct.  1952  –  11 Jan.  1954
Hon. William Ross Macdonald        12 Jan.  1954  –  21 June 1957

**Minister of Trade and Commerce**

Rt. Hon. Clarence Decatur Howe  27        15 Nov. 1948  –  21 June 1957

**Minister of Transport**

Hon. Lionel Chevrier  28        15 Nov. 1948  –  30 June 1954
Hon. George Carlyle Marler         1 July  1954  –  21 June 1957

**Minister of Veterans Affairs**

Hon. Milton Fowler Gregg  29        15 Nov. 1948  –   6 Aug. 1950
Hon. Hugues Lapointe  30         7 Aug. 1950  –  21 June 1957

16    See Note 7.

17    Winters was appointed Minister of Resources and Development on 18 Jan. 1950.

18    See Note 7.

19    Winters was appointed Minister of Public Works on 17 Sept. 1953.

20    Lesage was appointed Minister of Northern Affairs and National Resources on 16 Dec. 1953.

21    The Secretary of State of Canada was *ex officio* the Registrar General of Canada.

22    Gibson was appointed Minister of Mines and Resources on 1 Apr. 1949.

23    Pickersgill was appointed Minister of Citizenship and Immigration on 1 July 1954.

24    See Note 6.

      The National Defence Act of 1950 (Statute 14 Geo. VI, c. 43) provided for the designation by
      the Governor in Council of any other person in addition to the Minister of National Defence to
      exercise any power or perform any duty or function vested in the Minister of National Defence.
      By Order in Council dated 24 Nov. 1952 the Solicitor General of Canada was so designated
      and exercised that function until 12 Feb. 1953. See Associate Minister of National Defence.

25    Lapointe was appointed Minister of Veterans Affairs on 7 Aug. 1950.

26    Campney was also Associate Minister of National Defence.

27    Howe was also Minister of Defence Production.

28    Chevrier rejoined the Ministry as President of the Privy Council on 25 Apr. 1957.

29    Gregg was appointed Minister of Labour on 7 Aug. 1950.

30    Lapointe was also Postmaster General.

## Minister without Portfolio

| | |
|---|---|
| Hon. Wishart McLea Robertson  *Senator* | 15 Nov. 1948 – 13 Oct. 1953 |
| Hon. James Angus MacKinnon  *Senator* | 1 Apr. 1949 – 13 Dec. 1950 |
| Hon. William Ross Macdonald  31  *Senator* | 14 Oct. 1953 – 11 Jan. 1954 |

## PARLIAMENTARY ASSISTANTS
## NOT OF THE MINISTRY

### Agriculture

| | |
|---|---|
| Robert McCubbin | 15 Nov. 1948 – 30 Apr. 1949 |
| | 15 July 1949 – 13 June 1953 |
| | 26 Aug. 1953 – 12 Apr. 1957 |

### Defence Production

| | |
|---|---|
| George James McIlraith | 1 Apr. 1951 – 4 Feb. 1952 |
| | 12 Feb. 1952 – 13 June 1953 |
| John Horace Dickey | 27 Aug. 1953 – 12 Apr. 1957 |

### External Affairs

| | |
|---|---|
| Hugues Lapointe | 19 Jan. 1949 – 30 Apr. 1949 |
| | 12 July 1949 – 23 Aug. 1949 |
| Jean Lesage | 24 Jan. 1951 – 31 Dec. 1952 |
| Roch Pinard | 14 Oct. 1953 – 30 June 1954 |
| Louis Joseph Lucien Cardin | 9 Feb. 1956 – 12 Apr. 1957 |

### Finance

| | |
|---|---|
| Gleason Belzile | 15 Nov. 1948 – 30 Apr. 1949 |
| | 11 July 1949 – 25 July 1950 |
| James Sinclair | 19 Jan. 1949 – 30 Apr. 1949 |
| | 11 July 1949 – 14 Oct. 1952 |
| Jean Lesage | 1 Jan. 1953 – 13 June 1953 |
| | 24 Aug. 1953 – 16 Sept. 1953 |
| William Moore Benidickson | 14 Oct. 1953 – 12 Apr. 1957 |

### Fisheries

| | |
|---|---|
| John Watson MacNaught | 15 Nov. 1948 – 30 Apr. 1949 |
| | 11 July 1949 – 13 June 1953 |
| | 24 Aug. 1953 – 12 Apr. 1957 |

31    Macdonald was appointed Solicitor General of Canada on 12 Jan. 1954.

## Labour

| | |
|---|---|
| Paul-Émile Côté | 15 Nov. 1948 – 30 Apr. 1949 |
| | 11 July 1949 – 13 June 1953 |
| | 24 Aug. 1953 – 31 Dec. 1953 |
| Joseph Adéodat Blanchette | 9 Feb. 1956 – 12 Apr. 1957 |

## Mines and Resources

| | |
|---|---|
| Ralph Maybank | 25 Jan. 1949 – 30 Apr. 1949 |
| | 11 July 1949 – 17 Jan. 1950 |

## Mines and Technical Surveys

| | |
|---|---|
| Ralph Maybank | 18 Jan. 1950 – 23 Jan. 1951 |

## National Defence

| | |
|---|---|
| Hugues Lapointe | 15 Nov. 1948 – 18 Jan. 1949 |
| Loran Ellis Baker | 19 Jan. 1949 – 30 Apr. 1949 |
| Joseph Adéodat Blanchette | 19 Jan. 1949 – 30 Apr. 1949 |
| | 11 July 1949 – 13 June 1953 |
| | 24 Aug. 1953 – 8 Feb. 1956 |
| Ralph Osborne Campney | 24 Jan. 1951 – 14 Oct. 1952 |
| Paul Theodore Hellyer | 9 Feb. 1956 – 12 Apr. 1957 |

## National Health and Welfare

| | |
|---|---|
| Ralph Maybank | 15 Nov. 1948 – 24 Jan. 1949 |
| Thomas Reid | 25 Jan. 1949 – 30 Apr. 1949 |
| | 13 July 1949 – 6 Sept. 1949 |
| Emmet Andrew McCusker | 24 Jan. 1951 – 13 June 1953 |
| Frederick Greystock Robertson | 14 Oct. 1953 – 12 Apr. 1957 |

## National Revenue

| | |
|---|---|
| Thomas Reid | 15 Nov. 1948 – 24 Jan. 1949 |

## Postmaster General

| | |
|---|---|
| Léopold Langlois | 24 Jan. 1951 – 13 June 1953 |
| | 1 Sept. 1953 – 13 Oct. 1953 |
| Thomas Andrew Murray Kirk | 14 Oct. 1953 – 12 Apr. 1957 |

**Prime Minister**

Walter Edward Harris

15 Nov. 1948 – 30 Apr. 1949
18 July 1949 – 17 Jan. 1950

William Gilbert Weir

25 Aug. 1953 – 12 Apr. 1957

**Public Works**

Maurice Bourget

14 Oct. 1953 – 12 Apr. 1957

**Resources and Development**

George Prudham

1 Feb. 1950 – 12 Dec. 1950

Ralph Maybank

24 Jan. 1951 – 30 July 1951

**Trade and Commerce**

George James McIlraith

15 Nov. 1948 – 30 Apr. 1949
11 July 1949 – 13 June 1953

**Transport**

William Moore Benidickson

24 Jan. 1951 – 13 June 1953
31 Aug. 1953 – 13 Sept. 1953

Léopold Langlois

14 Oct. 1953 – 12 Apr. 1957

**Veterans Affairs**

Leslie Alexander Mutch

15 Nov. 1948 – 30 Apr. 1949
11 July 1949 – 13 June 1953

Colin Emerson Bennett

14 Oct. 1953 – 12 Apr. 1957

# Eighteenth Ministry

**PROGRESSIVE-CONSERVATIVE**  1

21 June 1957 to 22 April 1963

**PRIME MINISTER**

The Right Honourable John George Diefenbaker   2

**THE MINISTRY**

### Minister of Agriculture

| | |
|---|---|
| Hon. Douglas Scott Harkness   *Acting Minister* | 21 June 1957 −   6 Aug.  1957 |
| Hon. Douglas Scott Harkness   3 | 7 Aug.  1957 −  10 Oct.  1960 |
| Hon. Francis Alvin George Hamilton | 11 Oct.  1960 −  22 Apr.  1963 |

### Minister of Citizenship and Immigration

| | |
|---|---|
| Hon. Edmund Davie Fulton   *Acting Minister* | 21 June 1957 −  11 May  1958 |
| Hon. Ellen Louks Fairclough   4 | 12 May  1958 −   8 Aug.  1962 |
| Hon. Richard Albert Bell | 9 Aug.  1962 −  22 Apr.  1963 |

### Minister of Defence Production

| | |
|---|---|
| Hon. Howard Charles Green   *Acting Minister* | 21 June 1957 −  11 May  1958 |
| Hon. Raymond Joseph Michael O'Hurley | 12 May  1958 −  22 Apr.  1963 |

### Secretary of State for External Affairs

| | |
|---|---|
| Rt. Hon. John George Diefenbaker | 21 June 1957 −  12 Sept. 1957 |
| Hon. Sidney Earle Smith | 13 Sept. 1957 −  17 Mar.  1959 |
| Vacant | 18 Mar.  1959 |
| Rt. Hon. John George Diefenbaker   *Acting Minister* | 19 Mar.  1959 −   3 June 1959 |
| Hon. Howard Charles Green | 4 June 1959 −  22 Apr.  1963 |

### Minister of Finance and Receiver General

| | |
|---|---|
| Hon. Donald Methuen Fleming   5 | 21 June 1957 −   8 Aug.  1962 |
| Hon. George Clyde Nowlan | 9 Aug.  1962 −  22 Apr.  1963 |

### Minister of Fisheries

| | |
|---|---|
| Hon. John Angus MacLean | 21 June 1957 −  22 Apr.  1963 |

1   With the defeat of the Government in the general election of 10 June 1957, St-Laurent resigned on 21 June 1957 and the Eighteenth Ministry assumed office the same day.

2   Diefenbaker was also President of the Privy Council and Secretary of State for External Affairs.

3   Harkness was also Minister of Northern Affairs and National Resources. He was appointed Minister of National Defence on 11 Oct. 1960.

4   Fairclough was appointed Postmaster General on 9 Aug. 1962.

5   Fleming was appointed Minister of Justice and Attorney General on 9 Aug. 1962.

## Minister of Forestry  6

| | |
|---|---|
| Vacant | 1 Oct. 1960 — 10 Oct. 1960 |
| Hon. Hugh John Flemming  7. | 11 Oct. 1960 — 17 Mar. 1963 |
| Hon. Martial Asselin | 18 Mar. 1963 — 22 Apr. 1963 |

## Minister of Justice and Attorney General

| | |
|---|---|
| Hon. Edmund Davie Fulton  8 | 21 June 1957 —  8 Aug. 1962 |
| Hon. Donald Methuen Fleming | 9 Aug. 1962 — 22 Apr. 1963 |

## Minister of Labour

| | |
|---|---|
| Hon. Michael Starr | 21 June 1957 — 22 Apr. 1963 |

## Minister of Mines and Technical Surveys

| | |
|---|---|
| Hon. Léon Balcer   *Acting Minister* | 21 June 1957 —  6 Aug. 1957 |
| Hon. Paul Comtois | 7 Aug. 1957 —  6 Oct. 1961 |
| Vacant | 7 Oct. 1961 —  9 Oct. 1961 |
| Hon. Walter Gilbert Dinsdale   *Acting Minister* | 10 Oct. 1961 — 27 Dec. 1961 |
| Hon. Jacques Flynn | 28 Dec. 1961 — 12 July 1962 |
| Vacant | 13 July 1962 — 17 July 1962 |
| Hon. Hugh John Flemming   *Acting Minister* | 18 July 1962 —  8 Aug. 1962 |
| Hon. Paul Martineau | 9 Aug. 1962 — 22 Apr. 1963 |

## Minister of National Defence

| | |
|---|---|
| Hon. George Randolph Pearkes | 21 June 1957 — 10 Oct. 1960 |
| Hon. Douglas Scott Harkness | 11 Oct. 1960 —  3 Feb. 1963 |
| Vacant | 4 Feb. 1963 — 11 Feb. 1963 |
| Hon. Gordon Churchill | 12 Feb. 1963 — 22 Apr. 1963 |

## Associate Minister of National Defence

| | |
|---|---|
| Vacant | 21 June 1957 — 19 Aug. 1959 |
| Hon. Joseph Pierre Albert Sévigny | 20 Aug. 1959 —  8 Feb. 1963 |
| Vacant | 9 Feb. 1963 — 22 Apr. 1963 |

## Minister of National Health and Welfare

| | |
|---|---|
| Hon. Alfred Johnson Brooks   *Acting Minister* | 21 June 1957 — 21 Aug. 1957 |
| Hon. Jay Waldo Monteith | 22 Aug. 1957 — 22 Apr. 1963 |

6    The office of Minister of Forestry was created by Statute 8-9 Eliz. II, c. 41, assented to on 1 Aug. 1960 and proclaimed in force on 1 Oct. 1960.

7    Flemming was also Minister of National Revenue.

8    Fulton was appointed Minister of Public Works on 9 Aug. 1962.

## Minister of National Revenue

| | | |
|---|---|---|
| Hon. George Clyde Nowlan  9 | 21 June 1957 – | 8 Aug. 1962 |
| Hon. Hugh John Flemming   10 | 9 Aug. 1962 – | 22 Apr. 1963 |

## Minister of Northern Affairs and National Resources

| | | |
|---|---|---|
| Hon. Douglas Scott Harkness   11 | 21 June 1957 – | 18 Aug. 1957 |
| Vacant | 19 Aug. 1957 – | 21 Aug. 1957 |
| Hon. Francis Alvin George Hamilton   12 | 22 Aug. 1957 – | 10 Oct. 1960 |
| Hon. Walter Gilbert Dinsdale | 11 Oct. 1960 – | 22 Apr. 1963 |

## Postmaster General

| | | |
|---|---|---|
| Hon. William McLean Hamilton | 21 June 1957 – | 12 July 1962 |
| Vacant | 13 July 1962 – | 17 July 1962 |
| Hon. John Angus MacLean   *Acting Minister* | 18 July 1962 – | 8 Aug. 1962 |
| Hon. Ellen Louks Fairclough | 9 Aug. 1962 – | 22 Apr. 1963 |

## President of the Privy Council

| | | |
|---|---|---|
| Vacant | 21 June 1957 – | 27 Dec. 1961 |
| Hon. Noël Dorion   13 | 28 Dec. 1961 – | 5 July 1962 |
| Vacant | 6 July 1962 – | 20 Dec. 1962 |
| Rt. Hon. John George Diefenbaker | 21 Dec. 1962 – | 22 Apr. 1963 |

## Minister of Public Works

| | | |
|---|---|---|
| Hon. Howard Charles Green   14 | 21 June 1957 – | 19 Aug. 1959 |
| Hon. David James Walker | 20 Aug. 1959 – | 12 July 1962 |
| Vacant | 13 July 1962 – | 17 July 1962 |
| Hon. Howard Charles Green   *Acting Minister* | 18 July 1962 – | 8 Aug. 1962 |
| Hon. Edmund Davie Fulton | 9 Aug. 1962 – | 22 Apr. 1963 |

## Secretary of State of Canada   15

| | | |
|---|---|---|
| Hon. Ellen Louks Fairclough   16 | 21 June 1957 – | 11 May 1958 |
| Hon. Henri Courtemanche | 12 May 1958 – | 19 Jan. 1960 |
| Vacant | 20 Jan. 1960 | |
| Hon. Léon Balcer   *Acting Minister* | 21 Jan. 1960 – | 10 Oct. 1960 |
| Hon. Noël Dorion   17 | 11 Oct. 1960 – | 5 July 1962 |
| Vacant | 6 July 1962 – | 10 July 1962 |
| Hon. Léon Balcer   *Acting Minister* | 11 July 1962 – | 8 Aug. 1962 |
| Hon. George Ernest Halpenny | 9 Aug. 1962 – | 22 Apr. 1963 |

9    Nowlan was appointed Minister of Finance and Receiver General on 9 Aug. 1962.

10   Flemming was also Minister of Forestry.

11   Harkness was also Minister of Agriculture.

12   Hamilton was appointed Minister of Agriculture on 11 Oct. 1960.

13   Dorion was also Secretary of State of Canada.

14   Green was also Secretary of State for External Affairs.

15   The Secretary of State of Canada was *ex officio* the Registrar General of Canada.

16   Fairclough was appointed Minister of Citizenship and Immigration on 12 May 1958.

17   Dorion was also President of the Privy Council.

## Solicitor General of Canada

| | |
|---|---|
| Hon. Léon Balcer   18 | 21 June 1957 – 10 Oct. 1960 |
| Hon. William Joseph Browne | 11 Oct. 1960 – 9 Aug. 1962 |
| Vacant | 10 Aug. 1962 – 22 Apr. 1963 |

## Minister of Trade and Commerce

| | |
|---|---|
| Hon. Gordon Churchill   19 | 21 June 1957 – 10 Oct. 1960 |
| Hon. George Harris Hees | 11 Oct. 1960 – 8 Feb. 1963 |
| Vacant | 9 Feb. 1963 – 11 Feb. 1963 |
| Hon. Malcolm Wallace McCutcheon   *Senator* | 12 Feb. 1963 – 22 Apr. 1963 |

## Minister of Transport

| | |
|---|---|
| Hon. George Harris Hees   20 | 21 June 1957 – 10 Oct. 1960 |
| Hon. Léon Balcer | 11 Oct. 1960 – 22 Apr. 1963 |

## Minister of Veterans Affairs

| | |
|---|---|
| Hon. Alfred Johnson Brooks | 21 June 1957 – 10 Oct. 1960 |
| Hon. Gordon Churchill   21 | 11 Oct. 1960 – 11 Feb. 1963 |
| Hon. Marcel Joseph Aimé Lambert | 12 Feb. 1963 – 22 Apr. 1963 |

## Minister without Portfolio

| | |
|---|---|
| Hon. William Joseph Browne   22 | 21 June 1957 – 10 Oct. 1960 |
| Hon. James MacKerras Macdonnell | 21 June 1957 – 19 Aug. 1959 |
| Hon. John Thomas Haig   *Senator* | 9 Oct. 1957 – 11 May 1958 |
| Hon. George Ernest Halpenny   23 | 11 Oct. 1960 – 8 Aug. 1962 |
| Hon. Malcolm Wallace McCutcheon   24   *Senator* | 9 Aug. 1962 – 11 Feb. 1963 |
| Hon. Frank Charles McGee | 18 Mar. 1963 – 22 Apr. 1963 |
| Hon. Théogène Ricard | 18 Mar. 1963 – 22 Apr. 1963 |

## PARLIAMENTARY ASSISTANTS
## NOT OF THE MINISTRY

### Agriculture

| | |
|---|---|
| John Alpheus Charlton | 7 Aug. 1957 – 1 Feb. 1958 |

### Citizenship and Immigration

| | |
|---|---|
| John Borden Hamilton | 6 Nov. 1957 – 1 Feb. 1958 |

18    Balcer was appointed Minister of Transport on 11 Oct. 1960.

19    Churchill was appointed Minister of Veterans Affairs on 11 Oct. 1960.

20    Hees was appointed Minister of Trade and Commerce on 11 Oct. 1960.

21    Churchill was appointed Minister of National Defence on 12 Feb. 1963.

22    Browne was appointed Solicitor General of Canada on 11 Oct. 1960.

23    Halpenny was appointed Secretary of State of Canada on 9 Aug. 1962.

24    McCutcheon was appointed Minister of Trade and Commerce on 12 Feb. 1963.

**External Affairs**

Wallace Bickford Nesbitt                                            10 Jan. 1958  –  1 Feb. 1958

**Finance**

Richard Albert Bell                                                19 Aug. 1957  –  1 Feb. 1958

**Justice**

David James Walker                                                 19 Aug. 1957  –  1 Feb. 1958

**Labour**

Arthur Maloney                                                      7 Aug. 1957  –  1 Feb. 1958

**Mines and Technical Surveys**

Raymond Joseph Michael O'Hurley                                     7 Aug. 1957  –  1 Feb. 1958

**National Defence**

Marcel Joseph Aimé Lambert                                          7 Aug. 1957  –  1 Feb. 1958

**National Health and Welfare**

George Ernest Halpenny                                              7 Aug. 1957  –  1 Feb. 1958

**Prime Minister**

Wallace Bickford Nesbitt                                           19 Aug. 1957  –  9 Jan. 1958

**Public Works**

Clayton Wesley Hodgson                                              7 Aug. 1957  –  1 Feb. 1958

**Trade and Commerce**

Thomas Miller Bell                                                  7 Aug. 1957  –  9 Jan. 1958

**Transport**

Angus Ronald Macdonald                                             7 Aug. 1957  –  1 Feb. 1958

**Veterans Affairs**

Walter Gilbert Dinsdale                                            19 Aug. 1957  –  1 Feb. 1958

### Agriculture

| | |
|---|---|
| Lewis Elston Cardiff | 18 Nov. 1959 – 17 Nov. 1961 |
| Warner Herbert Jorgenson | 18 Oct. 1960 – 17 Oct. 1961 |
| | 18 Jan. 1962 – 19 Apr. 1962 |
| | 17 Aug. 1962 – 6 Feb. 1963 |
| John Alpheus Charlton | 18 Jan. 1962 – 19 Apr. 1962 |
| Louis-Joseph Pigeon | 17 Aug. 1962 – 6 Feb. 1963 |

### Citizenship and Immigration

| | |
|---|---|
| John Alpheus Charlton | 18 Nov. 1959 – 17 Nov. 1961 |
| Frank Charles McGee | 17 Aug. 1962 – 6 Feb. 1963 |

### External Affairs

| | |
|---|---|
| Wallace Bickford Nesbitt | 1 Sept. 1959 – 31 Aug. 1960 |
| | 18 Nov. 1960 – 17 Nov. 1961 |
| Heath Nelson Macquarrie | 17 Aug. 1962 – 6 Feb. 1963 |

### Finance

| | |
|---|---|
| Richard Albert Bell | 18 Nov. 1959 – 17 Nov. 1961 |
| | 18 Jan. 1962 – 19 Apr. 1962 |
| William Heward Grafftey | 17 Aug. 1962 – 6 Feb. 1963 |

### Fisheries

| | |
|---|---|
| Roland Léo English | 18 Nov. 1959 – 17 Nov. 1961 |
| | 18 Jan. 1962 – 19 Apr. 1962 |
| Albert Deburgo McPhillips | 17 Aug. 1962 – 6 Feb. 1963 |

### Justice

| | |
|---|---|
| Thomas Miller Bell | 18 Nov. 1959 – 17 Nov. 1961 |
| | 18 Jan. 1962 – 19 Apr. 1962 |
| | 17 Aug. 1962 – 6 Feb. 1963 |

### Labour

| | |
|---|---|
| Richard Devere Thrasher | 18 Nov. 1959 – 17 Nov. 1961 |
| | 18 Jan. 1962 – 19 Apr. 1962 |
| Alfred Dryden Hales | 17 Aug. 1962 – 6 Feb. 1963 |

25  Statute 7-8 Eliz. II, c. 15, assented to on 4 June 1959, created the office of Parliamentary Secretary, this office replacing that of Parliamentary Assistant.

## Mines and Technical Surveys

James Aloysius McGrath                    17 Aug. 1962 –   6 Feb. 1963

## National Defence

Egan Chambers                             18 Nov. 1959 –  17 Nov. 1961
                                          18 Jan. 1962 –  19 Apr. 1962

## National Health and Welfare

Lewis Elston Cardiff                      18 Jan. 1962 –  19 Apr. 1962
Jean Casselman                            17 Aug. 1962 –   6 Feb. 1963

## National Revenue

Marcel Joseph Aimé Lambert                18 Nov. 1959 –  17 Nov. 1961
                                          18 Jan. 1962 –  19 Apr. 1962

## Postmaster General

Edmund Leverett Morris                    18 Nov. 1959 –  17 Nov. 1960

## Prime Minister

Paul Martineau                            18 Nov. 1959 –  17 Nov. 1961
John Cameron Pallett                      18 Nov. 1960 –  17 Nov. 1961
                                          18 Jan. 1962 –  19 Apr. 1962
Théogène Ricard                           18 Jan. 1962 –  19 Apr. 1962
                                          17 Aug. 1962 –   6 Feb. 1963
Gerald William Baldwin                    17 Aug. 1962 –   6 Feb. 1963

## Public Works

Yvon-Roma Tassé                           18 Nov. 1959 –  17 Nov. 1961
                                          18 Jan. 1962 –  19 Apr. 1962
Robert Jardine McCleave                   17 Aug. 1962 –   6 Feb. 1963

## Trade and Commerce

John Cameron Pallett                      18 Nov. 1959 –  17 Nov. 1960
Edmund Leverett Morris                    18 Nov. 1960 –  17 Nov. 1961
                                          18 Jan. 1962 –  19 Apr. 1962
Wallace Bickford Nesbitt                  17 Aug. 1962 –   6 Feb. 1963

**Transport**

| | |
|---|---|
| Clayton Wesley Hodgson | 18 Nov. 1959 – 17 Nov. 1961 |
| Quinto Antonio Martini | 18 Nov. 1961 – 19 Apr. 1962 |
| James Alexander McBain | 17 Aug. 1962 – 6 Feb. 1963 |

**Veterans Affairs**

| | |
|---|---|
| Walter Gilbert Dinsdale | 18 Nov. 1959 – 10 Oct. 1960 |
| Henry Frank Jones | 16 Nov. 1960 – 15 Nov. 1961 |
| | 18 Jan. 1962 – 19 Apr. 1962 |
| | 17 Aug. 1962 – 6 Feb. 1963 |

# Nineteenth Ministry

**LIBERAL** 1

22 April 1963 to 20 April 1968

**PRIME MINISTER**

The Right Honourable Lester Bowles Pearson

**THE MINISTRY**

**Minister of Agriculture**

| | | |
|---|---|---|
| Hon. Harry William Hays | 22 Apr. 1963 | – 17 Dec. 1965 |
| Hon. John James Greene | 18 Dec. 1965 | – 20 Apr. 1968 |

**Minister of Citizenship and Immigration** 2

| | | |
|---|---|---|
| Hon. Guy Favreau 3 | 22 Apr. 1963 | – 2 Feb. 1964 |
| Hon. René Tremblay 4 | 3 Feb. 1964 | – 14 Feb. 1965 |
| Hon. John Robert Nicholson 5 | 15 Feb. 1965 | – 17 Dec. 1965 |
| Hon. Jean Marchand 6 | 18 Dec. 1965 | – 30 Sept. 1966 |

**Minister of Consumer and Corporate Affairs** 7

| | | |
|---|---|---|
| Hon. John Napier Turner | 21 Dec. 1967 | – 20 Apr. 1968 |

**Minister of Defence Production** 8

| | | |
|---|---|---|
| Hon. Charles Mills Drury | 22 Apr. 1963 | – 20 Apr. 1968 |

**Minister of Energy, Mines and Resources** 9

| | | |
|---|---|---|
| Hon. Jean-Luc Pepin | 1 Oct. 1966 | – 20 Apr. 1968 |

**Secretary of State for External Affairs**

| | | |
|---|---|---|
| Hon. Paul Joseph James Martin | 22 Apr. 1963 | – 20 Apr. 1968 |

**Minister of Finance and Receiver General**

| | | |
|---|---|---|
| Hon. Walter Lockhart Gordon 10 | 22 Apr. 1963 | – 10 Nov. 1965 |
| Hon. Mitchell William Sharp *Acting Minister* | 11 Nov. 1965 | – 17 Dec. 1965 |
| Hon. Mitchell William Sharp 11 | 18 Dec. 1965 | – 20 Apr. 1968 |

**Minister of Fisheries**

| | | |
|---|---|---|
| Hon. Hédard Robichaud | 22 Apr. 1963 | – 20 Apr. 1968 |

1       With the defeat of the Government in the general election of 8 Apr. 1963, on 22 Apr. the Governor General accepted Diefenbaker's resignation and the Nineteenth Ministry assumed office.

2       See Note 19.

3       Favreau was appointed Minister of Justice and Attorney General on 3 Feb. 1964.

4       Tremblay was appointed Postmaster General on 15 Feb. 1965.

5       Nicholson was appointed Minister of Labour on 18 Dec. 1965.

6       Marchand was appointed Minister of Manpower and Immigration on on 1 Oct. 1966.

7       The office of Minister of Consumer and Corporate Affairs was created by Statute 16 Eliz. II, c. 16, and assented to on 21 Dec. 1967. By this Act the Minister of Consumer and Corporate Affairs is to perform the duties of the Registrar General of Canada.

8       See Note 16.

9       The office of Minister of Mines and Technical Surveys was abolished and the office of Minister of Energy, Mines and Resources created by statute 14-15 Eliz. II, c. 25, assented to on 16 June 1966 and proclaimed in force on 1 Oct. 1966.

10      Gordon rejoined the Ministry as Minister without Portfolio on 9 Jan. 1967.

11      Sharp was also Minister of Trade and Commerce.

## Minister of Forestry  12

| | | |
|---|---|---|
| Hon. John Robert Nicholson   13 | 22 Apr.  1963 – | 2 Feb.  1964 |
| Hon. Maurice Sauvé   14 | 3 Feb.  1964 – | 30 Sept. 1966 |

## Minister of Forestry and Rural Development  12

| | | |
|---|---|---|
| Hon. Maurice Sauvé | 1 Oct.  1966 – | 20 Apr.  1968 |

## Minister of Indian Affairs and Northern Development  15

| | | |
|---|---|---|
| Hon. Arthur Laing | 1 Oct.  1966 – | 20 Apr.  1968 |

## Minister of Industry  16

| | | |
|---|---|---|
| Hon. Charles Mills Drury | 25 July  1963 – | 20 Apr.  1968 |

## Minister of Justice and Attorney General

| | | |
|---|---|---|
| Hon. Lionel Chevrier | 22 Apr.  1963 – | 2 Feb.  1964 |
| Hon. Guy Favreau   17 | 3 Feb.  1964 – | 29 June 1965 |
| Hon. George James McIlraith   *Acting Minister* | 30 June 1965 – | 6 July  1965 |
| Hon. Louis Joseph Lucien Cardin | 7 July  1965 – | 3 Apr.  1967 |
| Hon. Pierre Elliott Trudeau | 4 Apr.  1967 – | 20 Apr.  1968 |

## Minister of Labour

| | | |
|---|---|---|
| Hon. Allan Joseph MacEachen   18 | 22 Apr.  1963 – | 17 Dec.  1965 |
| Hon. John Robert Nicholson | 18 Dec.  1965 – | 20 Apr.  1968 |

## Minister of Manpower and Immigration  19

| | | |
|---|---|---|
| Hon. Jean Marchand | 1 Oct.  1966 – | 20 Apr.  1968 |

## Minister of Mines and Technical Surveys  20

| | | |
|---|---|---|
| Hon. William Moore Benidickson | 22 Apr.  1963 – | 6 July  1965 |
| Hon. John Watson MacNaught | 7 July  1965 – | 17 Dec.  1965 |
| Hon. Jean-Luc Pepin   21* | 18 Dec.  1965 – | 30 Sept. 1966 |

## Minister of National Defence

| | | |
|---|---|---|
| Hon. Paul Theodore Hellyer   22 | 22 Apr.  1963 – | 18 Sept. 1967 |
| Hon. Léo Alphonse Joseph Cadieux | 19 Sept. 1967 – | 20 Apr.  1968 |

## Associate Minister of National Defence

| | | |
|---|---|---|
| Hon. Louis Joseph Lucien Cardin   23 | 22 Apr.  1963 – | 14 Feb.  1965 |
| Hon. Léo Alphonse Joseph Cadieux   24 | 15 Feb.  1965 – | 18 Sept. 1967 |
| Vacant | 19 Sept. 1967 – | 20 Apr.  1968 |

12    The office of Minister of Forestry was abolished and the office of Minister of Forestry and Rural Development created by Statute 14-15 Eliz. II, c. 25, assented to on 16 June 1966 and proclaimed in force on 1 Oct. 1966.

13    Nicholson was appointed Postmaster General on 3 Feb. 1964.

14    Sauvé was appointed Minister of Forestry and Rural Development on 1 Oct. 1966.

15    The office of Minister of Northern Affairs and National Resources was abolished and the office of Minister of Indian Affairs and Northern Development was created by Statute 14-15 Eliz. II, c. 25, assented to on 16 June 1966 and proclaimed in force on 1 Oct. 1966.

16    The office of Minister of Industry was created by Statute 12 Eliz. II, c. 3, assented to on 22 July 1963 and proclaimed in force on 25 July 1963. By this Act the Minister of Industry was to exercise all the duties, powers and functions of the Minister of Defence Production.

17    Favreau was appointed President of the Privy Council on 7 July 1965.

18    MacEachen was appointed Minister of National Health and Welfare on 18 Dec. 1965.

19    The office of Minister of Citizenship and Immigration was abolished and the office of Minister of Manpower and Immigration created by Statute 14-15 Eliz. II, c. 25, assented to on 16 June 1966 and proclaimed in force 1 Oct. 1966.

20    See Note 9.

21    Pepin was appointed Minister of Energy, Mines and Resources on 1 Oct. 1966.

22    Hellyer was appointed Minister of Transport on 19 Sept. 1967.

23    Cardin was appointed Minister of Public Works on 15 Feb. 1965.

24    Cadieux was appointed Minister of National Defence on 19 Sept. 1967.

## Minister of National Health and Welfare

| | |
|---|---|
| Hon. Julia Verlyn LaMarsh   25 | 22 Apr.  1963  –  17 Dec.  1965 |
| Hon. Allan Joseph MacEachen | 18 Dec.  1965  –  20 Apr.  1968 |

## Minister of National Revenue

| | |
|---|---|
| Hon. John Richard Garland | 22 Apr.  1963  –  14 Mar.  1964 |
| Vacant | 15 Mar.  1964  –  18 Mar.  1964 |
| Hon. George James McIlraith   *Acting Minister* | 19 Mar.  1964  –  28 June 1964 |
| Hon. Edgar John Benson   26 | 29 June 1964  –  17 Jan.  1968 |
| Hon. Joseph Jacques Jean Chrétien | 18 Jan.  1968  –  20 Apr.  1968 |

## Minister of Northern Affairs and National Resources   27

| | |
|---|---|
| Hon. Arthur Laing   28 | 22 Apr.  1963  –  30 Sept. 1966 |

## Postmaster General

| | |
|---|---|
| Hon. Azellus Denis | 22 Apr.  1963  –   2 Feb.  1964 |
| Hon. John Robert Nicholson   29 | 3 Feb.  1964  –  14 Feb.  1965 |
| Hon. René Tremblay | 15 Feb.  1965  –  17 Dec.  1965 |
| Hon. Joseph Julien Jean-Pierre Côté | 18 Dec.  1965  –  20 Apr.  1968 |

## President of the Privy Council

| | |
|---|---|
| Hon. Maurice Lamontagne   30 | 22 Apr.  1963  –   2 Feb.  1964 |
| Hon. George James McIlraith   31 | 3 Feb.  1964  –   6 July  1965 |
| Hon. Guy Favreau   32 | 7 July  1965  –   3 Apr.  1967 |
| Hon. Walter Lockhart Gordon | 4 Apr.  1967  –  10 Mar.  1968 |
| Hon. Pierre Elliott Trudeau   *Acting Minister* | 11 Mar.  1968  –  20 Apr.  1968 |

## Minister of Public Works

| | |
|---|---|
| Hon. Jean-Paul Deschatelets | 22 Apr.  1963  –  11 Feb.  1965 |
| Vacant | 12 Feb.  1965  –  14 Feb.  1965 |
| Hon. Louis Joseph Lucien Cardin   33 | 15 Feb.  1965  –   6 July  1965 |
| Hon. George James McIlraith | 7 July  1965  –  20 Apr.  1968 |

## Registrar General of Canada   34

| | |
|---|---|
| Hon. Guy Favreau   35 | 1 Oct.  1966  –   3 Apr.  1967 |
| Hon. John Napier Turner   36 | 4 Apr.  1967  –  20 Dec.  1967 |

25    LaMarsh was appointed Secretary of State of Canada on 18 Dec. 1965.

26    Benson was also President of the Treasury Board.

27    See Note 15.

28    Laing was appointed Minister of Indian Affairs and Northern development on 1 Oct. 1966.

29    Nicholson was appointed Minister of Citizenship and Immigration on 15 Feb. 1965.

30    Lamontagne was appointed Secretary of State of Canada on 3 Feb. 1964.

31    McIlraith was appointed Minister of Public Works on 7 July 1965.

32    Favreau was also Registrar General of Canada.

33    Cardin was appointed Minister of Justice and Attorney General on 7 July 1965.

34    The separate ministerial office of Registrar General of Canada was created by Statute 14-15 Eliz. II, c. 25, assented to on 16 June 1966 and proclaimed in force on 1 Oct. 1966. Previously the Secretary of State of Canada was *ex officio* the Registrar General of Canada. See Note 7.

35    Favreau was also President of the Privy Council.

36    Turner was appointed Minister of Consumer and Corporate Affairs on 21 Dec. 1967.

### Secretary of State of Canada   37

| | |
|---|---|
| Hon. John Whitney Pickersgill   38 | 22 Apr. 1963 – 2 Feb. 1964 |
| Hon. Maurice Lamontagne | 3 Feb. 1964 – 17 Dec. 1965 |
| Hon. Julia Verlyn LaMarsh | 18 Dec. 1965 – 9 Apr. 1968 |
| Hon. John Joseph Connolly   *Acting Minister* | 10 Apr. 1968 – 20 Apr. 1968 |

### Solicitor General of Canada   39

| | |
|---|---|
| Hon. John Watson MacNaught   40 | 22 Apr. 1963 – 6 July 1965 |
| Hon. Lawrence Pennell | 7 July 1965 – 19 Apr. 1968 |

### Minister of Trade and Commerce

| | |
|---|---|
| Hon. Mitchell William Sharp   41 | 22 Apr. 1963 – 3 Jan. 1966 |
| Hon. Robert Henry Winters | 4 Jan. 1966 – 29 Mar. 1968 |
| Hon. Jean-Luc Pepin   *Acting Minister* | 30 Mar. 1968 – 20 Apr. 1968 |

### Minister of Transport

| | |
|---|---|
| Hon. George James McIlraith   42 | 22 Apr. 1963 – 2 Feb. 1964 |
| Hon. John Whitney Pickersgill | 3 Feb. 1964 – 18 Sept. 1967 |
| Hon. Paul Theodore Hellyer | 19 Sept. 1967 – 20 Apr. 1968 |

### President of the Treasury Board   43

| | |
|---|---|
| Hon. Edgar John Benson   44 | 1 Oct. 1966 – 20 Apr. 1968 |

### Minister of Veterans Affairs

| | |
|---|---|
| Hon. Roger Joseph Teillet | 22 Apr. 1963 – 20 Apr. 1968 |

37    See Note 34.

38    Pickersgill was appointed Minister of Transport on 3 Feb. 1964.

39    Statute 14-15 Eliz. II, c. 25, assented to on 16 June 1966 and proclaimed in force on 1 Oct. 1966, repealed the Solicitor General Act (R.S.C. 1952, c. 253) and created the ministerial office of the Solicitor General of Canada. Previously the office was not a cabinet portfolio *per se*, though frequently the incumbent was sworn of the Privy Council and attended Cabinet meetings. A unique procedure followed during the Nineteenth Ministry was the appointment and swearing of both MacNaught and Pennell as Minister without Portfolio at the same time each was appointed and sworn of the Privy Council and as Solicitor General of Canada. This apparently was done in order to leave no doubt that the appointees were considered members of the Cabinet.

40    MacNaught was appointed Minister of Mines and Technical Surveys on 7 July 1965.

41    Sharp was also Minister of Finance and Receiver General.

42    McIlraith was appointed President of the Privy Council on 3 Feb. 1964.

43    The office of President of the Treasury Board was created by Statute 14-15 Eliz. II, c. 25, assented to on 16 June 1966 and proclaimed in force on 1 Oct. 1966. Previously the Minister of Finance was *ex officio* the Chairman of the Treasury Board, which remained a committee of the Privy Council.

44    Benson was also Minister of National Revenue.

## Minister without Portfolio

| | |
|---|---|
| Hon. William Ross Macdonald   *Senator* | 22 Apr. 1963 –   2 Feb. 1964 |
| Hon. John Watson MacNaught   45 | 22 Apr. 1963 –   6 July 1965 |
| Hon. René Tremblay   46 | 22 Apr. 1963 –   2 Feb. 1964 |
| Hon. John Joseph Connolly   *Senator* | 3 Feb. 1964 – 20 Apr. 1968 |
| Hon. Yvon Dupuis | 3 Feb. 1964 – 21 Jan. 1965 |
| Hon. Lawrence Pennell   47 | 7 July 1965 – 30 Sept. 1966 |
| Hon. Jean-Luc Pepin   48 | 7 July 1965 – 17 Dec. 1965 |
| Hon. John Napier Turner   49 | 18 Dec. 1965 –   3 Apr. 1967 |
| Hon. Walter Lockhart Gordon   50 | 9 Jan. 1967 –   3 Apr. 1967 |
| Hon. Joseph Jacques Jean Chrétien   51 | 4 Apr. 1967 – 17 Jan. 1968 |
| Hon. Charles Ronald McKay Granger | 25 Sept. 1967 – 20 Apr. 1968 |
| Hon. Bryce Stuart Mackasey | 9 Feb. 1968 – 20 Apr. 1968 |

45  See Solicitor General of Canada.

46  Tremblay was appointed Minister of Citizenship and Immigration on 3 Feb. 1964.

47  Pennell was also Solicitor General of Canada.

48  Pepin was appointed Minister of Mines and Technical Surveys on 18 Dec. 1965.

49  Turner was appointed Registrar General of Canada on 4 April 1967.

50  Gordon was appointed President of the Privy Council on 4 Apr. 1967.

51  Chrétien was appointed Minister of National Revenue on 18 Jan. 1968.

## PARLIAMENTARY SECRETARIES
## NOT OF THE MINISTRY

**Agriculture**

| | | |
|---|---|---|
| Bruce Silas Beer | 14 May 1963 – | 8 Sept. 1965 |
| | 7 Jan. 1966 – | 20 Apr. 1968 |

**Citizenship and Immigration**

| | | |
|---|---|---|
| John Carr Munro | 14 May 1963 – | 19 Feb. 1964 |
| Hubert Badanai | 20 Feb. 1964 – | 8 Sept. 1965 |
| John Carr Munro | 7 Jan. 1966 – | 30 Sept. 1966 |

**Consumer and Corporate Affairs**

| | | |
|---|---|---|
| Ovide Laflamme | 7 Jan. 1968 – | 20 Apr. 1968 |

**Energy, Mines and Resources**

| | | |
|---|---|---|
| Jack Davis | 1 Oct. 1966 – | 20 Apr. 1968 |

**External Affairs**

| | | |
|---|---|---|
| John Benjamin Stewart | 14 May 1963 – | 19 Feb. 1964 |
| Stanley Haidasz | 20 Feb. 1964 – | 8 Sept. 1965 |
| Donald Stovel Macdonald | 7 Jan. 1966 – | 6 Jan. 1968 |
| Gérard Pelletier | 20 Apr. 1967 – | 20 Apr. 1968 |

**Finance**

| | | |
|---|---|---|
| Edgar John Benson | 14 May 1963 – | 28 June 1964 |
| Lawrence Pennell | 30 June 1964 – | 6 July 1965 |
| Donald Stovel Macdonald | 16 July 1965 – | 8 Sept. 1965 |
| Joseph Jacques Jean Chrétien | 7 Jan. 1966 – | 3 Apr. 1967 |

**Fisheries**

| | | |
|---|---|---|
| Charles Ronald McKay Granger | 7 Jan. 1966 – | 31 July 1966 |
| Richard Joseph Cashin | 4 Oct. 1966 – | 20 Apr. 1968 |

**Forestry**

| | | |
|---|---|---|
| Bruce Silas Beer | 20 Feb. 1964 – | 8 Sept. 1965 |

**Indian Affairs and Northern Development**

| | | |
|---|---|---|
| Stanley Haidasz | 1 Oct. 1966 – | 20 Apr. 1968 |

## Industry

| | |
|---|---|
| David George Hahn | 16 July 1965 – 8 Sept. 1965 |
| Donald Stovel Macdonald | 7 Jan. 1968 – 20 Apr. 1968 |

## Justice

| | |
|---|---|
| Donald Stovel Macdonald | 14 May 1963 – 15 July 1965 |
| Jean-Charles Cantin | 16 July 1965 – 8 Sept. 1965 |

## Labour

| | |
|---|---|
| James Allen Byrne | 14 May 1963 – 8 Sept. 1965 |
| Bryce Stuart Mackasey | 7 Jan. 1966 – 8 Feb. 1968 |

## Manpower and Immigration

| | |
|---|---|
| John Carr Munro | 1 Oct. 1966 – 20 Apr. 1968 |

## Mines and Technical Surveys

| | |
|---|---|
| Jack Davis | 7 Jan. 1966 – 30 Sept. 1966 |

## National Health and Welfare

| | |
|---|---|
| Stanley Haidasz | 14 May 1963 – 19 Feb. 1964 |
| John Carr Munro | 20 Feb. 1964 – 15 July 1965 |
| Bryce Stuart Mackasey | 16 July 1965 – 8 Sept. 1965 |
| Margaret Rideout | 7 Jan. 1966 – 20 Apr. 1968 |

## National Revenue

| | |
|---|---|
| James Edgar Walker | 7 Jan. 1966 – 6 Jan. 1968 |

## Northern Affairs and National Resources

| | |
|---|---|
| John Napier Turner | 14 May 1963 – 8 Sept. 1965 |
| Stanley Haidasz | 7 Jan. 1966 – 30 Sept. 1966 |

## Postmaster General

| | |
|---|---|
| George Roy McWilliam | 14 May 1963 – 19 Feb. 1964 |
| Alexis Caron | 20 Feb. 1964 – 8 Sept. 1965 |

## Prime Minister

| | | |
|---|---|---|
| Alexis Caron | 14 May 1963 – | 19 Feb. 1964 |
| Jack Davis | 14 May 1963 – | 8 Sept. 1965 |
| Guy Rouleau | 17 Feb. 1964 – | 23 Nov. 1964 |
| Joseph Jacques Jean Chrétien | 16 July 1965 – | 8 Sept. 1965 |
| Pierre Elliott Trudeau | 7 Jan. 1966 – | 3 Apr. 1967 |
| John Ross Matheson | 7 Jan. 1966 – | 20 Apr. 1968 |

## Public Works

| | | |
|---|---|---|
| Hubert Badanai | 14 May 1963 – | 19 Feb. 1964 |
| George Roy McWilliam | 20 Feb. 1964 – | 8 Sept. 1965 |
| John Benjamin Stewart | 7 Jan. 1966 – | 20 Apr. 1968 |

## Registrar General of Canada

| | | |
|---|---|---|
| Ovide Laflamme | 20 Apr. 1967 – | 6 Jan. 1968 |

## Secretary of State of Canada

| | | |
|---|---|---|
| Yvon Dupuis | 14 May 1963 – | 2 Feb. 1964 |
| John Benjamin Stewart | 20 Feb. 1964 – | 8 Sept. 1965 |
| Albert Béchard | 7 Jan. 1966 – | 20 Apr. 1968 |

## Trade and Commerce

| | | |
|---|---|---|
| Jean-Luc Pepin | 14 May 1963 – | 6 July 1965 |
| John Carr Munro | 16 July 1965 – | 8 Sept. 1965 |
| Jean-Charles Cantin | 7 Jan. 1966 – | 20 Apr. 1968 |

## Transport

| | | |
|---|---|---|
| Jean-Charles Cantin | 14 May 1963 – | 15 July 1965 |
| James Allen Byrne | 7 Jan. 1966 – | 20 Apr. 1968 |

## Treasury Board

| | | |
|---|---|---|
| James Edgar Walker | 7 Jan. 1968 – | 20 Apr. 1968 |

## Veterans Affairs

| | | |
|---|---|---|
| Chesley William Carter | 14 May 1963 – | 8 Sept. 1965 |

# Twentieth Ministry

**LIBERAL**  1

20 April 1968 to 3 June 1979

**PRIME MINISTER**

The Right Honourable Pierre Elliott Trudeau  2

**THE MINISTRY**

### Minister of Agriculture

| | | |
|---|---|---|
| Hon. John James Greene  3 | 20 Apr. 1968 – | 5 July 1968 |
| Hon. Horace Andrew Olson | 6 July 1968 – | 26 Nov. 1972 |
| Hon. Eugene Francis Whelan | 27 Nov. 1972 – | 3 June 1979 |

### Minister of Communications  4

| | | |
|---|---|---|
| Hon. Eric William Kierans | 1 Apr. 1969 – | 28 Apr. 1971 |
| Hon. Joseph Julien Jean-Pierre Côté  *Acting Minister* | 29 Apr. 1971 – | 10 May 1971 |
| Hon. Gérard Pelletier  *Acting Minister* | 11 May 1971 – | 11 Aug. 1971 |
| Hon. Robert Douglas George Stanbury  5 | 12 Aug. 1971 – | 26 Nov. 1972 |
| Hon. Gérard Pelletier | 27 Nov. 1972 – | 28 Aug. 1975 |
| Hon. Pierre Juneau | 29 Aug. 1975 – | 24 Oct. 1975 |
| Hon. Otto Emil Lang  *Acting Minister* | 25 Oct. 1975 – | 4 Dec. 1975 |
| Hon. Jeanne Sauvé | 5 Dec. 1975 – | 3 June 1979 |

### Minister of Consumer and Corporate Affairs  6

| | | |
|---|---|---|
| Hon. John Napier Turner  7 | 20 Apr. 1968 – | 5 July 1968 |
| Hon. Stanley Ronald Basford  8 | 6 July 1968 – | 27 Jan. 1972 |
| Hon. Robert Knight Andras  9 | 28 Jan. 1972 – | 26 Nov. 1972 |
| Hon. Herbert Eser Gray | 27 Nov. 1972 – | 7 Aug. 1974 |
| Hon. André Ouellet | 8 Aug. 1974 – | 15 Mar. 1976 |
| Hon. Bryce Stuart Mackasey  *Acting Minister* | 16 Mar. 1976 – | 7 Apr. 1976 |
| Hon. Bryce Stuart Mackasey  10 | 8 Apr. 1976 – | 13 Sept. 1976 |
| Hon. Anthony Chisholm Abbott  11 | 14 Sept. 1976 – | 15 Sept. 1977 |
| Hon. William Warren Allmand | 16 Sept. 1977 – | 3 June 1979 |

### Minister of Defence Production  12

| | | |
|---|---|---|
| Hon. Charles Mills Drury | 20 Apr. 1968 – | 5 July 1968 |
| Hon. Donald Campbell Jamieson  13 | 6 July 1968 – | 31 Mar. 1969 |

1   On 20 Apr. 1968, Pearson resigned as Prime Minister and the Twentieth Ministry assumed office. It was composed of twenty-one ministers from the Nineteenth Ministry and three additional Ministers without Portfolio. The Ministry resigned on 3 June 1979.

2   Trudeau was also Minister of Justice and Attorney General.

3   Greene was appointed Minister of Energy, Mines and Resources on 6 July 1968.

4   The office of Minister of Communications was created by Statute 17-18 Eliz. II, c. 28, assented to on 28 Mar. 1969 and proclaimed in force on 1 Apr. 1969. By this Act the Minister of Communications was *ex officio* the Postmaster General. The office of Postmaster General was recreated by Statute 1970-71 Eliz. II, c. 42, assented to on 26 May 1971 and in force on 11 June 1971.

5   Stanbury was appointed Minister of National Revenue on 27 Nov. 1972.

6   The Minister of Consumer and Corporate Affairs performs the duties of the Registrar General of Canada.

7   Turner was also Solicitor General of Canada. He was appointed Minister of Justice and Attorney General on 6 July 1968.

8   Basford was appointed Minister of State for Urban Affairs on 28 Jan. 1972.

9   Andras was appointed Minister of Manpower and Immigration on 27 Nov. 1972.

10  Mackasey was also Postmaster General. He resigned on 13 Sept. 1976.

11  Abbott was appointed Minister of State (Small Businesses) on 16 Sept. 1977.

12  From 25 July 1963 to 12 July 1968, pursuant to Statute 12 Eliz. II, c. 3, the Minister of Industry exercised all the duties, powers and functions of the Minister of Defence Production. On 12 July 1968, by Order in Council pursuant to the Public Service Rearrangement and Transfer of Duties Act, these powers were transferred back to the Minister of Defence Production. See Minister of Supply and Services.

13  Jamieson was appointed Minister of Supply and Services on 1 Apr. 1969.

## Minister of Energy, Mines and Resources

| | |
|---|---|
| Hon. Jean-Luc Pepin   14 | 20 Apr.  1968  –   5 July  1968 |
| Hon. John James Greene   . | 6 July  1968  –  27 Jan.  1972 |
| Hon. Donald Stovel Macdonald   15 | 28 Jan.  1972  –  25 Sept. 1975 |
| Hon. Alastair William Gillespie | 26 Sept. 1975  –   3 June 1979 |

## Secretary of State for External Affairs

| | |
|---|---|
| Hon. Mitchell William Sharp   16 | 20 Apr.  1968  –   7 Aug.  1974 |
| Hon. Allan Joseph MacEachen   17 | 8 Aug.  1974  –  13 Sept. 1976 |
| Hon. Donald Campbell Jamieson | 14 Sept. 1976  –   3 June 1979 |

## Minister of the Environment   18

| | |
|---|---|
| Hon. Jack Davis | 11 June 1971  –   7 Aug.  1974 |
| Hon. Jeanne Sauvé   19 | 8 Aug.  1974  –   4 Dec.  1975 |
| Hon. Roméo LeBlanc   *Acting Minister* | 5 Dec.  1975  –  21 Jan.  1976 |
| Hon. Jean Marchand   20 | 22 Jan.  1976  –  30 June 1976 |
| Hon. Roméo LeBlanc   *Acting Minister* | 1 July  1976  –  13 Sept. 1976 |
| Hon. Roméo LeBlanc   21         . | 14 Sept. 1976  –   1 Apr.  1979 |
| Hon. Leonard Stephen Marchand | 2 Apr.  1979  –   3 June 1979 |

## Minister of Finance   22

| | |
|---|---|
| Hon. Edgar John Benson   23 | 20 Apr.  1968  –  27 Jan.  1972 |
| Hon. John Napier Turner | 28 Jan.  1972  –   9 Sept. 1975 |
| Hon. Charles Mills Drury   *Acting Minister* | 10 Sept. 1975  –  25 Sept. 1975 |
| Hon. Donald Stovel Macdonald   24 | 26 Sept. 1975  –  15 Sept. 1977 |
| Hon. Joseph Jacques Jean Chrétien | 16 Sept. 1977  –   3 June 1979 |

## Minister of Fisheries   25

| | |
|---|---|
| Hon. Hédard Robichaud | 20 Apr.  1968  –   5 July  1968 |
| Hon. Jack Davis   26 | 6 July  1968  –  31 Mar.  1969 |

## Minister of Fisheries and Forestry   27

| | |
|---|---|
| Hon. Jack Davis   28 | 1 Apr.  1969  –  10 June 1971 |

14    Pepin was also Minister of Labour. He was appointed Minister of Industry and Minister of Trade and Commerce on 6 July 1968.

15    Macdonald was appointed Minister of Finance on 26 Sept. 1975.

16    Sharp was appointed President of the Privy Council on 8 Aug. 1974.

17    MacEachen was appointed President of the Privy Council on 14 Sept. 1976.

18    The office of Minister of the Environment was created by Statute 19-20 Eliz. II, c. 42 assented to on 26 May 1971 and in force 11 June 1971. By this Act the Minister of the Environment is the Minister of Fisheries. Government Organization Act 1979 deleted the duties of the Minister of Fisheries and created the Department of Fisheries and Oceans.

19    Sauvé was appointed Minister of Communications on 5 Dec. 1975.

20    Marchand resigned on 30 June 1976.

21    LeBlanc was given the title "Minister of Fisheries and the Environment" and became Minister of Fisheries and Oceans on 2 Apr. 1979.

22    See Minister of Supply and Services.

23    Benson was also President of the Treasury Board. He was appointed Minister of National Defence on 28 Jan. 1972.

24    Macdonald resigned on 15 Sept. 1977.

25    See Minister of Fisheries and Forestry.

26    Davis was appointed Minister of Fisheries and Forestry on 1 Apr. 1969.

27    The offices of Minister of Fisheries and Minister of Forestry and Rural Development were abolished and the office of Minister of Fisheries and Forestry created by Statute 17-18 Eliz. II, c. 28, assented to on 28 Mar. 1969 and in force on 1 Apr. 1969. See also Minister of the Environment.

28    Davis was appointed Minister of the Environment on 11 June 1971.

**Minister of Forestry and Rural Development**  29

| | |
|---|---|
| Hon. Maurice Sauvé | 20 Apr.  1968  –    5 July  1968 |
| Hon. Jean Marchand   30 | 6 July   1968  –  31 Mar.  1969 |

**Minister of Fisheries and Oceans**   31

| | |
|---|---|
| Hon. Roméo LeBlanc | 2 Apr.  1979  –    3 June 1979 |

**Minister of Indian Affairs and Northern Development**

| | |
|---|---|
| Hon. Arthur Laing   32 | 20 Apr.  1968  –    5 July  1968 |
| Hon. Joseph Jacques Jean Chrétien   33 | 6 July   1968  –    7 Aug.  1974 |
| Hon. J. Judd Buchanan   34 | 8 Aug.  1974  –  13 Sept. 1976 |
| Hon. William Warren Allmand   35 | 14 Sept. 1976  –  15 Sept. 1977 |
| Hon. James Hugh Faulkner | 16 Sept. 1977  –    3 June 1979 |

**Minister of Industry**   36

| | |
|---|---|
| Hon. Charles Mills Drury   37 | 20 Apr.  1968  –    5 July  1968 |
| Hon. Jean-Luc Pepin   38 | 6 July   1968  –  31 Mar.  1969 |

**Minister of Industry, Trade and Commerce**   39

| | |
|---|---|
| Hon. Jean-Luc Pepin | 1 Apr.  1969  –  26 Nov.  1972 |
| Hon. Alastair William Gillespie   40 | 27 Nov.  1972  –  25 Sept. 1975 |
| Hon. Donald Campbell Jamieson   41 | 26 Sept. 1975  –  13 Sept. 1976 |
| Hon. Joseph Jacques Jean Chrétien   42 | 14 Sept. 1976  –  15 Sept. 1977 |
| Hon. John Henry Horner | 16 Sept. 1977  –    3 June 1979 |

**Minister of Justice and Attorney General**

| | |
|---|---|
| Rt. Hon. Pierre Elliott Trudeau | 20 Apr.  1968  –    5 July  1968 |
| Hon. John Napier Turner   43 | 6 July   1968  –  27 Jan.  1972 |
| Hon. Otto Emil Lang   44 | 28 Jan.  1972  –  25 Sept. 1975 |
| Hon. Stanley Ronald Basford   45 | 26 Sept. 1975  –    2 Aug.  1978 |
| Hon. Otto Emil Lang   *Acting Minister* | 3 Aug.  1978  –    8 Aug.  1978 |
| Hon. Otto Emil Lang   46 | 9 Aug.  1978  –  23 Nov.  1978 |
| Hon. Marc Lalonde | 24 Nov.  1978  –    3 June 1979 |

29 See Minister of Fisheries and Forestry.

30 Marchand was appointed Minister of Regional Economic Expansion on 1 Apr. 1969.

31 This office was created by Government Organization Act 1979 and proclaimed in force on 2 Apr. 1979.

32 Laing was appointed Minister of Public Works on 6 July 1968.

33 Chrétien was appointed President of the Treasury Board on 8 Aug. 1974.

34 Buchanan was appointed Minister of Public Works on 14 Sept. 1976.

35 Allmand was appointed Minister of Consumer and Corporate Affairs on 16 Sept. 1977.

36 See Minister of Defence Production and Minister of Industry, Trade and Commerce.

37 Drury was also Minister of Trade and Commerce. He was appointed President of the Treasury Board on 6 July 1968.

38 Pepin was also Minister of Trade and Commerce. He was appointed Minister of Industry, Trade and Commerce on 1 Apr. 1969.

39 The offices of Minister of Industry and Minister of Trade and Commerce were abolished and the office of Minister of Industry, Trade and Commerce created by Statute 17-18 Eliz. II, c. 28, assented to on 28 Mar. 1969 and in force on 1 Apr. 1969.

40 Gillespie was appointed Minister of Energy, Mines and Resources on 26 Sept. 1975.

41 Jamieson was appointed Secretary of State for External Affairs on 14 Sept. 1976.

42 Chrétien was appointed Minister of Finance on 16 Sept. 1977.

43 Turner was appointed Minister of Finance on 28 Jan. 1972.

44 Lang was appointed Minister of Transport on 26 Sept. 1975.

45 Basford resigned on 2 Aug. 1978.

46 Lang was replaced by the Hon. Marc Lalonde on 24 Nov. 1978.

## Minister of Labour

| | |
|---|---|
| Hon. Jean-Luc Pepin   47 | 20 Apr.  1968  –   5 July  1968 |
| Hon. Bryce Stuart Mackasey   48 | 6 July  1968  –  27 Jan.  1972 |
| Hon. Martin Patrick O'Connell | 28 Jan.  1972  –  26 Nov.  1972 |
| Hon. John Carr Munro   49 | 27 Nov.  1972  –   7 Sept. 1978 |
| Hon. André Ouellet   *Acting Minister* | 8 Sept. 1978  –  23 Nov.  1978 |
| Hon. Martin Patrick O'Connell | 24 Nov.  1978  –   3 June 1979 |

## Minister of Manpower and Immigration

| | |
|---|---|
| Hon. Jean Marchand   50 | 20 Apr.  1968  –   5 July  1968 |
| Hon. Allan Joseph MacEachen   51 | 6 July  1968  –  23 Sept. 1970 |
| Hon. Otto Emil Lang   52 | 24 Sept. 1970  –  27 Jan.  1972 |
| Hon. Bryce Stuart Mackasey | 28 Jan.  1972  –  26 Nov.  1972 |
| Hon. Robert Knight Andras   53 | 27 Nov.  1972  –  13 Sept. 1976 |
| Hon. Jack Sydney George Cullen   54 | 14 Sept. 1976  –  14 Aug.  1977 |

## Minister of Employment and Immigration   55

| | |
|---|---|
| Hon. Jack Sydney George Cullen | 15 Aug.  1977  –   3 June 1979 |

## Minister of National Defence

| | |
|---|---|
| Hon. Léo Alphonse Joseph Cadieux | 20 Apr.  1968  –  16 Sept. 1970 |
| Hon. Charles Mills Drury   *Acting Minister* | 17 Sept. 1970  –  23 Sept. 1970 |
| Hon. Donald Stovel Macdonald   56 | 24 Sept. 1970  –  27 Jan.  1972 |
| Hon. Edgar John Benson | 28 Jan.  1972  –  31 Aug.  1972 |
| Hon. Jean-Eudes Dubé   *Acting Minister* | 1 Sept. 1972  –   6 Sept. 1972 |
| Hon. Charles Mills Drury   *Acting Minister* | 7 Sept. 1972  –  26 Nov.  1972 |
| Hon. James Armstrong Richardson   57 | 27 Nov.  1972  –  12 Oct.  1976 |
| Hon. Barnett Jerome Danson   *Acting Minister* | 13 Oct.  1976  –   2 Nov.  1976 |
| Hon. Barnett Jerome Danson | 3 Nov.  1976  –   3 June 1979 |

## Associate Minister of National Defence

| | |
|---|---|
| Vacant | 20 Apr.  1968  –   3 June 1979 |

## Minister of National Health and Welfare

| | |
|---|---|
| Hon. Allan Joseph MacEachen   58 | 20 Apr.  1968  –   5 July  1968 |
| Hon. John Carr Munro   59 | 6 July  1968  –  26 Nov.  1972 |
| Hon. Marc Lalonde   60 | 27 Nov.  1972  –  15 Sept. 1977 |
| Hon. Monique Bégin | 16 Sept. 1977  –   3 June 1979 |

47    Pepin was also Minister of Energy, Mines and Resources. He was appointed Minister of Industry and Minister of Trade and Commerce on 6 July 1968.

48    Mackasey was appointed Minister of Manpower and Immigration on 28 Jan. 1972.

49    Munro resigned on 7 Sept. 1978.

50    Marchand was also Secretary of State of Canada. He was appointed Minister of Forestry and Rural Development on 6 July 1968.

51    MacEachen was appointed President of the Privy Council on 24 Sept. 1970.

52    Lang was appointed Minister of Justice and Attorney General on 28 Jan. 1972.

53    Andras was appointed President of the Treasury Board on 14 Sept. 1976.

54    Cullen was appointed Minister of Employment and Immigration on 14 Aug. 1977.

55    The office of Minister of Employment and Immigration was created by Statute 25-26 Eliz. II, c. 54, assented to on 5 Aug. 1977 and in force on 15 Aug. 1977.

56    Macdonald was appointed Minister of Energy, Mines and Resources on 28 Jan. 1972.

57    Richardson resigned on 12 Oct. 1976.

58    MacEachen was appointed Minister of Manpower and Immigration on 6 July 1968.

59    Munro was appointed Minister of Labour on 27 Nov. 1972.

60    Lalonde was appointed Minister of State for Federal-Provincial Relations on 16 Sept. 1977.

## Minister of National Revenue

| | | |
|---|---|---|
| Hon. Joseph Jacques Jean Chrétien  61 | 20 Apr.  1968 – | 5 July  1968 |
| Hon. Joseph Julien Jean-Pierre Côté  62 | 6 July  1968 – | 23 Sept. 1970 |
| Hon. Herbert Eser Gray  63 | 24 Sept. 1970 – | 26 Nov.  1972 |
| Hon. Robert Douglas George Stanbury | 27 Nov.  1972 – | 7 Aug.  1974 |
| Hon. Stanley Ronald Basford  64 | 8 Aug.  1974 – | 25 Sept. 1975 |
| Hon. Jack Sydney George Cullen  65 | 26 Sept. 1975 – | 13 Sept. 1976 |
| Hon. Monique Bégin  66 | 14 Sept. 1976 – | 15 Sept. 1977 |
| Hon. Joseph-Philippe Guay  *Senator*  67 | 16 Sept. 1977 – | 23 Nov.  1978 |
| Hon. Anthony Chisholm Abbott  68 | 24 Nov.  1978 – | 3 June 1979 |

## Postmaster General  69

| | | |
|---|---|---|
| Hon. Joseph Julien Jean-Pierre Côté  70 | 20 Apr.  1968 – | 5 July  1968 |
| Hon. Eric William Kierans | 6 July  1968 – | 28 Apr.  1971 |
| Hon. Joseph Julien Jean-Pierre Côté  *Acting Minister* | 29 Apr.  1971 – | 10 June 1971 |
| Hon. Joseph Julien Jean-Pierre Côté | 11 June 1971 – | 26 Nov.  1972 |
| Hon. André Ouellet  71 | 27 Nov.  1972 – | 7 Aug.  1974 |
| Hon. Bryce Stuart Mackasey  72 | 8 Aug.  1974 – | 13 Sept. 1976 |
| Hon. Jean-Jacques Blais  73 | 14 Sept. 1976 – | 1 Feb.  1978 |
| Hon. Gilles Lamontagne | 2 Feb.  1978 – | 3 June 1979 |

## President of the Privy Council

| | | |
|---|---|---|
| Rt. Hon. Pierre Elliott Trudeau  *Acting Minister* | 20 Apr.ʼ 1968 – | 1 May  1968 |
| Hon. Allan Joseph MacEachen  *Acting Minister* | 2 May  1968 – | 5 July  1968 |
| Hon. Donald Stovel Macdonald  74 | 6 July  1968 – | 23 Sept. 1970 |
| Hon. Allan Joseph MacEachen  75 | 24 Sept. 1970 – | 7 Aug.  1974 |
| Hon. Mitchell William Sharp  76 | 8 Aug.  1974 – | 13 Sept. 1976 |
| Hon. Allan Joseph MacEachen  77 | 14 Sept. 1976 – | 3 June 1979 |

61    Chrétien was appointed Minister of Indian Affairs and Northern Development on 6 July 1968.

62    Côté was appointed Minister without Portfolio on 24 Sept. 1970.

63    Gray was appointed Minister of Consumer and Corporate Affairs on 27 Nov. 1972.

64    Basford was appointed Minister of Justice and Attorney General on 26 Sept. 1975.

65    Cullen was appointed Minister of Manpower and Immigration on 15 Sept. 1976.

66    Bégin was appointed Minister of National Health and Welfare on 16 Sept. 1977.

67    Guay was summoned to the Senate on 23 Mar. 1978. He resigned on 23 Nov. 1978.

68    Abbott was also Minister of State (Small Businesses).

69    See Minister of Communications.

70    Côté was appointed Minister of National Revenue on 6 July 1968.

71    Ouellet was appointed Minister of Consumer and Corporate Affairs on 8 Aug. 1974.

72    Mackasey was also Minister of Consumer and Corporate Affairs. He resigned on 13 Sept. 1976.

73    Blais was appointed Solicitor General on 2 Feb. 1978.

74    Macdonald was appointed Minister of National Defence on 24 Sept. 1970.

75    MacEachen was appointed Secretary of State for External Affairs on 8 Aug. 1974.

76    Sharp resigned on 14 Sept. 1976.

77    MacEachen was also given title "Deputy Prime Minister" on 16 Sept. 1977.

### Minister of Public Works

| | |
|---|---|
| Hon. George James McIlraith   78 | 20 Apr.  1968  –   5 July  1968 |
| Hon. Arthur Laing   79 | 6 July  1968  –  27 Jan.  1972 |
| Hon. Jean-Eudes Dubé | 28 Jan.  1972  –   7 Aug.  1974 |
| Hon. Charles Mills Drury   80 | 8 Aug.  1974  –  13 Sept. 1976 |
| Hon. J. Judd Buchanan   81 | 14 Sept. 1976  –  23 Nov.  1978 |
| Hon. André Ouellet | 24 Nov.  1978  –   3 June 1979 |

### Minister of Regional Economic Expansion   82

| | |
|---|---|
| Hon. Jean Marchand   83 | 1 Apr.  1969  –  26 Nov.  1972 |
| Hon. Donald Campbell Jamieson   84 | 27 Nov.  1972  –  25 Sept. 1975 |
| Hon. Marcel Lessard | 26 Sept. 1975  –   3 June 1979 |

### Minister of State for Science and Technology   85

| | |
|---|---|
| Hon. Alastair William Gillespie   86 | 12 Aug.  1971  –  26 Nov.  1972 |
| Hon. Jeanne Sauvé   87 | 27 Nov.  1972  –   7 Aug.  1974 |
| Hon. Charles Mills Drury   88 | 8 Aug.  1974  –  13 Sept. 1976 |
| Hon. James Hugh Faulkner   89 | 14 Sept. 1976  –  15 Sept. 1977 |
| Hon. J. Judd Buchanan   90 | 16 Sept. 1977  –  23 Nov.  1978 |
| Hon. Alastair William Gillespie | 24 Nov.  1978  –   3 June 1979 |

### Secretary of State of Canada

| | |
|---|---|
| Hon. Jean Marchand   91 | 20 Apr.  ·1968  –   5 July  1968 |
| Hon. Gérard Pelletier   92 | 6 July  1968  –  26 Nov.  1972 |
| Hon. James Hugh Faulkner   93 | 27 Nov.  1972  –  13 Sept. 1976 |
| Hon. John Roberts | 14 Sept. 1976  –   3 June 1979 |

78    McIlraith was appointed Solicitor General of Canada on 6 July 1968.

79    Laing was appointed Minister of Veterans Affairs on 28 Jan. 1972.

80    Drury resigned on 13 Sept. 1976.

81    Buchanan was also appointed Minister of State for Science and Technology on 16 Sept. 1977, and President of the Treasury Board on 24 Nov. 1978.

82    The office of Minister of Regional Economic Expansion was created by Statute 17-18 Eliz. II, c. 28, assented to on 28 Mar. 1969 and in force on 1 Apr. 1969.

83    Marchand was appointed Minister of Transport on 27 Nov. 1972.

84    Jamieson was appointed Minister of Industry, Trade and Commerce on 26 Sept. 1975.

85    The Ministry of State for Science and Technology was proclaimed on 12 Aug. 1971 under the Ministries and Ministers of State Act, 19-20 Eliz. II, 1970-71, c. 42, Part IV.

86    Gillespie was appointed Minister of Industry, Trade and Commerce on 27 Nov. 1972.

87    Sauvé was appointed Minister of the Environment on 8 Aug. 1974.

88    Drury was also Minister of Public Works. He resigned on 13 Sept. 1976.

89    Faulkner was appointed Minister of Indian Affairs and Northern Development on 16 Sept. 1977.

90    Buchanan was appointed President of the Treasury Board on 24 Nov. 1978.

91    Marchand was also Minister of Manpower and Immigration, and was appointed Minister of Forestry and Rural Development on 6 July 1968.

92    Pelletier was appointed Minister of Communications on 27 Nov. 1972.

93    Faulkner was appointed Minister of State for Science and Technology on 14 Sept. 1976.

## Leader of the Government in the Senate  94

| | | |
|---|---|---|
| Hon. Paul Joseph James Martin  *Senator* | 1 Apr.  1969 – | 7 Aug.  1974 |
| Hon. Raymond Joseph Perrault  *Senator* | 8 Aug.  1974 – | 3 June 1979 |

## Solicitor General of Canada

| | | |
|---|---|---|
| Hon. John Napier Turner  95 | 20 Apr.  1968 – | 5 July  1968 |
| Hon. George James McIlraith | 6 July  1968 – | 21 Dec.  1970 |
| Hon. Jean-Pierre Goyer  96 | 22 Dec.  1970 – | 26 Nov.  1972 |
| Hon. William Warren Allmand  97 | 27 Nov.  1972 – | 13 Sept. 1976 |
| Hon. Francis Fox  98 | 14 Sept. 1976 – | 27 Jan.  1978 |
| Hon. Stanley Ronald Basford  *Acting Minister* | 28 Jan.  1978 – | 1 Feb.  1978 |
| Hon. Jean-Jacques Blais | 2 Feb.  1978 – | 3 June 1979 |

## Minister of Supply and Services  99

| | | |
|---|---|---|
| Hon. Donald Campbell Jamieson  100 | 1 Apr.  1969 – | 4 May  1969 |
| Hon. James Armstrong Richardson  101 | 5 May  1969 – | 26 Nov.  1972 |
| Hon. Jean-Pierre Goyer  102 | 27 Nov.  1972 – | 23 Nov.  1978 |
| Hon. Pierre De Bané | 24 Nov.  1978 – | 3 June 1979 |

## Minister of Trade and Commerce  103

| | | |
|---|---|---|
| Hon. Charles Mills Drury  104 | 20 Apr.  1968 – | 5 July  1968 |
| Hon. Jean-Luc Pepin  105 | 6 July  1968 – | 31 Mar.  1969 |

94     The ministerial office of Leader of the Government in the Senate was recognized by the appointment of Martin by Commission under the Great Seal of Canada and by Section 97 of Statute 17-18 Eliz. II, c. 28, assented to on 28 Mar. 1969 and in force on 1 Apr. 1969. Previously the position was not *per se* a ministerial office, although occasionally the incumbent held a Cabinet portfolio while serving as Leader of the Government in the Senate.

95     Turner was also Minister of Consumer and Corporate Affairs. He was appointed Minister of Justice and Attorney General on 6 July 1968.

96     Goyer was appointed Minister of Supply and Services on 27 Nov. 1972.

97     Allmand was appointed Minister of Indian Affairs and Northern Development on 14 Sept. 1976.

98     Fox resigned on 27 Jan. 1978.

99     The office of Minister of Defence Production was abolished and the office of Minister of Supply and Services created by Statute 17-18 Eliz. II, c. 28, assented to on 28 Mar. 1969 and in force on 1 Apr. 1969. By this Act the Minister of Supply and Services is *ex officio* the Receiver General of Canada, the office having been previously held *ex officio* by the Minister of Finance.

100     Jamieson was appointed Minister of Transport on 5 May 1969.

101     Richardson was appointed Minister of National Defence on 27 Nov. 1972.

102     Goyer resigned on 23 Nov. 1978.

103     See Minister of Industry, Trade and Commerce.

104     Drury was also Minister of Industry. He was appointed President of the Treasury Board on 6 July 1968.

105     Pepin was also Minister of Industry. He was appointed Minister of Industry, Trade and Commerce on 1 Apr. 1969.

## Minister of Transport

| | |
|---|---|
| Hon. Paul Theodore Hellyer | 20 Apr. 1968 – 29 Apr. 1969 |
| Hon. James Armstrong Richardson *Acting Minister* | 30 Apr. 1969 – 4 May 1969 |
| Hon. Donald Campbell Jamieson 106 | 5 May 1969 – 26 Nov. 1972 |
| Hon. Jean Marchand 107 | 27 Nov. 1972 – 25 Sept. 1975 |
| Hon. Otto Emil Lang 108 | 26 Sept. 1975 – 3 June 1979 |

## President of the Treasury Board

| | |
|---|---|
| Hon. Edgar John Benson 109 | 20 Apr. 1968 – 5 July 1968 |
| Hon. Charles Mills Drury 110 | 6 July 1968 – 7 Aug. 1974 |
| Hon. Joseph Jacques Jean Chrétien 111 | 8 Aug. 1974 – 13 Sept. 1976 |
| Hon. Robert Knight Andras 112 | 14 Sept. 1976 – 23 Nov. 1978 |
| Hon. J. Judd Buchanan | 24 Nov. 1978 – 3 June 1979 |

## Minister of State for Urban Affairs 113

| | |
|---|---|
| Hon. Robert Knight Andras 114 | 30 June 1971 – 27 Jan. 1972 |
| Hon. Stanley Ronald Basford 115 | 28 Jan. 1972 – 7 Aug. 1974 |
| Hon. Barnett Jerome Danson 116 | 8 Aug. 1974 – 2 Nov. 1976 |
| Hon. André Ouellet 113 | 3 Nov. 1976 – 31 Mar. 1979 |

## Minister of Veterans Affairs

| | |
|---|---|
| Hon. Roger Joseph Teillet | 20 Apr. 1968 – 5 July 1968 |
| Hon. Jean-Eudes Dubé 117 | 6 July 1968 – 27 Jan. 1972 |
| Hon. Arthur Laing | 28 Jan. 1972 – 26 Nov. 1972 |
| Hon. Daniel Joseph MacDonald | 27 Nov. 1972 – 3 June 1979 |

## Minister of State for Economic Development 118

| | |
|---|---|
| Hon. Robert Knight Andras 119 | 24 Nov. 1978 – 3 June 1979 |

106  Jamieson was appointed Minister of Regional Economic Expansion on 27 Nov. 1972.

107  Marchand was appointed Minister without Portfolio on 26 Sept. 1975.

108  Lang was also Minister of Justice and Attorney General from 9 Aug. to 23 Nov. 1978.

109  Benson was also Minister of Finance.

110  Drury was appointed Minister of State for Science and Technology and Minister of Public Works on 8 Aug. 1974.

111  Chrétien was appointed Minister of Industry, Trade and Commerce on 14 Sept. 1976.

112  Andras was appointed Minister of State for Economic Development on 24 Nov. 1978.

113  The Ministry of State for Urban Affairs was proclaimed on 30 June 1971 under the Ministries and Ministers of State Act, 19-20 Eliz. II, 1970-71, c. 42, Part IV. The existence of the Ministry was terminated effective on 1 Apr. 1979 by proclamation.

114  Andras was appointed Minister of Consumer and Corporate Affairs on 28 Jan. 1972.

115  Basford was appointed Minister of National Revenue on 8 Aug. 1974.

116  Danson was appointed Minister of National Defence on 3 Nov. 1976.

117  Dubé was appointed Minister of Public Works on 28 Jan. 1972.

118  The Ministry of State for Economic Development was proclaimed on 19 Dec. 1978 under the Ministries and Ministers of State Act, 19-20 Eliz. II, 1970-1, c. 42 Part IV.

119  Andras was appointed to the new Ministry of State to be created on 24 Nov. 1978. He was also the President of the Board of Economic Development Ministers.

## Minister without Portfolio

| | | |
|---|---|---|
| Hon. Charles Ronald McKay Granger | 20 Apr. 1968 – | 5 July 1968 |
| Hon. Paul Joseph James Martin   120 | 20 Apr. 1968 – | 31 Mar. 1969 |
| Hon. Donald Stovel Macdonald   121 | 20 Apr. 1968 – | 5 July 1968 |
| Hon. Bryce Stuart Mackasey   122 | 20 Apr. 1968 – | 5 July 1968 |
| Hon. John Carr Munro   123 | 20 Apr. 1968 – | 5 July 1968 |
| Hon. Gérard Pelletier   124 | 20 Apr. 1968 – | 5 July 1968 |
| Hon. Jack Davis   125 | 26 Apr. 1968 – | 5 July 1968 |
| Hon. Robert Knight Andras   126 | 6 July 1968 – | 29 June 1971 |
| Hon. Otto Emil Lang   127 | 6 July 1968 – | 23 Sept. 1970 |
| Hon. James Armstrong Richardson   128 | 6 July 1968 – | 4 May 1969 |
| Hon. Herbert Eser Gray   129 | 20 Oct. 1969 – | 23 Sept. 1970 |
| Hon. Robert Douglas George Stanbury   130 | 20 Oct. 1969 – | 11 Aug. 1971 |
| Hon. Joseph Julien Jean-Pierre Côté   131 | 24 Sept. 1970 – | 10 June 1971 |
| Hon. Jean Marchand   132 | 26 Sept. 1975 – | 21 Jan. 1976 |
| Hon. Joseph-Philippe Guay   133 | 3 Nov. 1976 – | 20 Apr. 1977 |
| Hon. John Henry Horner   134 | 21 Apr. 1977 – | 15 Sept. 1977 |
| Hon. Gilles Lamontagne   135 | 19 Jan. 1978 – | 1 Feb. 1978 |

120  Martin was appointed Leader of the Government in the Senate on 1 Apr. 1969.

121  Macdonald was appointed President of the Privy Council on 6 July 1968.

122  Mackasey was appointed Minister of Labour on 6 July 1968.

123  Munro was appointed Minister of National Health and Welfare on 6 July 1968.

124  Pelletier was appointed Secretary of State of Canada on 6 July 1968.

125  Davis was appointed Minister of Fisheries on 6 July 1968.

126  Andras was appointed Minister of State for Urban Affairs on 30 June 1971.

127  Lang was appointed Minister of Manpower and Immigration on 24 Sept. 1970.

128  Richardson was appointed Minister of Supply and Services on 5 May 1969.

129  Gray was appointed Minister of National Revenue on 24 Sept. 1970.

130  Stanbury was appointed Minister of Communications on 12 Aug. 1971.

131  Côté was appointed Minister without Portfolio responsible for the Post Office on 24 Sept. 1970, and Postmaster General on 11 June 1971.

132  Marchand was appointed Minister of the Environment on 22 Jan. 1976.

133  Guay was appointed Minister of State on 21 Apr. 1977.

134  Horner was appointed Minister of Industry, Trade and Commerce on 16 Sept. 1977.

135  Lamontagne was appointed Postmaster General on 2 Feb. 1978.

## Minister of State 136

| | |
|---|---|
| Hon. Martin Patrick O'Connell   137 | 12 Aug. 1971 – 27 Jan. 1972 |
| Hon. Patrick Morgan Mahoney | 28 Jan. 1972 – 26 Nov. 1972 |
| Hon. Stanley Haidasz | 27 Nov. 1972 – 7 Aug. 1974 |
| Hon. Bryce Stuart Mackasey   138 | 3 June 1974 – 7 Aug. 1974 |
| Hon. Roméo LeBlanc   139 | 8 Aug. 1974 – 13 Sept. 1976 |
| Hon. Leonard Stephen Marchand   140 | 14 Sept. 1976 – 1 Apr. 1979 |
| Hon. Iona Campagnolo   141 | 15 Sept. 1976 – 3 June 1979 |

136 The title Minister of State was created under the Ministries and Ministers of State Act, 19-20 Eliz. II, 1970-71, c. 42, Part IV. While no specific duties are given to a Minister of State, he can be assigned by the Governor in Council to assist any Minister or Ministers having responsibilities for any department or other portion of the public service.

137 O'Connell was appointed Minister of Labour on 28 Jan. 1972.

138 Mackasey was appointed Postmaster General on 8 Aug. 1974.

139 LeBlanc was assigned by Order in Council P.C. 1974-1837 of 8 Aug. 1974 to assist the Minister of the Environment to carry out the latter's responsibilities as Minister of Fisheries. Also the powers, duties and functions of the Minister of the Environment under various Acts relating to fisheries were transferred to Mr. LeBlanc by Order in Council P.C. 1974-1839 of 8 Aug. 1974. Mr. LeBlanc was given the title "Minister of State (Fisheries)". He was appointed Minister of the Environment on 14 Sept. 1976 and given the title "Minister of Fisheries and Environment".

140 Marchand was assigned by Order in Council P.C. 1976-2424 of 30 Sept. 1976 to assist the Minister of Industry, Trade and Commerce in the carrying out of the latter's responsibilities in respect of the policies and programs related to small business firms and was given the title "Minister of State (Small Businesses)". He was assigned by Order in Council P.C. 1977-2796 of 29 Sept. 1977 to assist the Minister of Fisheries and the Environment in the carrying out of the latter's responsibilities in respect to the policies and programs related to Environment and was given the title "Minister of State (Environment)". He was appointed Minister of the Environment on 2 Apr. 1979.

141 Campagnolo was assigned by Order in Council P.C. 1976-2423 of 30 Sept. 1976 to assist the Minister of National Health and Welfare in carrying out the latter's responsibilities in respect of the policies and program related to fitness and amateur sport and was given the title "Minister of State (Fitness and Amateur Sport)".

**Minister of State**(continued)

| | |
|---|---|
| Hon. Joseph Philippe Guay   142 | 21 Apr.  1977  –  15 Sept. 1977 |
| Hon. Marc Lalonde   143 | 16 Sept. 1977  –  23 Nov.  1978 |
| Hon. Norman A. Cafik   144 | 16 Sept. 1977  –   3 June 1979 |
| Hon. Anthony Chisholm Abbott   145 | 16 Sept. 1977  –   3 June 1979 |
| Hon. John M. Reid   146 | 24 Nov.  1978  –   3 June 1979 |

142 Guay was assigned by Order in Council P.C. 1977-1129 of 21 Apr. 1977 to assist the Secretary of State of Canada in the carrying out of the latter's responsibilities in respect of the policies and programs related to Multiculturalism and was given the title "Minister of State (Multiculturalism)". He was appointed Minister of National Revenue on 16 Sept. 1977.

143 Lalonde was assigned to assist the Prime Minister in matters related to Federal-Provincial Relations and was given the title "Minister of State for Federal-Provincial Relations". He was appointed Minister of Justice and Attorney General on 24 Nov. 1978.

144 Cafik was assigned by Order in Council P.C. 1977-2798 of 29 Sept. 1977 to assist the Secretary of State of Canada in the carrying out of the latter's responsibilities in respect of the policies and programs related to Multiculturalism and was given the title "Minister of State (Multiculturalism)".

145 Abbott was assigned by Order in Council P.C. 1977-2797 of 29 Sept. 1977 to assist the Minister of Industry, Trade and Commerce in the carrying out of the latter's responsibilities in respect of the policies and programs related to small business firms and was given the title "Minister of State (Small Businesses)". On 24 Nov. 1978 he was also appointed Minister of National Revenue.

146 Reid was assigned to assist the Prime Minister in matters related to Federal-Provincial Relations and was given the title "Minister of State (Federal-Provincial Relations)".

## PARLIAMENTARY SECRETARIES
## NOT OF THE MINISTRY

### Agriculture

| | |
|---|---|
| Bruce Silas Beer | 20 Apr. 1968 – 23 Apr. 1968 |
| Florian Côté | 30 Aug. 1968 – 30 Sept. 1970 |
| Marcel Lessard | 1 Oct. 1970 – 1 Sept. 1972 |
| Léopold Corriveau | 22 Dec. 1972 – 21 Dec. 1973 |
| | 1 Jan. 1974 – 9 May 1974 |
| | 15 Sept. 1974 – 14 Sept. 1975 |
| Irénée Pelletier | 10 Oct. 1975 – 1 Oct. 1977 |
| Yves Caron | 1 Oct. 1977 – 1 Oct. 1978 |
| Yves Caron | 1 Oct. 1978 – 26 Mar. 1979 |

### Communications

| | |
|---|---|
| Joseph-Roland Comtois | 1 Oct. 1971 – 1 Sept. 1972 |
| James Sydney Clark Fleming | 10 Oct. 1975 – 30 Sept. 1976 |
| Ross Milne | 1 Oct. 1976 – 30 Sept. 1977 |
| Crawford Douglas | 1 Oct. 1977 – 30 Sept. 1978 |
| | 1 Oct. 1978 – 26 Mar. 1979 |

### Consumer and Corporate Affairs

| | |
|---|---|
| Ovide Laflamme | 20 Apr. 1968 – 23 Apr. 1968 |
| Stanley Haidasz | 30 Aug. 1968 – 19 Oct. 1969 |
| Paul Langlois | 20 Oct. 1969 – 30 Sept. 1970 |
| Donald Ross Tolmie | 1 Oct. 1971 – 1 Sept. 1972 |
| Pierre De Bané | 1 Jan. 1974 – 9 May 1974 |
| Norman A. Cafik | 15 Sept. 1974 – 14 Sept. 1975 |
| Arthur John Lee | 10 Oct. 1975 – 30 Sept. 1976 |
| Claude G. Lajoie | 1 Oct. 1976 – 30 Sept. 1977 |
| Alan A. Martin | 1 Oct. 1977 – 30 Sept. 1978 |
| Aideen Nicholson | 1 Oct. 1978 – 26 Mar. 1979 |

### Employment and Immigration

| | |
|---|---|
| Raymond Dupont | 1 Oct. 1977 – 30 Sept. 1978 |
| Frank Maine | 1 Oct. 1978 – 26 Mar. 1979 |

## Energy, Mines and Resources

| | | |
|---|---|---|
| Jack Davis | 20 Apr. 1968 | – 23 Apr. 1968 |
| Robert John Orange | 30 Aug. 1968 | – 30 Sept. 1970 |
| Allen B. Sulatycky | 1 Oct. 1971 | – 2 Feb. 1972 |
| Jack Sydney George Cullen | 3 Feb. 1972 | – 1 Sept. 1972 |
| Herb Breau | 1 Jan. 1974 | – 9 May 1974 |
| Maurice Brydon Foster | 15 Sept. 1974 | – 14 Sept. 1975 |
| | 10 Oct. 1975 | – 30 Sept. 1976 |
| Maurice Dupras | 1 Oct. 1976 | – 30 Sept. 1977 |
| Gilles Lamontagne | 1 Oct. 1977 | – 18 Jan. 1978 |
| Pierre Bussières | 1 Oct. 1978 | – 26 Mar. 1979 |

## Environment

| | | |
|---|---|---|
| Eymard Georges Corbin | 11 June 1971 | – 1 Sept. 1972 |
| William Rompkey | 22 Dec. 1972 | – 21 Dec. 1973 |
| | 1 Jan. 1974 | – 9 May 1974 |
| Leonard Stephen Marchand | 15 Sept. 1974 | – 14 Sept. 1975 |
| George S. Baker | 10 Oct. 1975 | – 30 Sept. 1976 |
| James Sydney Clark Fleming | 1 Oct. 1976 | – 30 Sept. 1977 |
| Jack Pearsall | 1 Oct. 1978 | – 26 Mar. 1979 |

## External Affairs

| | | |
|---|---|---|
| Jean-Pierre Goyer | 30 Aug. 1968 | – 30 Sept. 1970 |
| André Ouellet | 1 Oct. 1970 | – 12 Aug. 1971 |
| Gaston Joseph Isabelle | 1 Oct. 1971 | – 1 Sept. 1972 |
| Paul St-Pierre | 1 Oct. 1971 | – 1 Sept. 1972 |
| Pierre De Bané | 22 Dec. 1972 | – 21 Dec. 1973 |
| Herb Breau | 15 Sept. 1974 | – 14 Sept. 1975 |
| Monique Bégin | 10 Oct. 1975 | – 14 Sept. 1976 |
| Fernand E. Leblanc | 1 Oct. 1976 | – 30 Sept. 1977 |
| Maurice Dupras | 1 Oct. 1977 | – 30 Sept. 1978 |
| Louis Duclos | 1 Oct. 1978 | – 26 Mar. 1979 |

## Finance

| | |
|---|---|
| Herbert Eser Gray | 30 Aug. 1968 – 19 Oct. 1969 |
| Patrick Morgan Mahoney | 1 Oct. 1970 – 27 Jan. 1972 |
| J. Judd Buchanan | 3 Feb. 1972 – 1 Sept. 1972 |
| Joseph-Roland Comtois | 22 Dec. 1972 – 21 Dec. 1973 |
| | 1 Jan. 1974 – 9 May 1974 |
| Jack Sydney George Cullen | 15 Sept. 1974 – 14 Sept. 1975 |
| Jacques L. Trudel | 10 Oct. 1975 – 30 Sept. 1976 |
| Robert Phillip Kaplan | 1 Oct. 1976 – 30 Sept. 1977 |
| Edward Lumley | 1 Oct. 1977 – 30 Sept. 1978 |
| Alan A. Martin | 1 Oct. 1978 – 26 Mar. 1979 |

## Fisheries

| | |
|---|---|
| Richard Joseph Cashin | 20 Apr. 1968 – 23 Apr. 1968 |
| Eugene Francis Whelan | 30 Aug. 1968 – 31 Mar. 1969 |

## Fisheries and Forestry

| | |
|---|---|
| Eugene Francis Whelan | 1 Aug. 1969 – 30 Sept. 1970 |
| Eymard Georges Corbin | 1 Oct. 1970 – 10 June 1971 |

## Forestry and Rural Development

| | |
|---|---|
| Russell Clayton Honey | 30 Aug. 1968 – 31 Mar. 1969 |

## Indian Affairs and Northern Development

| | |
|---|---|
| Stanley Haidasz | 20 Apr. 1968 – 23 Apr. 1968 |
| Russell Clayton Honey | 20 Oct. 1969 – 30 Sept. 1970 |
| J. Judd Buchanan | 1 Oct. 1970 – 2 Feb. 1972 |
| Allen B. Sulatycky | 3 Feb. 1972 – 1 Sept. 1972 |
| Leonard Stephen Marchand | 22 Dec. 1972 – 21 Dec. 1973 |
| | 1 Jan. 1974 – 9 May 1974 |
| Iona Campagnolo | 15 Sept. 1974 – 14 Sept. 1975 |
| | 10 Oct. 1975 – 13 Sept. 1976 |
| Keith Penner | 1 Oct. 1976 – 30 Sept. 1977 |
| Ross Milne | 1 Oct. 1977 – 30 Sept. 1978 |
| Hugh Anderson | 1 Oct. 1978 – 26 Mar. 1979 |

## Industry, Trade and Commerce

| | | |
|---|---|---|
| Bruce Andrew Thomas Howard | 1 Oct. 1970 – | 1 Sept. 1972 |
| Herb Breau | 22 Dec. 1972 – | 21 Dec. 1973 |
| Raynald J.A. Guay | 1 Jan. 1974 – | 9 May 1974 |
| Gaston Clermont | 15 Sept. 1974 – | 14 Sept. 1975 |
| Marcel Claude Roy | 10 Oct. 1975 – | 30 Sept. 1976 |
| Hugh Poulin | 1 Oct. 1976 – | 30 Sept. 1977 |
| Bernard Loiselle | 1 Oct. 1977 – | 30 Sept. 1978 |
| Bernard Loiselle | 1 Oct. 1978 – | 26 Mar. 1979 |

## Justice

| | | |
|---|---|---|
| Jean-Charles Cantin | 30 Aug. 1968 – | 30 Sept. 1970 |
| Albert Béchard | 1 Oct. 1970 – | 1 Sept. 1972 |
| Raynald J.A. Guay | 22 Dec. 1972 – | 21 Dec. 1973 |
| Gilles Marceau | 1 Jan. 1974 – | 9 May 1974 |
| Gilles Marceau | 15 Sept. 1974 – | 14 Sept. 1975 |
| Francis Fox | 10 Oct. 1975 – | 13 Sept. 1976 |
| Michael Landers | 1 Oct. 1976 – | 30 Sept. 1977 |
| Roger Young | 1 Oct. 1977 – | 30 Sept. 1978 |
| Claude-André Lachance | 1 Oct. 1978 – | 26 Mar. 1979 |

## Labour

| | | |
|---|---|---|
| James Carroll Patrick McNulty | 30 Aug. 1968 – | 30 Sept. 1970 |
| Raymond Joseph Perrault | 1 Oct. 1970 – | 2 Feb. 1972 |
| Charles Turner | 22 Dec. 1972 – | 21 Dec. 1973 |
| Charles Turner | 1 Jan. 1974 – | 9 May 1974 |
| Mark MacGuigan | 15 Sept. 1974 – | 14 Sept. 1975 |
| Fernand E. Leblanc | 10 Oct. 1975 – | 30 Sept. 1976 |
| Jacques Olivier | 1 Oct. 1976 – | 30 Sept. 1977 |
| Jacques Olivier | 1 Oct. 1977 – | 30 Sept. 1978 |
| Dennis M. Dawson | 1 Oct. 1978 – | 26 Mar. 1979 |

## Manpower and Immigration

| | |
|---|---|
| Gérard Loiselle | 30 Aug. 1968 – 19 Oct. 1969 |
| Rosaire Gendron | 20 Oct. 1969 – 30 Sept. 1970 |
| Charles L. Caccia | 1 Oct. 1970 – 30 Sept. 1971 |
| Marcel Prud'homme | 1 Oct. 1971 – 2 Feb. 1972 |
| Raymond Joseph Perrault | 3 Feb. 1972 – 1 Sept. 1972 |
| Mark MacGuigan | 22 Dec. 1972 – 21 Dec. 1973 |
| | 1 Jan. 1974 – 9 May 1974 |
| William Rompkey | 15 Sept. 1974 – 14 Sept. 1975 |
| Arthur Portelance | 10 Oct. 1975 – 30 Sept. 1976 |
| | 1 Oct. 1976 – 30 Sept. 1977 |

## National Defence

| | |
|---|---|
| David Walter Groos | 30 Aug. 1968 – 30 Sept. 1970 |
| Jack Sydney George Cullen | 1 Oct. 1971 – 2 Feb. 1972 |
| Joseph-Roland Comtois | 3 Feb. 1972 – 1 Sept. 1972 |
| Leonard Hopkins | 22 Dec. 1972 – 21 Dec. 1973 |
| | 1 Jan. 1974 – 9 May 1974 |
| | 15 Sept. 1974 – 14 Sept. 1975 |
| Maurice Adrian Dionne | 10 Oct. 1975 – 30 Sept. 1976 |
| Maurice Adrian Dionne | 1 Oct. 1976 – 30 Sept. 1977 |
| Jacques Guilbault | 1 Oct. 1977 – 30 Sept. 1978 |
| Raymond Dupont | 1 Oct. 1978 – 26 Mar. 1979 |

## National Health and Welfare

| | |
|---|---|
| Margaret Rideout | 20 Apr. 1968 – 23 Apr. 1968 |
| Rosaire Gendron | 30 Aug. 1968 – 19 Oct. 1969 |
| Stanley Haidasz | 20 Oct. 1969 – 30 Sept. 1970 |
| Gaston Joseph Isabelle | 1 Oct. 1970 – 30 Sept. 1971 |
| André Ouellet | 13 Aug. 1971 – 1 Sept. 1972 |
| Norman A. Cafik | 22 Dec. 1972 – 21 Dec. 1973 |
| | 1 Jan. 1974 – 9 May 1974 |
| Coline Campbell | 15 Sept. 1974 – 14 Sept. 1975 |
| Robert Phillip Kaplan | 10 Oct. 1975 – 30 Sept. 1976 |
| Paul McRae | 1 Oct. 1976 – 30 Sept. 1977 |
| William Kenneth Robinson | 1 Oct. 1977 – 30 Sept. 1978 |
| | 1 Oct. 1978 – 26 Mar. 1979 |

## National Revenue

| | | |
|---|---|---|
| Ian Watson | 3 Feb. 1972 – | 1 Sept. 1972 |
| Claude G. Lajoie | 10 Oct. 1975 – | 30 Sept. 1975 |
| George S. Baker | 1 Oct. 1976 – | 30 Sept. 1977 |
| Yves Demers | 1 Oct. 1977 – | 30 Sept. 1978 |
| | 1 Oct. 1978 – | 26 Mar. 1979 |

## Postmaster General

| | | |
|---|---|---|
| Gerald Richard Cobbe | 1 Oct. 1971 – | 1 Sept. 1972 |
| Raynald J.A. Guay | 15 Sept. 1974 – | 14 Sept. 1975 |
| Paul McRae | 10 Oct. 1975 – | 30 Sept. 1976 |
| Walter Smith | 1 Oct. 1976 – | 30 Sept. 1977 |
| David Collenette | 1 Oct. 1978 – | 26 Mar. 1979 |

## Prime Minister

| | | |
|---|---|---|
| John Ross Matheson | 20 Apr. 1968 – | 23 Apr. 1968 |
| James Edgar Walker | 30 Aug. 1968 – | 30 Sept. 1970 |
| Barnett Jerome Danson | 1 Oct. 1970 – | 1 Sept. 1972 |

## Privy Council

| | | |
|---|---|---|
| Yves Forest | 30 Aug. 1968 – | 30 Sept. 1970 |
| James Alexander Jerome | 1 Oct. 1970 – | 1 Sept. 1972 |
| John M. Reid | 22 Dec. 1972 – | 21 Dec. 1973 |
| | 1 Jan. 1974 – | 9 May 1974 |
| Maurice Brydon Foster | 1 Jan. 1974 – | 9 May 1974 |
| John M. Reid | 15 Sept. 1974 – | 14 Sept. 1975 |
| Jean-Jacques Blais | 10 Oct. 1975 – | 30 Sept. 1976 |
| Ralph Goodale | 1 Oct. 1976 – | 30 Sept. 1977 |
| Yvon Pinard | 1 Oct. 1977 – | 30 Sept. 1978 |
| | 1 Oct. 1978 – | 26 Mar. 1979 |

## Public Works

| | | |
|---|---|---|
| John Benjamin Stewart | 20 Apr. 1968 – | 23 Apr. 1968 |
| Paul Langlois | 30 Aug. 1968 – | 19 Oct. 1969 |
| Gustave Blouin | 1 Oct. 1971 – | 1 Sept. 1972 |
| Charles Turner | 15 Sept. 1974 – | 14 Sept. 1975 |
| Alexandre Cyr | 10 Oct. 1975 – | 30 Sept. 1976 |
| | 1 Oct. 1976 – | 30 Sept. 1977 |
| Frank Maine | 1 Oct. 1977 – | 30 Sept. 1978 |
| Harold Thomas Herbert | 1 Oct. 1978 – | 26 Mar. 1979 |

## Regional Economic Expansion

| | | |
|---|---|---|
| Russell Clayton Honey | 1 Apr. 1969 – | 19 Oct. 1969 |
| Martin Patrick O'Connell | 20 Oct. 1969 – | 11 Aug. 1971 |
| John Roberts | 1 Oct. 1971 – | 1 Sept. 1972 |
| Marcel Prud'homme | 22 Dec. 1972 – | 21 Dec. 1973 |
| | 1 Jan. 1974 – | 9 May 1974 |
| Joseph-Philippe Guay | 15 Sept. 1974 – | 14 Sept. 1975 |
| Joseph Clifford McIsaac | 10 Oct. 1975 – | 30 Sept. 1976 |
| Edward Lumley | 1 Oct. 1976 – | 30 Sept. 1977 |
| Donald Wood | 1 Oct. 1977 – | 30 Sept. 1978 |
| | 1 Oct. 1978 – | 26 Mar. 1979 |

## Science and Technology

| | | |
|---|---|---|
| Charles Turner | 15 Sept. 1974 – | 14 Sept. 1975 |
| Keith Penner | 10 Oct. 1975 – | 30 Sept. 1976 |
| Frank Maine | 1 Oct. 1977 – | 30 Sept. 1978 |
| Pierre Bussières | 1 Oct. 1978 – | 26 Mar. 1979 |

## Secretary of State of Canada

| | | |
|---|---|---|
| Albert Béchard | 20 Apr. 1968 – | 23 Apr. 1968 |
| Robert Douglas George Stanbury | 30 Aug. 1968 – | 19 Oct. 1969 |
| James Hugh Faulkner | 1 Oct. 1970 – | 1 Sept. 1972 |
| Marcel Prud'homme | 3 Feb. 1972 – | 1 Sept. 1972 |
| Gilles Marceau | 22 Dec. 1972 – | 21 Dec. 1973 |
| Gustave Blouin | 15 Sept. 1974 – | 14 Sept. 1975 |
| Coline Campbell | 10 Oct. 1975 – | 30 Sept. 1976 |
| Jacques Guilbault | 1 Oct. 1976 – | 30 Sept. 1977 |
| Robert Daudlin | 1 Oct. 1977 – | 30 Sept. 1978 |
| | 1 Oct. 1978 – | 26 Mar. 1979 |

## Solicitor General

| | | |
|---|---|---|
| Charles L. Caccia | 20 Oct. 1969 – | 4 Mar. 1970 |
| Douglas Aird Hogarth | 1 Oct. 1971 – | 1 Sept. 1972 |
| Hugh Poulin | 10 Oct. 1975 – | 30 Sept. 1976 |
| Arthur John Lee | 1 Oct. 1976 – | 30 Sept. 1977 |
| Roderick Blaker | 1 Oct. 1977 – | 30 Sept. 1978 |
| Roger Young | 1 Oct. 1978 – | 26 Mar. 1979 |

## Supply and Services

| | | |
|---|---|---|
| Steven Otto | 1 Oct. 1971 – | 1 Sept. 1972 |
| Walter Smith | 10 Oct. 1975 – | 30 Sept. 1976 |
| Roderick Blaker | 1 Oct. 1976 – | 30 Sept. 1977 |
| Aideen Nicholson | 1 Oct. 1977 – | 30 Sept. 1978 |
| Maurice Harquail | 1 Oct. 1978 – | 26 Mar. 1979 |

## Trade and Commerce

| | | |
|---|---|---|
| Jean-Charles Cantin | 20 Apr. 1968 – | 23 Apr. 1968 |

## Transport

| | | |
|---|---|---|
| James Allen Byrne | 20 Apr. 1968 – | 23 Apr. 1968 |
| Gérard Loiselle | 20 Oct. 1969 – | 30 Sept. 1970 |
| Gérard Duquet | 1 Oct. 1970 – | 1 Sept. 1972 |
| Joseph-Philippe Guay | 22 Dec. 1972 – | 21 Dec. 1973 |
| Joseph-Philippe Guay | 1 Jan. 1974 – | 9 May 1974 |
| Joseph Clifford McIsaac | 15 Sept. 1974 – | 14 Sept. 1975 |
| Ralph Goodale | 10 Oct. 1975 – | 30 Sept. 1976 |
| Marcel Claude Roy | 1 Oct. 1976 – | 30 Sept. 1977 |
| Charles Lapointe | 1 Oct. 1977 – | 30 Sept. 1978 |
| Charles Lapointe | 1 Oct. 1978 – | 26 Mar. 1979 |

## Treasury Board

| | | |
|---|---|---|
| James Edgar Walker | 20 Apr. 1968 – | 23 Apr. 1968 |
| Charles L. Caccia | 5 Mar. 1970 – | 30 Sept. 1970 |
| Alastair William Gillespie | 1 Oct. 1970 – | 11 Aug. 1971 |
| Gaston Clermont | 1 Oct. 1971 – | 1 Sept. 1972 |
| Cyril Lloyd Francis | 10 Oct. 1975 – | 30 Sept. 1976 |
| Jacques L. Trudel | 1 Oct. 1976 – | 30 Sept. 1977 |
| Thomas-Henri Lefebvre | 1 Oct. 1977 – | 30 Sept. 1978 |
| Thomas-Henri Lefebvre | 1 Oct. 1978 – | 26 Mar. 1979 |

## Urban Affairs

| | | |
|---|---|---|
| David Bennington Weatherhead | 1 Oct. 1971 – | 1 Sept. 1972 |
| Ian Watson | 22 Dec. 1972 – | 21 Dec. 1973 |
| | 1 Jan. 1974 – | 9 May 1974 |
| Pierre De Bané | 15 Sept. 1974 – | 14 Sept. 1975 |
| Jean-Robert Gauthier | 10 Oct. 1975 – | 30 Sept. 1976 |
| | 1 Oct. 1976 – | 30 Sept. 1977 |
| Maurice Harquail | 1 Oct. 1977 – | 30 Sept. 1978 |
| Harold Thomas Herbert | 1 Oct. 1978 – | 26 Mar. 1979 |

## Veterans Affairs

| | | |
|---|---|---|
| Cyril Lloyd Francis | 1 Oct. 1971 – | 1 Sept. 1972 |
| Sammuel Victor Railton | 10 Oct. 1975 – | 30 Sept. 1976 |
| | 1 Oct. 1976 – | 30 Sept. 1977 |
| Gilbert Parent | 1 Oct. 1977 – | 30 Sept. 1978 |
| | 1 Oct. 1978 – | 26 Mar. 1979 |

## Minister of State for Federal-Provincial Relations

| | | |
|---|---|---|
| Gus MacFarlane | 1 Oct. 1978 – | 26 Mar. 1979 |

## Minister of State (Multiculturalism)

| | | |
|---|---|---|
| William Andres | 1 Oct. 1977 – | 30 Sept. 1978 |
| | 1 Oct. 1978 – | 26 Mar. 1979 |

## Minister of State (Environment)

| | | |
|---|---|---|
| Michael Landers | 1 Oct. 1977 – | 30 Sept. 1978 |

# Twenty-First Ministry

**PROGRESSIVE CONSERVATIVE** 1

4 June 1979 to 2 March 1980

**PRIME MINISTER**

The Right Honourable Charles Joseph Clark

**THE MINISTRY**

**Minister of Agriculture**
Hon. John Wise                                    4 June 1979 –    2 Mar. 1980

**Minister of Communications**
Hon. David S. H. MacDonald   2                    4 June 1979 –    2 Mar. 1980

**Minister of Consumer and Corporate Affairs**
Hon. Allan Frederick Lawrence   3                 4 June 1979 –    2 Mar. 1980

**Minister of Employment and Immigration**
Hon. Ronald George Atkey                          4 June 1979 –    2 Mar. 1980

**Minister of Energy, Mines and Resources**
Hon. Ramon John Hnatyshyn   4                     4 June 1979 –    2 Mar. 1980

**Secretary of State for External Affairs**
Hon. Flora Isabel MacDonald                       4 June 1979 –    2 Mar. 1980

**Minister of the Environment**
Hon. John Allen Fraser   5                        4 June 1979 –    2 Mar. 1980

**Minister of Finance**
Hon. John C. Crosbie                              4 June 1979 –    2 Mar. 1980

**Minister of Fisheries and Oceans**
Hon. James Aloysius McGrath                       4 June 1979 –    2 Mar. 1980

1   On 4 June 1979 Trudeau resigned as Prime Minister and the Twenty-First Ministry assumed office. It was composed of 30 ministers.

2   MacDonald was also Secretary of State of Canada.

3   Lawrence was also Solicitor General of Canada.

4   Hnatyshyn was also Minister of State for Science and Technology.

5   Fraser was also Postmaster General.

**Minister of Indian Affairs and Northern Development**
Hon. Arthur Jacob Epp                                    4 June 1979  –    2 Mar.  1980

**Minister of Industry, Trade and Commerce**
Hon. Robert R. de Cotret   *Senator*  6                  4 June 1979  –    2 Mar.  1980

**Minister of Justice and Attorney General**
Hon. Jacques Flynn   *Senator*  7                        4 June 1979  –    2 Mar.  1980

**Minister of Labour**
Hon. Lincoln Alexander                                   4 June 1979  –    2 Mar.  1980

**Minister of National Defence**
Hon. Allan Bruce McKinnon   8                            4 June 1979  –    2 Mar.  1980

**Associate Minister of National Defence**
Vacant                                                   4 June 1969  –    2 Mar.  1980

**Minister of National Health and Welfare**
Hon. David Crombie                                       4 June 1979  –    2 Mar.  1980

**Minister of National Revenue**
Hon. Walter David Baker   9                              4 June 1979  –    2 Mar.  1980

**Postmaster General**
Hon. John Allen Fraser   10                              4 June 1979  –    2 Mar.  1980

**President of the Privy Council**
Hon. Walter David Baker   11                             4 June 1979  –    2 Mar.  1980

**Minister of Public Works**
Hon. Erik H. Nielsen                                     4 June 1979  –    2 Mar.  1980

**Minister of Regional Economic Expansion**
Hon. Elmer MacIntosh MacKay                              4 June 1979  –    2 Mar.  1980

**Minister of State for Science and Technology**
Hon. Ramon John Hnatyshyn   12                           4 June 1979  –    7 Oct.  1979
Hon. William Heward Grafftey                             8 Oct.  1979  –    2 Mar.  1980

**Minister of State for Economic Development**
Hon. Robert R. de Cotret   *Senator*  13                 4 June 1979  –    2 Mar.  1980

6       De Cotret was also Minister of State for Economic Development. He was summoned to the
        Senate on 5 June 1979.

7       Flynn was also Leader of the Government in the Senate.

8       McKinnon was also Minister of Veterans Affairs.

9       Baker was also President of the Privy Council.

10      Fraser was also Minister of the Environment.

11      Baker was also Minister of National Revenue.

12      Hnatyshyn was also Minister of Energy, Mines and Resources.

13      De Cotret was also Minister of Industry, Trade and Commerce.

### Secretary of State of Canada

Hon. David S. H. MacDonald   14                4 June 1979 –   2 Mar. 1980

### Leader of the Government in the Senate

Hon. Jacques Flynn   *Senator*   15            4 June 1979 –   2 Mar. 1980

### Solicitor General of Canada

Hon. Allan Frederick Lawrence   16             4 June 1979 –   2 Mar. 1980

### Minister of Supply and Services

Hon. Roch LaSalle                              4 June 1979 –   2 Mar. 1980

### Minister of Transport

Hon. Donald F. Mazankowski                     4 June 1979 –   2 Mar. 1980

### President of the Treasury Board

Hon. Sinclair McKnight Stevens                 4 June 1979 –   2 Mar. 1980

### Minister of Veterans Affairs

Hon. Allan Bruce McKinnon   17                 4 June 1979 –   2 Mar. 1980

### Minister of State

| | | |
|---|---|---|
| Hon. Martial Asselin   *Senator*   18 | 4 June 1979 – | 2 Mar. 1980 |
| Hon. William Jarvis   19 | 4 June 1979 – | 2 Mar. 1980 |
| Hon. William Heward Grafftey   20 | 4 June 1979 – | 7 Oct. 1979 |
| Hon. Perrin Beatty   21 | 4 June 1979 – | 2 Mar. 1980 |
| Hon. J. Robert Howie   22 | 4 June 1979 – | 2 Mar. 1980 |
| Hon. Steven Eugene Paproski   23 | 4 June 1979 – | 2 Mar. 1980 |
| Hon. Ronald Huntington   24 | 4 June 1979 – | 2 Mar. 1980 |
| Hon. Michael H. Wilson   25 | 4 June 1979 – | 2 Mar. 1980 |

14    MacDonald was also Minister of Communications.

15    Flynn was also Minister of Justice and Attorney General of Canada.

16    Lawrence was also Minister of Consumer and Corporate Affairs.

17    McKinnon was also Minister of National Defence.

18    Asselin was assigned by Order in Council P.C. 1979-1630 of 5 June 1979 to assist the Secretary of State for External Affairs in the carrying out of the latter's responsibilities in respect of the Canadian International Development Agency and matters related thereto. He was given the title "Minister of State for the Canadian International Development Agency".

19    Jarvis was assigned by Order in Council P.C. 1979-1631 of 5 June 1979 to assist the Prime Minister in respect of matters relating to federal-provincial relations. He was given the title "Minister of State for Federal-Provincial Relations".

20    Grafftey was assigned by Order in Council P.C. 1979-1632 of 5 June 1979 to assist the Minister of National Health and Welfare in the carrying out of the latter's responsibilities in respect of social programs. He was given the title "Minister of State for Social Programmes". He was appointed Minister of State for Science and Technology on 8 Oct. 1979.

21    Beatty was assigned by Order in Council P.C. 1979-1633 of 5 June 1979 to assist the President of the Treasury Board. He was given the title "Minister of State (Treasury Board)".

22    Howie was assigned by Order in Council P.C. 1979-1634 of 5 June 1979 to assist the Minister of Transport. He was given the title "Minister of State (Transport)".

23    Paproski was assigned by Order in Council P.C. 1979-1635 of 5 June 1979 to assist the Secretary of State of Canada in carrying out of the latter's responsibilities in respect of the policies and programs related to fitness and amateur sport and to multiculturalism. He was given the title "Minister of State for Fitness and Amateur Sport and Multiculturalism".

24    Huntington was assigned by Order in Council P.C. 1979-1636 of 5 June 1979 to assist the Minister of Industry, Trade and Commerce in the carrying out of the latter's responsibilities in respect of small businesses and industry. He was given the title "Minister of State for Small Businesses and Industry".

25    Wilson was assigned by Order in Council P.C. 1979-1637 of 5 June 1979 to assist the Minister of Industry, Trade and Commerce in the carrying out of the latter's responsibilities in respect of international trade. He was given the title "Minister of State for International Trade".

## PARLIAMENTARY SECRETARIES
## NOT OF THE MINISTRY

**Agriculture**

Herbert Thomas Hargrave                    1 Oct. 1979 – 14 Dec. 1979

**Communications**

Scott Fennell                              1 Oct. 1979 – 14 Dec. 1979

**Consumer and Corporate Affairs**

Gary Gurbin                                1 Oct. 1979 – 14 Dec. 1979

**Employment and Immigration**

Paul McCrossan                             1 Oct. 1979 – 14 Dec. 1979

**Energy, Mines and Resources**

Robert Jarvis                              1 Oct. 1979 – 14 Dec. 1979

**Environment and Postmaster General**

Joseph Reid                                1 Oct. 1979 – 14 Dec. 1979

**External Affairs**

Douglas James Roche                        1 Oct. 1979 – 14 Dec. 1979

**Finance**

Ronald Ritchie                             1 Oct. 1979 – 14 Dec. 1979

**Fisheries and Oceans**

Thomas Siddon                              1 Oct. 1979 – 14 Dec. 1979

**Indian Affairs and Northern Development**

John Robert Holmes                         1 Oct. 1979 – 14 Dec. 1979

**Justice**

George Cooper                              1 Oct. 1979 – 14 Dec. 1979

**Labour**

William Wightman                           1 Oct. 1979 – 14 Dec. 1979

**National Defence and Veterans Affairs**
A. Daniel McKenzie                                            1 Oct. 1979 – 14 Dec. 1979

**National Health and Welfare**
Stanley Kenneth Schellenberger                                1 Oct. 1979 – 14 Dec. 1979

**Prime Minister**
John Bosley                                                   1 Oct. 1979 – 14 Dec. 1979

**Privy Council**
David Kilgour                                                 1 Oct. 1979 – 14 Dec. 1979

**Regional Economic Expansion**
Richard Janelle                                               1 Oct. 1979 – 14 Dec. 1979

**Secretary of State of Canada**
Diane Stratas                                                 1 Oct. 1979 – 14 Dec. 1979

**Solicitor General**
Christopher Speyer                                            1 Oct. 1979 – 14 Dec. 1979

**Supply and Services**
Douglas Lewis                                                 1 Oct. 1979 – 14 Dec. 1979

**Transport**
Otto John Jelinek                                             1 Oct. 1979 – 14 Dec. 1979

**Treasury Board**
Jack Murta                                                    1 Oct. 1979 – 14 Dec. 1979

# Twenty-Second Ministry

**LIBERAL**   1

3 March 1980 –

**PRIME MINISTER**

The Right Honourable Pierre Elliott Trudeau

**THE MINISTRY**

**Minister of Agriculture**
Hon. Eugene Francis Whelan                                    3 Mar. 1980 –

**Minister of Communications**
Hon. Francis Fox   2                                          3 Mar. 1980 –

**Minister of Consumer and Corporate Affairs**
Hon. André Ouellet   3                                       3 Mar. 1980 –

**Minister of Employment and Immigration**
Hon. Lloyd Axworthy                                          3 Mar. 1980 –

**Minister of Energy, Mines and Resources**
Hon. Marc Lalonde                                            3 Mar. 1980 –

**Secretary of State for External Affairs**
Hon. Mark MacGuigan                                          3 Mar. 1980 –

**Minister of State for Economic Development**
Hon. Horace Andrew Olson   *Senator*                         3 Mar. 1980 –

**Minister of the Environment**
Hon. John Roberts   4                                        3 Mar. 1980 –

**Minister of Finance**
Hon. Allan Joseph MacEachen   5                              3 Mar. 1980 –

**Minister of Fisheries and Oceans**
Hon. Roméo LeBlanc                                           3 Mar. 1980 –

**Minister of Indian Affairs and Northern Development**
Hon. John Carr Munro                                         3 Mar. 1980 –

1   After the defeat of the Government in the general election of 18 Feb. 1980, Clark formally tendered his resignation on 3 Mar. 1980. On the same day the Twenty-Second Ministry took office. It was composed of 33 ministers.

2   Fox was also Secretary of State for Canada until 21 Sept. 1981.

3   Ouellet was also Postmaster General until 15 Oct. 1981.

4   Roberts was also Minister of State for Science and Technology.

5   MacEachen was also given the title "Deputy Prime Minister".

**Minister of Industry, Trade and Commerce**
Hon. Herbert Eser Gray   6                                    3 Mar. 1980 –

**Minister of Justice and Attorney General**
Hon. Joseph Jacques Jean Chrétien   7                         3 Mar. 1980 –

**Minister of Labour**
Hon. Gerald Regan   8                                        3 Mar. 1980 – 21 Sept. 1981
Hon. Charles L. Caccia                                       22 Sept. 1981 –

**Minister of National Defence**
Hon. Gilles Lamontagne                                       3 Mar. 1980 –

**Associate Minister of National Defence**
Vacant                                                       3 Mar. 1980 –

**Minister of National Health and Welfare**
Hon. Monique Bégin                                           3 Mar. 1980 –

**Minister of National Revenue**
Hon. William Rompkey                                         3 Mar. 1980 –

**Postmaster General**
Hon. André Ouellet   9                                       3 Mar. 1980 – 15 Oct. 1981

**President of the Privy Council**
Hon. Yvon Pinard                                             3 Mar. 1980 –

**Minister of Public Works**
Hon. Paul James Cosgrove                                     3 Mar. 1980 –

**Minister of Regional Economic Expansion**
Hon. Pierre De Bané   10                                     3 Mar. 1980 – 11 Jan. 1982
Herbert Eser Gray   11                                       12 Jan. 1982 –

**Minister of State for Science and Technology**
Hon. John Roberts   12                                       3 Mar. 1980 –

**Minister of State for Social Development**   13
Hon. Joseph Jacques Jean Chrétien   14                       3 Mar. 1980 –

6       As of 12 Jan. 1982, Gray was also Minister of Regional Economic Expansion.

7       Chrétien was also Minister of State for Social Development.

8       Regan was also Minister of State (Sports) until 5 Mar. 1980. He was appointed Secretary of State of Canada on 22 Sept. 1981.

9       Ouellet was also Minister of Consumer and Corporate Affairs. He ceased to be Postmaster General on 15 Oct. 1981. The Canada Post Corporation was created by the Canada Post Corporation Act, Chapter 54, 29-30 Eliz. II and proclaimed in force on 16 Oct. 1981.

10      De Bané was appointed Minister of State (External Relations) as of 12 Jan. 1982.

11      Gray was also Minister of Industry, Trade and Commerce as of 12 Jan. 1982.

12      Roberts was also Minister of the Environment.

13      The Ministry of State for Social Development was proclaimed on 19 June, 1980, under the Ministries and Ministers of State Act  19-20 Eliz. II, 1970-71, c. 42 Part IV.

14      Chrétien was also Minister of Justice and Attorney General of Canada.

## Secretary of State of Canada

| | |
|---|---|
| Hon. Francis Fox   15 | 3 Mar. 1980 – 21 Sept. 1981 |
| Hon. Gerald Regan   16 | 22 Sept. 1981 – |

## Leader of the Government in the Senate

| | |
|---|---|
| Hon. Raymond Joseph Perrault | 3 Mar. 1980 – |

## Solicitor General of Canada

| | |
|---|---|
| Hon. Robert Phillip Kaplan | 3 Mar. 1980 – |

## Minister of Supply and Services

| | |
|---|---|
| Hon. Jean-Jacques Blais | 3 Mar. 1980 – |

## Minister of Transport

| | |
|---|---|
| Hon. Jean-Luc Pepin | 3 Mar. 1980 – |

## President of the Treasury Board

| | |
|---|---|
| Hon. Donald Johnston | 3 Mar. 1980 – |

## Minister of Veterans Affairs

| | |
|---|---|
| Hon. Daniel Joseph MacDonald   17 | 3 Mar. 1980 – 30 Sept. 1980 |
| Hon. Gilles Lamontagne,   *Acting Minister* | 1 Oct. 1980 – 21 Sept. 1981 |
| Hon. W. Bennett Campbell | 22 Sept. 1981 – |

15    Fox was also Minister of Communications.

16    By Order in Council P.C. 1981-2680 of 24 Sept. 1981, the powers, duties and functions of the Minister of National Health and Welfare under the Fitness and Amateur Sport Act were transferred to the Secretary of State. That part of the Public Service of Canada known as the Fitness and Amateur Sport Branch of the Department of Labour was also transferred to the Secretary of State of Canada.

17    MacDonald died on 30 Sept., 1980.

## Minister of State

| | | |
|---|---|---|
| Hon. Hazen Argue  *Senator*  18 | 3 Mar. 1980 – | |
| Hon. Gerald Regan  19 | 3 Mar. 1980 – | 5 Mar. 1980 |
| Hon. James Sydney Clark Fleming  20 | 3 Mar. 1980 – | |
| Hon. Pierre Bussières  21 | 3 Mar. 1980 – | |
| Hon. Charles Lapointe  22 | 3 Mar. 1980 – | |
| Hon. Edward Lumley  23 | 3 Mar. 1980 – | |

18   Argue was assigned by Order in Council P.C. 1980-605 of 4 Mar. 1980, to assist the Minister of Transport in the carrying out of the latter's responsibilities in respect of the Canadian Wheat Board and as Minister for the purposes of the Two-Price Wheat Act and the Western Grain Stabilization Act. He was given the title "Minister of State (Canadian Wheat Board)".

19   By Order in Council P.C. 1980-613 of 6 Mar. 1980, the powers, duties and functions of the Minister of National Health and Welfare under the Fitness and Amateur Sport Act were transferred to the Minister of Labour. That part of the Public Service of Canada known as the Fitness and Amateur Sport Branch of the Department of the Secretary of State of Canada was also transferred to the Minister of Labour. Therefore the Hon. Gerald Regan ceased to hold the title of Minister of State (Sports) on 5 Mar. 1980, as he was also the Minister of Labour.

20   Fleming was assigned by Order in Council P.C. 1980-606 of 4 Mar. 1980, to assist the Secretary of State of Canada in carrying out of the latter's responsibilities in respect of the policies and programs related to multiculturalism. He was given the title "Minister of State (Multiculturalism)".

21   Bussières was assigned by Order in Council P.C. 1980-607 of 4 Mar. 1980, to assist the Minister of Finance. He was given the title "Minister of State (Finance)".

22   Lapointe was assigned by Order in Council P.C. 1980-608 of 4 Mar. 1980, to assist the Minister of Industry, Trade and Commerce in the carrying out of the latter's responsibilities in respect of small businesses. He was given the title "Minister of State (Small Businesses)". This Order in Council was amended by Order in Council P.C. 1981-472 of 24 Feb. 1981, adding to his responsibilities to assist the Minister of Industry, Trade and Commerce in the carrying out of the latter's responsibilities in respect of tourism. He was therefore given the new title "Minister of State (Small Businesses and Tourism)".

23   Lumley was assigned by Order in Council P.C. 1980-609 of 4 Mar. 1980, to assist the Minister of Industry, Trade and Commerce in the carrying out of the latter's responsibilities in respect to trade. He was given the title "Minister of State (Trade)". Order in Council P.C. 1982-18 of 12 Jan. 1982, assigned the Hon. Edward Lumley, a Minister of State, to assist the Secretary of State for External Affairs in the carrying out of the latter's responsibilities in respect of international trade and export promotion. He was given the title "Minister of State (International Trade)".

**Minister of State** (continued)

| | |
|---|---|
| Hon. Judy Erola  24 | 3 Mar.  1980 – |
| Hon. Jacob Austin | 22 Sept. 1981 – |
| Hon. Serge Joyal | 22 Sept. 1981 – |
| Hon. Pierre De Bané  25 | 12 Jan.  1982 – |

24 Erola was assigned by Order in Council P.C. 1980-610 of 4 Mar. 1980, to assist the Minister of Energy, Mines and Resources in respect of matters relating to mines. She was given the title "Minister of State (Mines)".

25 De Bané was assigned by Order in Council P.C. 1982-17 of 12 Jan. 1982, a Minister of State, to assist the Secretary of State for External Affairs in the carrying out of the latter's responsibilities relating to the conduct of international relations. He was given the title "Minister of State (External Relations)".

## PARLIAMENTARY SECRETARIES
## NOT OF THE MINISTRY

**Agriculture**

| | |
|---|---|
| Marcel Ostiguy | 4 Mar. 1980  –  30 Sept. 1980 |
| | 1 Oct.  1980  –  30 Sept. 1981 |
| | 1 Oct.  1981  – |

**Communications**

| | |
|---|---|
| Peter Stollery | 4 Mar. 1980  –  30 Sept. 1980 |
| | 1 Oct.  1980  –  30 Sept. 1981 |
| Jack Masters | 1 Oct.  1981  – |

**Consumer and Corporate Affairs**

| | |
|---|---|
| Aideen Nicholson | 4 Mar. 1980  –  30 Sept. 1980 |
| Gary McCauley | 1 Oct.  1980  –  30 Sept. 1981 |
| | 1 Oct.  1981  – |

**Employment and Immigration**

| | |
|---|---|
| Dennis M. Dawson | 4 Mar. 1980  –  30 Sept. 1980 |
| | 1 Oct.  1980  –  30 Sept. 1981 |
| Rémi Bujold | 1 Oct.  1981  – |

**Energy, Mines and Resources**

| | |
|---|---|
| Roy MacLaren | 4 Mar. 1980  –  30 Sept. 1980 |
| | 1 Oct.  1980  –  30 Sept. 1981 |
| | 1 Oct.  1981  – |

**Environment**

| | |
|---|---|
| Roger Simmons | 4 Mar. 1980  –  30 Sept. 1980 |
| | 1 Oct.  1980  –  30 Sept. 1981 |
| | 1 Oct.  1981  – |

**External Affairs**

| | |
|---|---|
| Louis Duclos | 4 Mar. 1980  –  30 Sept. 1980 |
| | 1 Oct.  1980  –  30 Sept. 1981 |
| Ron Irwin | 1 Oct.  1981  – |

## Finance

| | | |
|---|---|---|
| John Evans | 4 Mar. 1980 – 30 Sept. 1980 |
| | 1 Oct. 1980 – 30 Sept. 1981 |
| | 1 Oct. 1981 – |

## Fisheries and Oceans

| | |
|---|---|
| George Henderson | 4 Mar. 1980 – 30 Sept. 1980 |
| | 1 Oct. 1980 – 30 Sept. 1981 |
| Brian Tobin | 1 Oct. 1981 – |

## Indian Affairs and Northern Development

| | |
|---|---|
| Bernard Loiselle | 4 Mar. 1980 – 30 Sept. 1980 |
| Raymond Chénier | 1 Oct. 1980 – 30 Sept. 1981 |
| | 1 Oct. 1981 – |

## Industry, Trade and Commerce

| | |
|---|---|
| Gérald Laniel | 4 Mar. 1980 – 30 Sept. 1980 |
| | 1 Oct. 1980 – 30 Sept. 1981 |
| | 1 Oct. 1981 – |

## Justice and Attorney General of Canada

| | |
|---|---|
| William Kenneth Robinson | 4 Mar. 1980 – 30 Sept. 1980 |
| Ron Irwin | 1 Oct. 1980 – 30 Sept. 1981 |
| Jim Peterson | 1 Oct. 1981 – |

## Labour

| | |
|---|---|
| Gilbert Parent | 4 Mar. 1980 – 30 Sept. 1980 |
| Louis Desmarais | 1 Oct. 1980 – 13 May 1981 |
| Gilbert Parent | 26 May 1981 – 30 Sept. 1981 |
| Antonio Yanakis | 1 Oct. 1981 – |

## National Defence
Ursula Appolloni

| | | |
|---|---|---|
| 4 Mar. 1980 | – | 30 Sept. 1980 |
| 1 Oct. 1980 | – | 30 Sept. 1981 |
| 1 Oct. 1981 | – | |

## National Health and Welfare
David Bennington Weatherhead
Doug Frith

| | | |
|---|---|---|
| 4 Mar. 1980 | – | 30 Sept. 1980 |
| 1 Oct. 1980 | – | 30 Sept. 1981 |
| 1 Oct. 1981 | – | |

## National Revenue
Yves Demers
Claude Tessier

| | | |
|---|---|---|
| 4 Mar. 1980 | – | 30 Sept. 1980 |
| 1 Oct. 1980 | – | 30 Sept. 1981 |
| 1 Oct. 1981 | – | |

## Postmaster General
Aideen Nicholson
Gary McCauley

| | | |
|---|---|---|
| 4 Mar. 1980 | – | 30 Sept. 1980 |
| 1 Oct. 1980 | – | 30 Sept. 1981 |
| 1 Oct. 1981 | – | 15 Oct. 1981 |

## Privy Council
David Collenette

David Smith

| | | |
|---|---|---|
| 4 Mar. 1980 | – | 30 Sept. 1980 |
| 1 Oct. 1980 | – | 30 Sept. 1981 |
| 1 Oct. 1981 | – | |

## Public Works
Raymond Savard

| | | |
|---|---|---|
| 4 Mar. 1980 | – | 30 Sept. 1980 |
| 1 Oct. 1980 | – | 30 Sept. 1981 |
| 1 Oct. 1981 | – | |

## Regional Economic Expansion
Maurice Harquail
Russell MacLellan

| | | |
|---|---|---|
| 4 Mar. 1980 | – | 30 Sept. 1980 |
| 1 Oct. 1980 | – | 30 Sept. 1981 |
| 1 Oct. 1981 | – | |

## Science and Technology
Roger Simmons

| | | |
|---|---|---|
| 4 Mar. 1980 | – | 30 Sept. 1980 |
| 1 Oct. 1980 | – | 30 Sept. 1981 |
| 1 Oct. 1981 | – | |

## Secretary of State of Canada

Peter Stollery

4 Mar. 1980  —  30 Sept. 1980
1 Oct.  1980  —  30 Sept. 1981

Jean Lapierre

1 Oct.  1981  —

## Solicitor General

Céline Hervieux-Payette

4 Mar. 1980  —  30 Sept. 1980
1 Oct.  1980  —  30 Sept. 1981
1 Oct.  1981  —

## Supply and Services

Raymond Dupont

4 Mar. 1980  —  30 Sept. 1980

Norman Kelly

1 Oct.  1980  —  30 Sept. 1981

## Transport

Robert Bockstael

4 Mar. 1980  —  30 Sept. 1980
1 Oct.  1980  —  30 Sept. 1981
1 Oct.  1981  —

## Treasury Board

Robert Daudlin

4 Mar. 1980  —  30 Sept. 1980

Serge Joyal

1 Oct.  1980  —  21 Sept. 1981

Norman Kelly

1 Oct.  1981  —

## Veterans Affairs

John Campbell

4 Mar. 1980  —  30 Sept. 1980
1 Oct.  1980  —  30 Sept. 1981
1 Oct.  1981  —

## Minister of State (Mines)

Russell MacLellan

4 Mar. 1980  —  30 Sept. 1980

Jack Masters

1 Oct.  1980  —  30 Sept. 1981

Thérèse Killens

1 Oct.  1981  —

## Minister of State (Multiculturalism)

Pierre Deniger

4 Mar. 1980  —  30 Sept. 1980
1 Oct.  1980  —  30 Sept. 1981
1 Oct.  1981  —

**Minister of State (Small Businesses)**

Ralph Ferguson

| | | |
|---|---|---|
| 4 Mar. 1980 | – | 30 Sept. 1980 |
| 1 Oct. 1980 | – | 30 Sept. 1981 |
| 1 Oct. 1981 | – | |

**Minister of State (Social Development)**

William Kenneth Robinson     4 Mar. 1980 – 30 Sept. 1980
Ron Irwin     1 Oct. 1980 – 30 Sept. 1981
Jim Peterson     1 Oct. 1981 –

**Minister of State (Trade)**

Claude-André Lachance

| | | |
|---|---|---|
| 4 Mar. 1980 | – | 30 Sept. 1980 |
| 1 Oct. 1980 | – | 30 Sept. 1981 |

# Appendix

**ABBOTT, Hon. Anthony Chisholm**
26 Nov. 1930 –

| | |
|---|---|
| Sworn of the Privy Council | 14 Sept. 1976 |
| Minister of Consumer and Corporate Affairs | 14 Sept. 1976 – 15 Sept. 1977 |
| Minister of State (Small Businesses)  *Ministry Resigned* | 16 Sept. 1977 – 3 June 1979 |
| Minister of National Revenue  *Ministry Resigned* | 24 Nov. 1978 – 3 June 1979 |

**ABBOTT, Hon. Douglas Charles**
29 May 1899 –

| | |
|---|---|
| Parliamentary Assistant – Finance | 1 Apr. 1943 – 7 Mar. 1945 |
| Parliamentary Assistant – National Defence | 8 Mar. 1945 – 16 Apr. 1945 |
| Sworn of the Privy Council | 18 Apr. 1945 |
| Minister of National Defence for Naval Services | 18 Apr. 1945 – 11 Dec. 1946 |
| Minister of National Defence | 21 Aug. 1945 – 11 Dec. 1946 |
| Minister of Finance and Receiver General | 10 Dec. 1946 – 30 June 1954 |

**ABBOTT, Hon. Sir John Joseph Caldwell**
12 Mar. 1821 – 30 Oct. 1893

| | |
|---|---|
| Member of the Senate | 12 May 1887 – 30 Oct. 1893 |
| Leader of the Government in the Senate | 12 May 1887 – 30 Oct. 1893 |
| Sworn of the Privy Council | 13 May 1887 |
| Minister without Portfolio  *Ministry Dissolved* | 13 May 1887 – 15 June 1891 |
| Prime Minister | 16 June 1891 – 23 Nov. 1892 |
| President of the Privy Council  *Ministry Resigned* | 16 June 1891 – 4 Dec. 1892 |

**AIKINS, Hon. James Cox**
30 Mar. 1823 – 6 Aug. 1904

| | |
|---|---|
| Member of the Senate | 23 Oct. 1867 – 30 May 1882 |
| Sworn of the Privy Council | 8 Dec. 1869 |
| Secretary of State of Canada  *Ministry Resigned* | 8 Dec. 1869 – 6 Nov. 1873 |
| Acting Secretary of State for the Provinces | 7 May 1873 – 13 June 1873 |
| Acting Superintendent-General of Indian Affairs | 7 May 1873 – 13 June 1873 |
| Secretary of State of Canada | 19 Oct. 1878 – 7 Nov. 1880 |
| Minister of Inland Revenue | 8 Nov. 1880 – 22 May 1882 |
| Member of the Senate | 7 Jan. 1896 – 6 Aug. 1904 |

## ALEXANDER, Hon. Lincoln
21 Jan. 1922 –

| | | |
|---|---|---|
| Sworn of the Privy Council | 4 June 1979 | |
| Minister of Labour *Ministry Resigned* | 4 June 1979 – | 2 Mar. 1980 |

## ALLMAND, Hon. William Warren
19 Sept. 1932 –

| | | |
|---|---|---|
| Sworn of the Privy Council | 27 Nov. 1972 | |
| Solicitor General of Canada | 27 Nov. 1972 – | 13 Sept. 1976 |
| Minister of Indian Affairs and Northern Development | 14 Sept. 1976 – | 15 Sept. 1977 |
| Minister of Consumer and Corporate Affairs | | |
| *Ministry Resigned* | 16 Sept. 1977 – | 3 June 1979 |

## ANDRAS, Hon. Robert Knight
20 Feb. 1921 –

| | | |
|---|---|---|
| Sworn of the Privy Council | 6 July 1968 | |
| Minister without Portfolio | 6 July 1968 – | 29 June 1971 |
| Minister of State for Urban Affairs | 30 June 1971 – | 27 Jan. 1972 |
| Minister of Consumer and Corporate Affairs | 28 Jan. 1972 – | 26 Nov. 1972 |
| Minister of Manpower and Immigration | 27 Nov. 1972 – | 13 Sept. 1976 |
| President of the Treasury Board | 14 Sept. 1976 – | 23 Nov. 1978 |
| Minister of State for Economic Development | | |
| *Ministry Resigned* | 24 Nov. 1978 – | 3 June 1979 |

## ANGERS, Hon. Sir Auguste Réal
4 Oct. 1838 – 15 Apr. 1919

| | | |
|---|---|---|
| Sworn of the Privy Council | 7 Dec. 1892 | |
| Minister of Agriculture | 7 Dec. 1892 – | 12 July 1895 |
| Member of the Senate | 16 Dec. 1892 – | 10 June 1896 |
| President of the Privy Council *Ministry Resigned* | 1 May 1896 – | 10 July 1896 |

## ARCHIBALD, Hon. Sir Adams George
18 May 1814 – 14 Dec. 1892

| | | |
|---|---|---|
| Sworn of the Privy Council | 1 July 1867 | |
| Secretary of State for the Provinces | 1 July 1867 – | 30 Apr. 1868 |

**ARGUE, Hon. Hazen**
6 Jan. 1921 –

| | | |
|---|---|---|
| Member of the Senate | 24 Feb. 1966 | |
| Sworn of the Privy Council | 3 Mar. 1980 | |
| Minister of State (Canadian Wheat Board) | 3 Mar. 1980 – | |

**ASSELIN, Hon. Martial**
3 Feb. 1924 –

| | | |
|---|---|---|
| Sworn of the Privy Council | 18 Mar. 1963 | |
| Minister of Forestry   *Ministry Resigned* | 18 Mar. 1963 – | 21 Apr. 1963 |
| Member of the Senate | 1 Sept. 1972 – | |
| Minister of State (CIDA)   *Ministry Resigned* | 4 June 1979 – | 2 Mar. 1980 |

**ATKEY, Hon. Ronald George**
15 Feb. 1942 –

| | | |
|---|---|---|
| Sworn of the Privy Council | 4 June 1979 | |
| Minister of Employment and Immigration   *Ministry Resigned* | 4 June 1979 – | 2 Mar. 1980 |

**AUSTIN, Hon. Jacob**
2 Mar. 1932 –

| | |
|---|---|
| Member of the Senate | 19 Aug. 1975 – |
| Sworn of the Privy Council | 22 Sept. 1981 |
| Minister of State | 22 Sept. 1981 – |

**AXWORTHY, Hon. Lloyd**
21 Dec. 1939 –

| | |
|---|---|
| Sworn of the Privy Council | 3 Mar. 1980 |
| Minister of Employment and Immigration | 3 Mar. 1980 – |

**AYLESWORTH, Hon. Sir Allen Bristol**
27 Nov. 1854 – 13 Feb. 1952

| | | |
|---|---|---|
| Sworn of the Privy Council | 16 Oct. 1905 | |
| Postmaster General | 16 Oct. 1905 – | 3 June 1906 |
| Minister of Justice and Attorney General   *Ministry Resigned* | 4 June 1906 – | 9 Oct. 1911 |
| Member of the Senate | 11 Jan. 1923 – | 13 Feb. 1952 |

**BABY, Hon. Louis François Georges**
26 Aug. 1834 – 13 May 1906

| | | |
|---|---|---|
| Sworn of the Privy Council | 26 Oct. 1878 | |
| Minister of Inland Revenue | 26 Oct. 1878 – | 28 Oct. 1880 |

**BAKER, Hon. Walter David**
22 Aug. 1930 –

| | | |
|---|---|---|
| Sworn of the Privy Council | 4 June 1979 | |
| Minister of National Revenue   *Ministry Resigned* | 4 June 1979 – | 2 Mar. 1980 |
| President of the Privy Council   *Ministry Resigned* | 4 June 1979 – | 2 Mar. 1980 |

**BALCER, Hon. Léon**
13 Oct. 1917 –

| | | |
|---|---|---|
| Sworn of the Privy Council | 21 June 1957 | |
| Solicitor General of Canada | 21 June 1957 – | 10 Oct. 1960 |
| Acting Minister of Mines and Technical Surveys | 21 June 1957 – | 6 Aug. 1957 |
| Acting Secretary of State of Canada | 21 Jan. 1960 – | 10 Oct. 1960 |
| Minister of Transport   *Ministry Resigned* | 11 Oct. 1960 – | 21 Apr. 1963 |
| Acting Secretary of State of Canada | 11 July 1962 – | 8 Aug. 1962 |

**BALLANTYNE, Hon. Charles Colquhoun**
9 Aug. 1867 – 19 Oct. 1950

| | | |
|---|---|---|
| Sworn of the Privy Council | 3 Oct. 1917 | |
| Minister of Public Works | 3 Oct. 1917 – | 12 Oct. 1917 |
| Minister of Marine and Fisheries   *Ministry Resigned* | 13 Oct. 1917 – | 28 Dec. 1921 |
| Minister of the Naval Service   *Ministry Resigned* | 13 Oct. 1917 – | 28 Dec. 1921 |
| Member of the Senate | 3 Feb. 1932 – | 19 Oct. 1950 |

**BASFORD, Hon. Stanley Ronald**
22 Apr. 1932 –

| | | |
|---|---|---|
| Sworn of the Privy Council | 6 July 1968 | |
| Minister of Consumer and Corporate Affairs | 6 July 1968 – | 27 Jan. 1972 |
| Minister of State for Urban Affairs | 28 Jan. 1972 – | 7 Aug. 1974 |
| Minister of National Revenue | 8 Aug. 1974 – | 25 Sept. 1975 |
| Minister of Justice and Attorney General | 26 Sept. 1975 – | 2 Aug. 1978 |
| Acting Minister Solicitor General of Canada | 28 Jan. 1978 – | 1 Feb. 1978 |

**BAXTER, Hon. John Babington Macaulay**
16 Feb. 1868 – 27 Dec. 1946

| | |
|---|---|
| Sworn of the Privy Council | 21 Sept. 1921 |
| Minister of Customs and Excise   *Ministry Resigned* | 21 Sept. 1921 – 28 Dec. 1921 |

**BEATTY, Hon. Perrin**
1 June 1950 –

| | |
|---|---|
| Sworn of the Privy Council | 4 June 1979 |
| Minister of State (Treasury Board)   *Ministry Resigned* | 4 June 1979 – 2 Mar. 1980 |

**BÉGIN, Hon. Monique**
1 Mar. 1936 –

| | |
|---|---|
| Parliamentary Secretary – External Affairs | 10 Oct.  1975 – 13 Sept. 1976 |
| Sworn of the Privy Council | 14 Sept. 1976 |
| Minister of National Revenue | 14 Sept. 1976 – 15 Sept. 1977 |
| Minister of National Health and Welfare   *Ministry Resigned* | 16 Sept. 1977 –  3 June 1979 |
| Minister of National Health and Welfare | 3 Mar. 1980 – |

**BÉLAND, Hon. Henri Sévérin**
11 Oct. 1869 – 22 Apr. 1935

| | |
|---|---|
| Sworn of the Privy Council | 19 Aug. 1911 |
| Postmaster General   *Ministry Resigned* | 19 Aug. 1911 –  9 Oct.  1911 |
| Minister of Soldiers' Civil Re-establishment | 29 Dec. 1921 – 14 Apr.  1926 |
| Member of the Senate | 5 Sept. 1925 – 22 Apr.  1935 |

**BELL, Hon. Richard Albert**
4 Sept. 1913 –

| | |
|---|---|
| Parliamentary Assistant – Finance | 19 Aug.  1957 –  1 Feb.  1958 |
| Parliamentary Secretary – Finance | 18 Nov.  1959 – 17 Nov.  1961 |
| | 18 Jan.  1962 – 19 Apr.  1962 |
| Sworn of the Privy Council | 9 Aug.  1962 |
| Minister of Citizenship and Immigration   *Ministry Resigned* | 9 Aug.  1962 – 21 Apr.  1963 |

**BELLEY, Hon. Louis-de-Gonzague**
3 Feb. 1863 – 9 July 1930

| | |
|---|---|
| Sworn of the Privy Council | 21 Sept. 1921 |
| Postmaster General   *Ministry Resigned* | 21 Sept. 1921 – 28 Dec. 1921 |

**BENIDICKSON, Hon. William Moore**
8 Apr. 1911 –

| | |
|---|---|
| Parliamentary Assistant – Transport | 24 Jan. 1951 – 13 June 1953 |
| | 31 Aug. 1953 – 13 Sept. 1953 |
| Parliamentary Assistant – Finance | 14 Oct. 1953 – 12 Apr. 1957 |
| Sworn of the Privy Council | 22 Apr. 1963 |
| Minister of Mines and Technical Surveys | 22 Apr. 1963 – 6 July 1965 |
| Member of the Senate | 7 July 1965 – |

**BENNETT, Rt. Hon. Richard Bedford**
3 July 1870 – 27 June 1947

| | |
|---|---|
| Sworn of the Privy Council | 4 Oct. 1921 |
| Minister of Justice and Attorney General   *Ministry* | |
| *Resigned* | 4 Oct. 1921 – 28 Dec. 1921 |
| Minister without Portfolio | 7 July 1926 – 12 July 1926 |
| Minister of Finance and Receiver General   *Ministry* | |
| *Resigned* | 13 July 1926 – 24 Sept. 1926 |
| Acting Superintendent-General of Indian Affairs   *Ministry* | |
| *Resigned* | 13 July 1926 – 24 Sept. 1926 |
| Acting Minister of the Interior   *Ministry Resigned* | 13 July 1926 – 24 Sept. 1926 |
| Acting Minister of Mines   *Ministry Resigned* | 13 July 1926 – 24 Sept. 1926 |
| Prime Minister   *Ministry Resigned* | 7 Aug. 1930 – 22 Oct. 1935 |
| Secretary of State for External Affairs   *Ministry Resigned* | 7 Aug. 1930 – 22 Oct. 1935 |
| Minister of Finance and Receiver General | 7 Aug. 1930 – 2 Feb. 1932 |
| President of the Privy Council   *Ministry Resigned* | 7 Aug. 1930 – 22 Oct. 1935 |
| Member of the United Kingdom Privy Council | 27 Oct. 1930 |

**BENSON, Hon. Edgar John**
28 May 1923 –

| | |
|---|---|
| Parliamentary Secretary – Finance | 14 May 1963 – 28 June 1964 |
| Sworn of the Privy Council | 29 June 1964 |
| Minister of National Revenue | 29 June 1964 – 17 Jan. 1968 |
| President of the Treasury Board | 1 Oct. 1966 – 5 July 1968 |
| Minister of Finance | 20 Apr. 1968 – 27 Jan. 1972 |
| Minister of National Defence | 28 Jan. 1972 – 31 Aug. 1972 |

**BERNIER, Hon. Michel Esdras**
28 Sept. 1841 – 27 July 1921

| | |
|---|---|
| Sworn of the Privy Council | 22 June 1900 |
| Minister of Inland Revenue | 22 June 1900 – 18 Jan. 1904 |

**BERTRAND, Hon. Ernest**
14 Dec. 1888 – 11 Oct. 1958

| | |
|---|---|
| Sworn of the Privy Council | 7 Oct. 1942 |
| Minister of Fisheries | 7 Oct. 1942 – 28 Aug. 1945 |
| Postmaster General | 29 Aug. 1945 – 23 Aug. 1949 |
| Acting Minister of Fisheries | 14 Aug. 1947 – 1 Sept. 1947 |

**BLACK, Hon. William Anderson**
9 Oct. 1847 – 1 Sept. 1934

| | |
|---|---|
| Sworn of the Privy Council | 29 June 1926 |
| Acting Minister of Marine and Fisheries | 29 June 1926 – 12 July 1926 |
| Minister of Railways and Canals   *Ministry Resigned* | 13 July 1926 – 24 Sept. 1926 |

**BLAIR, Hon. Adam Johnston Fergusson**
4 Nov. 1815 – 29 Dec. 1867

| | |
|---|---|
| Sworn of the Privy Council | 1 July 1867 |
| President of the Privy Council | 1 July 1867 – 29 Dec. 1867 |
| Member of the Senate | 23 Oct. 1867 – 29 Dec. 1867 |

**BLAIR, Hon. Andrew George**
7 Mar. 1844 – 25 Jan. 1907

| | |
|---|---|
| Sworn of the Privy Council | 20 July 1896 |
| Minister of Railways and Canals | 20 July 1896 – 20 July 1903 |

**BLAIS, Hon. Jean-Jacques**
27 June 1940 –

| | |
|---|---|
| Parliamentary Secretary – Privy Council | 10 Oct. 1975 – 13 Sept. 1976 |
| Sworn of the Privy Council | 14 Sept. 1976 |
| Postmaster General | 14 Sept. 1976 – 1 Feb. 1978 |
| Solicitor General   *Ministry Resigned* | 2 Feb. 1978 – 3 June 1979 |
| Minister of Supply and Services | 3 Mar. 1980 – |

## BLAKE, Hon. Dominick Edward
13 Oct. 1833 – 1 Mar. 1912

| | | |
|---|---|---|
| Sworn of the Privy Council | 7 Nov. 1873 | |
| Minister without Portfolio | 7 Nov. 1873 – | 13 Feb. 1874 |
| Minister of Justice and Attorney General | 19 May 1875 – | 7 June 1877 |
| President of the Privy Council | 8 June 1877 – | 17 Jan. 1878 |

## BLONDIN, Hon. Pierre Edouard
14 Dec. 1874 – 29 Oct. 1943

| | | |
|---|---|---|
| Sworn of the Privy Council | 20 Oct. 1914 | |
| Minister of Inland Revenue | 20 Oct. 1914 – | 5 Oct. 1915 |
| Minister of Mines | 6 Oct. 1915 – | 7 Jan. 1917 |
| Secretary of State of Canada | 6 Oct. 1915 – | 7 Jan. 1917 |
| Postmaster General | 8 Jan. 1917 – | 20 Sept. 1921 |
| Member of the Senate | 20 July 1918 – | 29 Oct. 1943 |

## BOIVIN, Hon. Georges-Henri
26 Dec. 1882 – 7 Aug. 1926

| | | |
|---|---|---|
| Sworn of the Privy Council | 5 Sept. 1925 | |
| Minister of Customs and Excise   *Ministry Resigned* | 5 Sept. 1925 – | 28 June 1926 |

## BORDEN, Hon. Sir Frederick William
14 May 1847 – 6 Jan. 1917

| | | |
|---|---|---|
| Sworn of the Privy Council | 13 July 1896 | |
| Minister of Militia and Defence   *Ministry Resigned* | 13 July 1896 – | 9 Oct. 1911 |

## BORDEN, Rt. Hon. Sir Robert Laird
26 June 1854 – 10 June 1937

| | | |
|---|---|---|
| Sworn of the Privy Council | 10 Oct. 1911 | |
| Prime Minister   *Ministry Resigned* | 10 Oct. 1911 – | 9 July 1920 |
| President of the Privy Council   *Ministry Resigned* | 10 Oct. 1911 – | 11 Oct. 1917 |
| Secretary of State for External Affairs   *Ministry Resigned* | 1 Apr. 1912 – | 9 July 1920 |
| Member of the United Kingdom Privy Council | 19 July 1912 | |

## BOSTOCK, Hon. Hewitt
31 May 1864 – 28 Apr. 1930

| | | |
|---|---|---|
| Member of the Senate | 6 June 1904 – | 28 Apr. 1930 |
| Sworn of the Privy Council | 29 Dec. 1921 | |
| Minister of Public Works | 29 Dec. 1921 – | 2 Feb. 1922 |
| Acting Minister of Immigration and Colonization | 3 Jan. 1922 – | 2 Feb. 1922 |

## BOWELL, Hon. Sir Mackenzie
27 Dec. 1823 – 10 Dec. 1917

| | | |
|---|---|---|
| Sworn of the Privy Council | 19 Oct. 1878 | |
| Minister of Customs | 19 Oct. 1878 – | 24 Jan. 1892 |
| Acting Minister of Railways and Canals | 17 June 1891 – | 10 Jan. 1892 |
| Minister of Militia and Defence   *Ministry Resigned* | 25 Jan. 1892 – | 4 Dec. 1892 |
| Minister of Trade and Commerce   *Ministry Dissolved* | 5 Dec. 1892 – | 20 Dec. 1894 |
| Member of the Senate | 5 Dec. 1892 – | 10 Dec. 1917 |
| Leader of the Government in the Senate | 1893 – | 1896 |
| Prime Minister | 21 Dec. 1894 – | 26 Apr. 1896 |
| President of the Privy Council   *Ministry Resigned* | 21 Dec. 1894 – | 30 Apr. 1896 |
| Acting Minister of Finance and Receiver General | 6 Jan. 1896 – | 14 Jan. 1896 |
| Acting Minister of Militia and Defence | 6 Jan. 1896 – | 14 Jan. 1896 |

## BRADLEY, Hon. Frederick Gordon
21 Mar. 1888 – 30 Mar. 1966

| | | |
|---|---|---|
| Sworn of the Privy Council | 1 Apr. 1949 | |
| Secretary of State of Canada | 1 Apr. 1949 – | 11 June 1953 |
| Member of the Senate | 12 June 1953 – | 30 Mar. 1966 |

## BRIDGES, Hon. Hedley Francis Gregory
7 Apr. 1902 – 10 Aug. 1947

| | | |
|---|---|---|
| Sworn of the Privy Council | 30 Aug. 1945 | |
| Minister of Fisheries | 30 Aug. 1945 – | 10 Aug. 1947 |

## BRISTOL, Hon. Edmund James
4 Sept. 1961 – 14 July 1927

| | | |
|---|---|---|
| Sworn of the Privy Council | 21 Sept. 1921 | |
| Minister without Portfolio   *Ministry Resigned* | 21 Sept. 1921 – | 28 Dec. 1921 |

## BRODEUR, Hon. Louis-Philippe
21 Aug. 1862 – 1 Jan. 1924

| | | | |
|---|---|---|---|
| Sworn of the Privy Council | 19 Jan. 1904 | | |
| Minister of Inland Revenue | 19 Jan. 1904 – | 5 Feb. 1906 | |
| Minister of Marine and Fisheries | 6 Feb. 1906 – | 10 Aug. 1911 | |
| Minister of the Naval Service | 4 May 1910 – | 10 Aug. 1911 | |

## BROOKS, Hon. Alfred Johnson
14 Nov. 1890 – 7 Dec. 1967

| | | | |
|---|---|---|---|
| Sworn of the Privy Council | 21 June 1957 | | |
| Minister of Veterans Affairs | 21 June 1957 – | 10 Oct. 1960 | |
| Acting Minister of National Health and Welfare | 21 June 1957 – | 21 Aug. 1957 | |
| Member of the Senate | 12 Sept. 1960 – | 7 Nov. 1967 | |
| Leader of the Government in the Senate | 1 Sept. 1962 – | 21 Apr. 1963 | |

## BROWNE, Hon. William Joseph
3 May 1897 –

| | | | |
|---|---|---|---|
| Sworn of the Privy Council | 21 June 1957 | | |
| Minister without Portfolio | 21 June 1957 – | 10 Oct. 1960 | |
| Solicitor General of Canada | 11 Oct. 1960 – | 9 Aug. 1962 | |

## BUCHANAN, Hon. J. Judd
25 July 1929 –

| | | | |
|---|---|---|---|
| Parliamentary Secretary – Indian and Northern Affairs | 1 Oct. 1970 – | 2 Feb. 1972 | |
| Parliamentary Secretary – Finance | 3 Feb. 1972 – | 1 Sept. 1972 | |
| Sworn of the Privy Council | 8 Aug. 1974 | | |
| Minister of Indian Affairs and Northern Development | 8 Aug. 1974 – | 13 Sept. 1976 | |
| Minister of Public Works | 14 Sept. 1976 – | 23 Nov. 1978 | |
| Minister of State for Science and Technology | 16 Sept. 1977 – | 23 Nov. 1978 | |
| President of the Treasury Board   *Ministry Resigned* | 24 Nov. 1978 – | 3 June 1979 | |

## BUREAU, Hon. Jacques
9 July 1860 – 23 Jan. 1933

| | | | |
|---|---|---|---|
| Solicitor General of Canada   *Ministry Resigned* | 14 Feb. 1907 – | 9 Oct. 1911 | |
| Sworn of the Privy Council | 29 Dec. 1921 | | |
| Minister of Customs and Excise | 29 Dec. 1921 – | 4 Sept. 1925 | |
| Member of the Senate | 5 Sept. 1925 – | 23 Jan. 1933 | |

## BURPEE, Hon. Isaac
28 Nov. 1825 – 1 Mar. 1885

| | |
|---|---|
| Sworn of the Privy Council | 7 Nov. 1873 |
| Minister of Customs   *Ministry Resigned* | 7 Nov. 1873 – 16 Oct. 1878 |
| Acting Minister of Agriculture | 15 Dec. 1876 – 25 Jan. 1877 |

## BURRELL, Hon. Martin
14 Oct. 1858 – 20 Mar. 1938

| | |
|---|---|
| Sworn of the Privy Council | 16 Oct. 1911 |
| Minister of Agriculture   *Ministry Resigned* | 16 Oct. 1911 – 11 Oct. 1917 |
| Minister of Mines | 12 Oct. 1917 – 30 Dec. 1919 |
| Secretary of State of Canada | 12 Oct. 1917 – 30 Dec. 1919 |
| Minister of Customs and Inland Revenue | 31 Dec. 1919 – 7 July 1920 |

## BUSSIÈRES, Hon. Pierre
8 July 1939 –

| | |
|---|---|
| Parliamentary Secretary – Energy, Mines and Resources | 1 Oct. 1978 – 26 Mar. 1979 |
| Parliamentary Secretary – Science and Technology | 1 Oct. 1978 – 26 Mar. 1979 |
| Sworn of the Privy Council | 3 Mar. 1980 |
| Minister of State (Finance) | 3 Mar. 1980 – |

## CACCIA, Hon. Charles L.
28 Apr. 1930 –

| | |
|---|---|
| Parliamentary Secretary – Solicitor General | 20 Oct. 1969 – 4 Mar. 1970 |
| Parliamentary Secretary – Treasury Board | 5 Mar. 1970 – 30 Sept. 1970 |
| Parliamentary Secretary – Manpower and Immigration | 1 Oct. 1970 – 30 Sept. 1971 |
| Sworn of the Privy Council | 22 Sept. 1981 |
| Minister of Labour | 22 Sept. 1981 – |

## CADIEUX, Hon. Léo Alphonse Joseph
28 May 1908 –

| | |
|---|---|
| Sworn of the Privy Council | 15 Feb. 1965 |
| Associate Minister of National Defence | 15 Feb. 1965 – 18 Sept. 1967 |
| Minister of National Defence | 19 Sept. 1967 – 16 Sept. 1970 |

## CAFIK, Hon. Norman A.
29 Dec. 1928 –

| | | |
|---|---|---|
| Parliamentary Secretary – National Health and Welfare | 22 Dec. 1972 – | 21 Dec. 1973 |
| | 1 Jan. 1974 – | 9 May 1974 |
| Parliamentary Secretary – Consumer and Corporate Affairs | 15 Sept. 1974 – | 14 Sept. 1975 |
| Sworn of the Privy Council | 16 Sept. 1977 | |
| Minister of State (Multiculturalism)   *Ministry Resigned* | 16 Sept. 1977 – | 3 June 1979 |

## CAHAN, Hon. Charles Hazlitt
31 Oct. 1861 – 15 Aug. 1944

| | | |
|---|---|---|
| Sworn of the Privy Council | 7 Aug. 1930 | |
| Secretary of State of Canada   *Ministry Resigned* | 7 Aug. 1930 – | 22 Oct. 1935 |

## CALDER, Hon. James Alexander
17 Sept. 1868 – 20 July 1956

| | | |
|---|---|---|
| Sworn of the Privy Council | 12 Oct. 1917 | |
| Minister of Immigration and Colonization | 12 Oct. 1917 – | 20 Sept. 1921 |
| Acting Minister of Agriculture | 18 June 1919 – | 11 Aug. 1919 |
| Acting Minister of Militia and Defence | 16 Jan. 1920 – | 23 Jan. 1920 |
| President of the Privy Council | 10 July 1920 – | 20 Sept. 1921 |
| Member of the Senate | 22 Sept. 1921 – | 20 July 1956 |

## CAMPAGNOLO, Hon. Iona
18 Oct. 1932 –

| | | |
|---|---|---|
| Parliamentary Secretary – Indian and Northern Affairs | 15 Sept. 1974 – | 14 Sept. 1975 |
| | 10 Oct. 1975 – | 13 Sept. 1976 |
| Sworn of the Privy Council | 14 Sept. 1976 | |
| Minister of State (Fitness and Amateur Sport)   *Ministry Resigned* | 14 Sept. 1976 – | 3 June 1979 |

## CAMPBELL, Hon. Sir Alexander
9 Mar. 1822 – 24 May 1892

| | | |
|---|---|---|
| Sworn of the Privy Council | 1 July 1867 | |
| Postmaster General | 1 July 1867 – | 30 June 1873 |
| Member of the Senate | 23 Oct. 1867 – | 7 Feb. 1887 |
| Leader of the Government in the Senate | 1867 – | 1873 |
| Acting Minister of Inland Revenue | 15 July 1868 – | 15 Nov. 1869 |
| Superintendent-General of Indian Affairs *Ministry Resigned* | 1 July 1873 – | 6 Nov. 1873 |
| Minister of the Interior *Ministry Resigned* | 1 July 1873 – | 6 Nov. 1873 |
| Leader of the Government in the Senate | 1878 – | 1887 |
| Receiver General | 8 Nov. 1878 – | 19 May 1879 |
| Postmaster General | 20 May 1879 – | 15 Jan. 1880 |
| Minister of Militia and Defence | 16 Jan. 1880 – | 7 Nov. 1880 |
| Postmaster General | 8 Nov. 1880 – | 19 May 1881 |
| Minister of Justice and Attorney General | 20 May 1881 – | 24 Sept. 1885 |
| Postmaster General | 25 Sept. 1885 – | 26 Jan. 1887 |

## CAMPBELL, Hon. W. Bennett
27 Aug. 1943 –

| | |
|---|---|
| Sworn of the Privy Council | 22 Sept. 1981 |
| Minister of Veterans Affairs | 22 Sept. 1981 – |

## CAMPNEY, Hon. Ralph Osborne
6 June 1894 – 6 Oct. 1967

| | | |
|---|---|---|
| Parliamentary Assistant – National Defence | 24 Jan. 1951 – | 14 Oct. 1952 |
| Sworn of the Privy Council | 15 Oct. 1952 | |
| Solicitor General of Canada | 15 Oct. 1952 – | 11 Jan. 1954 |
| Associate Minister of National Defence | 12 Feb. 1953 – | 30 June 1954 |
| Minister of National Defence *Ministry Resigned* | 1 July 1954 – | 20 June 1957 |

## CANNON, Hon. Lucien
16 Jan. 1887 – 14 Feb. 1950

| | | |
|---|---|---|
| Solicitor General of Canada *Ministry Resigned* | 5 Sept. 1925 – | 28 June 1926 |
| Sworn of the Privy Council | 25 Sept. 1926 | |
| Solicitor General of Canada *Ministry Resigned* | 25 Sept. 1926 – | 6 Aug. 1930 |

**CARDIN, Hon. Louis Joseph Lucien**
1 Mar. 1919 –

| | | |
|---|---|---|
| Parliamentary Assistant – External Affairs | 9 Feb. 1956 – | 12 Apr. 1957 |
| Sworn of the Privy Council | 22 Apr. 1963 | |
| Associate Minister of National Defence | 22 Apr. 1963 – | 14 Feb. 1965 |
| Minister of Public Works | 15 Feb. 1965 – | 6 July 1965 |
| Minister of Justice and Attorney General | 7 July 1965 – | 3 Apr. 1967 |

**CARDIN, Hon. Pierre Joseph Arthur**
28 June 1879 – 20 Oct. 1946

| | | |
|---|---|---|
| Sworn of the Privy Council | 30 Jan. 1924 | |
| Minister of Marine and Fisheries  *Ministry Resigned* | 30 Jan. 1924 – | 28 June 1926 |
| Minister of Marine and Fisheries | 25 Sept. 1926 – | 13 June 1930 |
| Minister of Marine  *Ministry Resigned* | 14 June 1930 – | 6 Aug. 1930 |
| Minister of Public Works | 23 Oct. 1935 – | 12 May 1942 |
| Minister of Transport | 8 July 1940 – | 12 May 1942 |

**CARLING, Hon. Sir John**
23 Jan. 1828 – 6 Nov. 1911

| | | |
|---|---|---|
| Sworn of the Privy Council | 23 May 1882 | |
| Postmaster General | 23 May 1882 – | 24 Sept. 1885 |
| Minister of Agriculture  *Ministry Resigned* | 25 Sept. 1885 – | 4 Dec. 1892 |
| Acting Postmaster General | 11 July 1888 – | 5 Aug. 1888 |
| Member of the Senate | 27 Apr. 1891 – | 17 Feb. 1892 |
| Minister without Portfolio  *Ministry Dissolved* | 5 Dec. 1892 – | 20 Dec. 1894 |
| Member of the Senate | 23 Apr. 1896 – | 6 Nov. 1911 |

**CARON, Hon. Sir Joseph Philippe René Adolphe**
24 Dec. 1843 – 20 Apr. 1908

| | | |
|---|---|---|
| Sworn of the Privy Council | 8 Nov. 1880 | |
| Minister of Militia and Defence | 8 Nov. 1880 – | 24 Jan. 1892 |
| Postmaster General  *Ministry Resigned* | 25 Jan. 1892 – | 30 Apr. 1896 |

**CARROLL, Hon. Henry George**
31 Jan. 1866 – 20 Aug. 1939

| | | |
|---|---|---|
| Solicitor General of Canada | 10 Feb. 1902 – | 28 Jan. 1904 |

**CARTIER, Hon. Sir George Étienne**
6 Sept. 1814 – 20 May 1873

| | |
|---|---|
| Sworn of the Privy Council | 1 July 1867 |
| Minister of Militia and Defence | 1 July 1867 – 20 May 1873 |

**CARTWRIGHT, Rt. Hon. Sir Richard John**
14 Dec. 1835 – 24 Sept. 1912

| | |
|---|---|
| Sworn of the Privy Council | 7 Nov. 1873 |
| Minister of Finance  *Ministry Resigned* | 7 Nov. 1873 – 16 Oct. 1878 |
| Minister of Trade and Commerce  *Ministry Resigned* | 13 July 1896 – 9 Oct. 1911 |
| Member of the United Kingdom Privy Council | 9 Nov. 1902 |
| Member of the Senate | 30 Sept. 1904 – 24 Sept. 1912 |
| Leader of the Government in the Senate | 1909 – 1911 |

**CARVELL, Hon. Frank Broadstreet**
14 Aug. 1862 – 9 Aug. 1924

| | |
|---|---|
| Sworn of the Privy Council | 13 Oct. 1917 |
| Minister of Public Works | 13 Oct. 1917 – 1 Aug. 1919 |

**CASGRAIN, Hon. Pierre-François**
4 Aug. 1886 – 2 Aug. 1950

| | |
|---|---|
| Sworn of the Privy Council | 2 May 1940 |
| Secretary of State of Canada | 9 May 1940 – 14 Dec. 1941 |

**CASGRAIN, Hon. Thomas Chase**
28 July 1852 – 29 Dec. 1916

| | |
|---|---|
| Sworn of the Privy Council | 20 Oct. 1914 |
| Postmaster General | 20 Oct. 1914 – 29 Dec. 1916 |

**CAUCHON, Hon. Joseph Édouard**
31 Dec. 1816 – 24 Feb. 1885

| | |
|---|---|
| Member of the Senate | 2 Nov. 1867 – 30 June 1872 |
| Sworn of the Privy Council | 7 Dec. 1875 |
| President of the Privy Council | 7 Dec. 1875 – 7 June 1877 |
| Minister of Inland Revenue | 8 June 1877 – 7 Oct. 1877 |

## CHAPAIS, Hon. Jean-Charles
21 Dec. 1811 – 17 July 1885

| | | |
|---|---|---|
| Sworn of the Privy Council | 1 July 1867 | |
| Minister of Agriculture | 1 July 1867 – | 15 Nov. 1869 |
| Member of the Senate | 30 Jan. 1868 – | 17 July 1885 |
| Receiver General | 16 Nov. 1869 – | 29 Jan. 1873 |

## CHAPLEAU, Hon. Sir Joseph Adolphe
9 Nov. 1840 – 13 June 1898

| | | |
|---|---|---|
| Sworn of the Privy Council | 29 July 1882 | |
| Secretary of State of Canada | 29 July 1882 – | 24 Jan. 1892 |
| Minister of Customs | 25 Jan. 1892 – | 2 Dec. 1892 |

## CHAPLIN, Hon. James Dew
20 Mar. 1863 – 23 Aug. 1937

| | | |
|---|---|---|
| Sworn of the Privy Council | 13 July 1926 | |
| Minister of Trade and Commerce   *Ministry Resigned* | 13 July 1926 – | 24 Sept. 1926 |

## CHEVRIER, Hon. Lionel
2 Apr. 1903 –

| | | |
|---|---|---|
| Parliamentary Assistant – Munitions and Supply | 1 Apr. 1943 – | 16 Apr. 1945 |
| Sworn of the Privy Council | 18 Apr. 1945 | |
| Minister of Transport | 18 Apr. 1945 – | 30 June 1954 |
| President of the Privy Council   *Ministry Resigned* | 25 Apr. 1957 – | 20 June 1957 |
| Minister of Justice and Attorney General | 22 Apr. 1963 – | 2 Feb. 1964 |

## CHRÉTIEN, Hon. Joseph Jacques Jean
11 Jan. 1934 –

| | | |
|---|---|---|
| Parliamentary Secretary – Prime Minister | 16 July 1965 – | 8 Sept. 1965 |
| Parliamentary Secretary – Finance | 7 Jan. 1966 – | 3 Apr. 1967 |
| Sworn of the Privy Council | 4 Apr. 1967 | |
| Minister without Portfolio | 4 Apr. 1967 – | 17 Jan. 1968 |
| Minister of National Revenue | 20 Apr. 1968 – | 5 July 1968 |
| Minister of Indian Affairs and Northern Development | 6 July 1968 – | 7 Aug. 1974 |
| President of the Treasury Board | 8 Aug. 1974 – | 13 Sept. 1976 |
| Minister of Industry, Trade and Commerce | 14 Sept. 1976 – | 15 Sept. 1977 |
| Minister of Finance   *Ministry Resigned* | 16 Sept. 1977 – | 3 June 1979 |
| Minister of Justice and Attorney General | 3 Mar. 1980 – | |
| Minister of State (Social Development) | 3 Mar. 1980 – | |

**CHRISTIE, Hon. David**
Oct. 1818 – 15 Dec. 1880

| | | | | |
|---|---|---|---|---|
| Member of the Senate | 23 Oct. | 1867 | – | 15 Dec. 1880 |
| Sworn of the Privy Council | 7 Nov. | 1873 | | |
| Secretary of State of Canada | 7 Nov. | 1873 | – | 8 Jan. 1874 |

**CHURCHILL, Hon. Gordon**
8 Nov. 1898 –

| | | | | |
|---|---|---|---|---|
| Sworn of the Privy Council | 21 June | 1957 | | |
| Minister of Trade and Commerce | 21 June | 1957 | – | 10 Oct. 1960 |
| Minister of Veterans Affairs | 11 Oct. | 1960 | – | 11 Feb. 1963 |
| Minister of National Defence   *Ministry Resigned* | 12 Feb. | 1963 | – | 21 Apr. 1963 |

**CLARK, Rt. Hon. Charles Joseph**
5 June 1939 –

| | | | | |
|---|---|---|---|---|
| Sworn of the Privy Council | 4 June | 1979 | | |
| Prime Minister   *Ministry Resigned* | 4 June | 1979 | – | 2 Mar. 1980 |

**CLARK, Hugh**
6 May 1867 – 13 May 1959

| | | | | |
|---|---|---|---|---|
| Parliamentary Under Secretary of State for External Affairs | 21 Oct. | 1916 | – | 6 Nov. 1918 |
| Parliamentary Secretary of Militia and Defence | 7 Nov. | 1918 | – | 1 July 1920 |

**CLAXTON, Hon. Brooke**
23 Aug. 1898 – 13 June 1960

| | | | | |
|---|---|---|---|---|
| Parliamentary Assistant – Privy Council | 6 May | 1943 | – | 12 Oct. 1944 |
| Sworn of the Privy Council | 13 Oct. | 1944 | | |
| Minister of National Health and Welfare | 18 Oct. | 1944 | – | 11 Dec. 1946 |
| Minister of National Defence | 12 Dec. | 1946 | – | 30 June 1954 |

**COCHRANE, Hon. Francis**
18 Nov. 1852 – 22 Sept. 1919

| | | | | |
|---|---|---|---|---|
| Sworn of the Privy Council | 10 Oct. | 1911 | | |
| Minister of Railways and Canals   *Ministry Resigned* | 10 Oct. | 1911 | – | 11 Oct. 1917 |
| Minister without Portfolio | 12 Oct. | 1917 | – | 22 Sept. 1919 |

**CODERRE, Hon. Louis**
1 Nov. 1865 – 29 Mar. 1935

| | | |
|---|---|---|
| Sworn of the Privy Council | 29 Oct. 1912 | |
| Secretary of State of Canada | 29 Oct. 1912 – | 5 Oct. 1915 |
| Minister of Mines | 10 Feb. 1913 – | 5 Oct. 1915 |

**COFFIN, Hon. Thomas**
1817 – 12 July 1890

| | | |
|---|---|---|
| Sworn of the Privy Council | 7 Nov. 1873 | |
| Receiver General   *Ministry Resigned* | 7 Nov. 1873 – | 16 Oct. 1878 |

**COLBY, Hon. Charles Carrol**
10 Dec. 1827 – 10 Dec. 1907

| | | |
|---|---|---|
| Sworn of the Privy Council | 28 Nov. 1889 | |
| President of the Privy Council | 28 Nov. 1889 – | 30 Apr. 1891 |

**COMTOIS, Hon. Paul**
22 Aug. 1895 – 21 Feb. 1966

| | | |
|---|---|---|
| Sworn of the Privy Council | 7 Aug. 1957 | |
| Minister of Mines and Technical Surveys | 7 Aug. 1957 – | 6 Oct. 1961 |

**CONNOLLY, Hon. John Joseph**
31 Oct. 1906 –

| | | |
|---|---|---|
| Member of the Senate | 12 June 1953 | |
| Sworn of the Privy Council | 3 Feb. 1964 | |
| Minister without Portfolio   *Ministry Resigned* | 3 Feb. 1964 – | 19 Apr. 1968 |
| Leader of the Government in the Senate   *Ministry Resigned* | 3 Feb. 1964 – | 19 Apr. 1968 |
| Acting Secretary of State of Canada   *Ministry Resigned* | 10 Apr. 1968 – | 19 Apr. 1968 |

**COPP, Hon. Arthur Bliss**
10 July 1870 – 5 Dec. 1949

| | | |
|---|---|---|
| Sworn of the Privy Council | 29 Dec. 1921 | |
| Secretary of State of Canada | 29 Dec. 1921 – | 24 Sept. 1925 |
| Member of the Senate | 25 Sept. 1925 – | 5 Dec. 1949 |

**COSGROVE, Hon. Paul James**
30 Dec. 1934 –

| | |
|---|---|
| Sworn of the Privy Council | 3 Mar. 1980 |
| Minister of Public Works | 3 Mar. 1980 – |

**COSTIGAN, Hon. John**
1 Feb. 1835 – 29 Sept. 1916

| | | | |
|---|---|---|---|
| Sworn of the Privy Council | 23 May | 1882 | |
| Minister of Inland Revenue | 23 May | 1882 – | 2 Dec. 1892 |
| Secretary of State of Canada *Ministry Dissolved* | 5 Dec. | 1892 – | 20 Dec. 1894 |
| Minister of Marine and Fisheries *Ministry Resigned* | 21 Dec. | 1894 – | 10 July 1896 |
| Acting Minister of Trade and Commerce | 6 Jan. | 1896 – | 14 Jan. 1896 |
| Member of the Senate | 15 Jan. | 1907 – | 29 Sept. 1916 |

**CÔTÉ, Hon. Alcide**
19 May 1903 – 7 Aug. 1955

| | | | |
|---|---|---|---|
| Sworn of the Privy Council | 13 Feb. | 1952 | |
| Postmaster General | 13 Feb. | 1952 – | 7 Aug. 1955 |

**CÔTÉ, Hon. Joseph-Julien-Jean-Pierre**
9 Jan. 1926 –

| | | | |
|---|---|---|---|
| Sworn of the Privy Council | 18 Dec. | 1965 | |
| Postmaster General | 18 Dec. | 1965 – | 5 July 1968 |
| Minister of National Revenue | 6 July | 1968 – | 23 Sept. 1970 |
| Minister without Portfolio | 24 Sept. | 1970 – | 10 June 1971 |
| Acting Minister of Communications | 29 Apr. | 1971 – | 10 May 1971 |
| Acting Postmaster General | 29 Apr. | 1971 – | 10 June 1971 |
| Postmaster General | 11 June | 1971 – | 26 Nov. 1972 |
| Member of the Senate | 1 Sept. | 1972 – | 19 Apr. 1978 |

**COURTEMANCHE, Hon. Henri**
7 Aug. 1916 –

| | | | |
|---|---|---|---|
| Sworn of the Privy Council | 12 May | 1958 | |
| Secretary of State of Canada | 12 May | 1958 – | 19 Jan. 1960 |
| Member of the Senate | 20 Jan. | 1960 – | 22 Dec. 1961 |

**CRERAR, Hon. Thomas Alexander**
17 June 1876 – 11 Apr. 1975

| | | |
|---|---|---|
| Sworn of the Privy Council | 12 Oct. 1917 | |
| Minister of Agriculture | 12 Oct. 1917 – | 11 June 1919 |
| Minister of Railways and Canals   *Ministry Resigned* | 30 Dec. 1929 – | 6 Aug. 1930 |
| Minister of Immigration and Colonization | 23 Oct. 1935 – | 30 Nov. 1936 |
| Superintendent-General of Indian Affairs | 23 Oct. 1935 – | 30 Nov. 1936 |
| Minister of the Interior | 23 Oct. 1935 – | 30 Nov. 1936 |
| Minister of Mines | 23 Oct. 1935 – | 30 Nov. 1936 |
| Acting Minister of Agriculture | 25 Oct. 1935 – | 3 Nov. 1935 |
| Minister of Mines and Resources | 1 Dec. 1936 – | 17 Apr. 1945 |
| Member of the Senate | 18 Apr. 1945 – | 31 May 1966 |

**CROMBIE, Hon. David**
24 Apr. 1936 –

| | | |
|---|---|---|
| Sworn of the Privy Council | 4 June 1979 | |
| Minister of National Health and Welfare   *Ministry Resigned* | 4 June 1979 – | 2 Mar. 1980 |

**CROSBIE, Hon. John C.**
30 Jan. 1931 –

| | | |
|---|---|---|
| Sworn of the Privy Council | 4 June 1979 | |
| Minister of Finance   *Ministry Resigned* | 4 June 1979 – | 2 Mar. 1980 |

**CROTHERS, Hon. Thomas Wilson**
1 Jan. 1850 – 10 Dec. 1921

| | | |
|---|---|---|
| Sworn of the Privy Council | 10 Oct. 1911 | |
| Minister of Labour | 10 Oct. 1911 – | 6 Nov. 1918 |
| Member of the Senate | 3 Oct. 1921 – | 10 Dec. 1921 |

**CULLEN, Hon. Jack Sydney George**
20 Apr. 1927 –

| | | |
|---|---|---|
| Parliamentary Secretary – National Defence | 1 Oct. 1971 – | 2 Feb. 1972 |
| Parliamentary Secretary – Energy, Mines and Resources | 3 Feb. 1972 – | 1 Sept. 1972 |
| Parliamentary Secretary – Finance | 15 Sept. 1974 – | 14 Sept. 1975 |
| Sworn of the Privy Council | 26 Sept. 1975 | |
| Minister of National Revenue | 26 Sept. 1975 – | 13 Sept. 1976 |
| Minister of Manpower and Immigration | 14 Sept. 1976 – | 14 Aug. 1977 |
| Minister of Employment and Immigration   *Ministry Resigned* | 15 Aug. 1977 – | 3 June 1979 |

**CURRAN, Hon. John Joseph**
22 Feb. 1842 – 1 Oct. 1909

| | |
|---|---|
| Solicitor General of Canada | 5 Dec. 1892 – 17 Oct. 1895 |

**DALY, Hon. Thomas Mayne**
16 Aug. 1852 – 24 June 1911

| | |
|---|---|
| Sworn of the Privy Council | 17 Oct. 1892 |
| Superintendent-General of Indian Affairs *Ministry Resigned* | 17 Oct. 1892 – 30 Apr. 1896 |
| Minister of the Interior *Ministry Resigned* | 17 Oct. 1892 – 30 Apr. 1896 |
| Acting Minister of Justice and Attorney General | 6 Jan. 1896 – 14 Jan. 1896 |
| Acting Secretary of State of Canada | 6 Jan. 1896 – 14 Jan. 1896 |

**DANDURAND, Rt. Hon. Raoul**
4 Nov. 1861 – 11 Mar. 1942

| | |
|---|---|
| Member of the Senate | 22 Jan. 1898 – 11 Mar. 1942 |
| Sworn of the Privy Council | 20 Jan. 1909 |
| Leader of the Government in the Senate *Ministry Resigned* | 29 Dec. 1921 – 28 June 1926 |
| Minister without Portfolio *Ministry Resigned* | 29 Dec. 1921 – 28 June 1926 |
| Minister without Portfolio *Ministry Resigned* | 25 Sept. 1926 – 6 Aug. 1930 |
| Leader of the Government in the Senate *Ministry Resigned* | 25 Sept. 1926 – 6 Aug. 1930 |
| Minister without Portfolio | 23 Oct. 1935 – 11 Mar. 1942 |
| Leader of the Government in the Senate | 23 Oct. 1935 – 11 Mar. 1942 |
| Member of the United Kingdom Privy Council | 1 July 1941 |

**DANSON, Hon. Barnett Jerome**
8 Feb. 1921 –

| | |
|---|---|
| Parliamentary Secretary – Prime Minister | 1 Oct. 1970 – 1 Sept. 1972 |
| Sworn of the Privy Council | 8 Aug. 1974 |
| Minister of State for Urban Affairs | 8 Aug. 1974 – 2 Nov. 1976 |
| Acting Minister of National Defence | 13 Oct. 1976 – 2 Nov. 1976 |
| Minister of National Defence *Ministry Resigned* | 3 Nov. 1976 – 3 June 1979 |

**DAVIES, Rt. Hon. Sir Louis Henry**
4 May 1845 – 1 May 1924

| | |
|---|---|
| Sworn of the Privy Council | 13 July 1896 |
| Minister of Marine and Fisheries | 13 July 1896 – 24 Sept. 1901 |
| Member of the United Kingdom Privy Council | 14 July 1921 |

**DAVIS, Hon. Jack**

31 July 1916 –

| | | |
|---|---|---|
| Parliamentary Secretary – Prime Minister | 14 May 1963 – | 8 Sept. 1965 |
| Parliamentary Secretary – Mines and Technical Surveys | 7 Jan. 1966 – | 30 Sept. 1966 |
| Parliamentary Secretary – Energy, Mines and Resources | 1 Oct. 1966 – | 23 Apr. 1968 |
| Sworn of the Privy Council | 26 Apr. 1968 | |
| Minister without Portfolio | 26 Apr. 1968 – | 5 July 1968 |
| Minister of Fisheries | 6 July 1968 – | 31 Mar. 1969 |
| Minister of Fisheries and Forestry | 1 Apr. 1969 – | 10 June 1971 |
| Minister of the Environment | 11 June 1971 – | 7 Aug. 1974 |

**DE BANÉ, Hon. Pierre**

| | | |
|---|---|---|
| Parliamentary Secretary – External Affairs | 22 Dec. 1972 – | 21 Dec. 1973 |
| Parliamentary Secretary – Urban Affairs | 15 Sept. 1974 – | 14 Sept. 1975 |
| Sworn of the Privy Council | 24 Nov. 1978 | |
| Minister of Supply and Services   *Ministry Resigned* | 24 Nov. 1978 – | 3 June 1979 |
| Minister of Regional Economic Expansion | 3 Mar. 1980 – | 11 Jan. 1982 |
| Minister of State (External Relations) | 12 Jan. 1982 – | |

**DE COTRET, Hon. Robert R.**

20 Feb. 1944 –

| | | |
|---|---|---|
| Appointed to the Senate | 5 June 1979 | |
| Minister of Industry, Trade and Commerce   *Ministry Resigned* | 4 June 1979 – | 2 Mar. 1980 |
| Resigned from the Senate | 14 Jan. 1980 | |

**DENIS, Hon. Azellus**

26 Mar. 1907 –

| | | |
|---|---|---|
| Sworn of the Privy Council | 22 Apr. 1963 | |
| Postmaster General | 22 Apr. 1963 – | 2 Feb. 1964 |
| Member of the Senate | 3 Feb. 1964 – | |

**DESCHATELETS, Hon. Jean-Paul**

9 Oct. 1912 –

| | | |
|---|---|---|
| Sworn of the Privy Council | 22 Apr. 1963 | |
| Minister of Public Works | 22 Apr. 1963 – | 11 Feb. 1965 |
| Member of the Senate | 24 Feb. 1966 – | |

## DESJARDINS, Hon. Alphonse
6 May 1841 – 4 June 1912

| | |
|---|---|
| Member of the Senate | 1 Oct. 1892 – 10 June 1896 |
| Sworn of the Privy Council | 15 Jan. 1896 |
| Minister of Militia and Defence *Ministry Resigned* | 15 Jan. 1896 – 30 Apr. 1896 |
| Minister of Public Works *Ministry Resigned* | 1 May 1896 – 10 July 1896 |

## DEWDNEY, Hon. Edgar
5 Nov. 1835 – 8 Aug. 1916

| | |
|---|---|
| Sworn of the Privy Council | 25 Sept. 1888 |
| Superintendent-General of Indian Affairs | 25 Sept. 1888 – 16 Oct. 1892 |
| Minister of the Interior | 25 Sept. 1888 – 16 Oct. 1892 |

## DICKEY, Hon. Arthur Rupert
18 Aug. 1854 – 3 July 1900

| | |
|---|---|
| Sworn of the Privy Council | 21 Dec. 1894 |
| Secretary of State of Canada | 21 Dec. 1894 – 25 Mar. 1895 |
| Minister of Militia and Defence | 26 Mar. 1895 – 5 Jan. 1896 |
| Minister of Justice and Attorney General *Ministry Resigned* | 15 Jan. 1896 – 10 July 1896 |

## DIEFENBAKER, Rt. Hon. John George
18 Sept. 1895 – 16 Aug. 1979

| | |
|---|---|
| Sworn of the Privy Council | 21 June 1957 |
| Prime Minister *Ministry Resigned* | 21 June 1957 – 21 Apr. 1963 |
| Secretary of State for External Affairs | 21 June 1957 – 12 Sept. 1957 |
| Acting Secretary of State for External Affairs | 19 Mar. 1959 – 3 June 1959 |
| President of the Privy Council *Ministry Resigned* | 21 Dec. 1962 – 21 Apr. 1963 |
| Member of the United Kingdom Privy Council | Sept. 1957 |

## DINSDALE, Hon. Walter Gilbert
3 April. 1916 –

| | |
|---|---|
| Parliamentary Assistant – Veterans Affairs | 19 Aug. 1957 – 1 Feb. 1958 |
| Parliamentary Secretary – Veterans Affairs | 18 Nov. 1959 – 10 Oct. 1960 |
| Sworn of the Privy Council | 11 Oct. 1960 |
| Minister of Northern Affairs and National Resources *Ministry Resigned* | 11 Oct. 1960 – 21 Apr. 1963 |
| Acting Minister of Mines and Technical Surveys | 10 Oct. 1961 – 27 Dec. 1961 |

**DOBELL, Hon. Richard Reid**
1837 – 11 Jan. 1902

| | | |
|---|---|---|
| Sworn of the Privy Council | 13 July 1896 | |
| Minister without Portfolio | 13 July 1896 – | 11 Jan. 1902 |

**DOHERTY, Rt. Hon. Charles Joseph**
11 May 1855 – 28 July 1931

| | | |
|---|---|---|
| Sworn of the Privy Council | 10 Oct. 1911 | |
| Minister of Justice and Attorney General | 10 Oct. 1911 – | 20 Sept. 1921 |
| Member of the United Kingdom Privy Council | 11 Oct. 1921 | |

**DORION, Hon. Sir Antoine-Aimé**
17 Jan. 1818 – 31 May 1891

| | | |
|---|---|---|
| Sworn of the Privy Council | 7 Nov. 1873 | |
| Minister of Justice and Attorney General | 7 Nov. 1873 – | 31 May 1874 |

**DORION, Hon. Noël**
24 July 1904 – 8 Mar. 1980

| | | |
|---|---|---|
| Sworn of the Privy Council | 11 Oct. 1960 | |
| Secretary of State of Canada | 11 Oct. 1960 – | 5 July 1962 |
| President of the Privy Council | 28 Dec. 1961 – | 5 July 1962 |

**DRAYTON, Hon. Sir Henry Lumley**
27 Apr. 1869 – 28 Aug. 1950

| | | |
|---|---|---|
| Sworn of the Privy Council | 2 Aug. 1919 | |
| Minister of Finance and Receiver General  *Ministry Resigned* | 2 Aug. 1919 – | 28 Dec. 1921 |
| Acting Secretary of State of Canada | 24 Jan. 1921 – | 20 Sept. 1921 |
| Acting Minister of Finance and Receiver General | 29 June 1926 – | 12 July 1926 |
| Acting Minister of Railways and Canals | 29 June 1926 – | 12 July 1926 |
| Minister without Portfolio  *Ministry Resigned* | 13 July 1926 – | 24 Sept. 1926 |
| Acting Minister of Immigration and Colonization  *Ministry Resigned* | 13 July 1926 – | 24 Sept. 1926 |

**DRURY, Hon. Charles Mills**

7 May 1912 –

| | | |
|---|---|---|
| Sworn of the Privy Council | 22 Apr. 1963 | |
| Minister of Defence Production | 22 Apr. 1963 – | 5 July 1968 |
| Minister of Industry | 25 July 1963 – | 5 July 1968 |
| Minister of Trade and Commerce | 20 Apr. 1968 – | 5 July 1968 |
| President of the Treasury Board | 6 July 1968 – | 7 Aug. 1974 |
| Acting Minister of National Defence | 17 Sept. 1970 – | 23 Sept. 1970 |
| | 7 Sept. 1972 – | 26 Nov. 1972 |
| Minister of Public Works | 8 Aug. 1974 – | 13 Sept. 1976 |
| Minister of State for Science and Technology | 8 Aug. 1974 – | 13 Sept. 1976 |
| Acting Minister of Finance | 10 Sept. 1975 – | 25 Sept. 1975 |

**DUBÉ, Hon. Jean-Eudes**

6 Nov. 1926 –

| | | |
|---|---|---|
| Sworn of the Privy Council | 6 July 1968 | |
| Minister of Veterans Affairs | 6 July 1968 – | 27 Jan. 1972 |
| Minister of Public Works | 28 Jan. 1972 – | 7 Aug. 1974 |
| Acting Minister of National Defence | 1 Sept. 1972 – | 6 Sept. 1972 |

**DUNKIN, Hon. Christopher**

25 Sept. 1812 – 6 Jan. 1881

| | | |
|---|---|---|
| Sworn of the Privy Council | 16 Nov. 1869 | |
| Minister of Agriculture | 16 Nov. 1869 – | 24 Oct. 1871 |

**DUNNING, Hon. Charles Avery**

31 July 1885 – 2 Oct. 1958

| | | |
|---|---|---|
| Sworn of the Privy Council | 1 Mar. 1926 | |
| Minister of Railways and Canals   *Ministry Resigned* | 1 Mar. 1926 – | 28 June 1926 |
| Minister of Railways and Canals | 25 Sept. 1926 – | 25 Nov. 1929 |
| Minister of Finance and Receiver General   *Ministry Resigned* | 26 Nov. 1929 – | 6 Aug. 1930 |
| Acting Minister of Railways and Canals | 26 Nov. 1929 – | 29 Dec. 1929 |
| Minister of Finance and Receiver General | 23 Oct. 1935 – | 5 Sept. 1939 |

**DUPRÉ, Hon. Maurice**

20 Mar. 1888 – 3 Oct. 1941

| | | |
|---|---|---|
| Sworn of the Privy Council | 7 Aug. 1930 | |
| Solicitor General of Canada   *Ministry Resigned* | 7 Aug. 1930 – | 22 Oct. 1935 |

**DUPUIS, Hon. Yvon**
11 Oct. 1926 –

| | | |
|---|---|---|
| Parliamentary Secretary – Secretary of State of Canada | 14 May 1963 – | 2 Feb. 1964 |
| Sworn of the Privy Council | 3 Feb. 1964 | |
| Minister without Portfolio | 3 Feb. 1964 – | 21 Jan. 1965 |

**DURANLEAU, Hon. Alfred**
1 Nov. 1871 – 11 Mar. 1951

| | | |
|---|---|---|
| Sworn of the Privy Council | 7 Aug. 1930 | |
| Minister of Marine | 7 Aug. 1930 – | 19 July 1935 |
| Acting Minister of Fisheries | 3 Feb. 1932 – | 16 Nov. 1934 |

**EDWARDS, Hon. John Wesley**
25 May 1865 – 18 Apr. 1929

| | | |
|---|---|---|
| Sworn of the Privy Council | 21 Sept. 1921 | |
| Minister of Immigration and Colonization *Ministry Resigned* | 21 Sept. 1921 – | 28 Dec. 1921 |

**ELLIOTT, Hon. John Campbell**
25 July 1872 – 20 Dec. 1941

| | | |
|---|---|---|
| Sworn of the Privy Council | 8 Mar. 1926 | |
| Minister of Labour *Ministry Resigned* | 8 Mar. 1926 – | 28 June 1926 |
| Minister of Soldiers' Civil Re-establishment | | |
| *Ministry Resigned* | 15 Apr. 1926 – | 28 June 1926 |
| Minister of Public Works *Ministry Resigned* | 25 Sept. 1926 – | 6 Aug. 1930 |
| Postmaster General | 23 Oct. 1935 – | 22 Jan. 1939 |
| Member of the Senate | 29 Jan. 1940 – | 20 Dec. 1941 |

**EMMERSON, Hon. Henry Robert**
25 Sept. 1853 – 9 July 1914

| | | |
|---|---|---|
| Sworn of the Privy Council | 15 Jan. 1904 | |
| Minister of Railways and Canals | 15 Jan. 1904 – | 2 Apr. 1907 |

**EPP, Hon. Arthur Jacob**
1 Sept. 1939 –

| | | |
|---|---|---|
| Sworn of the Privy Council | 4 June 1979 | |
| Minister of Indian Affairs and Northern Development | | |
| *Ministry Resigned* | 4 June 1979 – | 2 Mar. 1980 |

**ERNST, Hon. William Gordon**
18 Oct. 1897 – 12 July 1939

| | |
|---|---|
| Sworn of the Privy Council | 14 Aug. 1935 |
| Minister of Fisheries  *Ministry Resigned* | 14 Aug. 1935 – 22 Oct. 1935 |

**EROLA, Hon. Judy**
16 Jan. 1934 –

| | |
|---|---|
| Sworn of the Privy Council | 3 Mar. 1980 |
| Minister of State (Mines) | 3 Mar. 1980 – |

**EULER, Hon. William Daum**
10 July 1875 – 15 July 1961

| | |
|---|---|
| Sworn of the Privy Council | 25 Sept. 1926 |
| Minister of Customs and Excise | 26 Sept. 1926 – 30 Mar. 1927 |
| Minister of National Revenue  *Ministry Resigned* | 31 Mar. 1927 –  6 Aug. 1930 |
| Minister of Trade and Commerce | 23 Oct.  1935 –  8 May  1940 |
| Member of the Senate | 9 May  1940 – 15 July  1961 |

**FAIRCLOUGH, Hon. Ellen Louks**
28 Jan. 1905 –

| | |
|---|---|
| Sworn of the Privy Council | 21 June 1957 |
| Secretary of State of Canada | 21 June 1957 – 11 May  1958 |
| Minister of Citizenship and Immigration | 12 May  1958 –  8 Aug. 1962 |
| Postmaster General  *Ministry Resigned* | 9 Aug.  1962 – 21 Apr.  1963 |

**FAULKNER, Hon. James Hugh**
9 Mar. 1933 –

| | |
|---|---|
| Parliamentary Secretary – Secretary of State of Canada | 1 Oct.  1970 –  1 Sept. 1971 |
| Sworn of the Privy Council | 27 Nov.  1972 |
| Secretary of State of Canada | 27 Nov.  1972 – 13 Sept. 1976 |
| Minister of State for Science and Technology | 14 Sept. 1976 – 15 Sept. 1977 |
| Minister of Indian Affairs and Northern Development   *Ministry Resigned* | 16 Sept. 1977 –  3 June 1979 |

**FAUTEUX, Hon. Guillaume André**
20 Oct. 1874 – 10 Sept. 1940

| | |
|---|---|
| Solicitor General of Canada  *Ministry Resigned* | 1 Oct.  1921 – 28 Dec.  1921 |
| Sworn of the Privy Council | 23 Aug.  1926 |
| Solicitor General of Canada  *Ministry Resigned* | 23 Aug.  1926 – 24 Sept. 1926 |
| Member of the Senate | 30 Dec.  1933 – 10 Sept. 1940 |

## FAVREAU, Hon. Guy
20 May 1917 – 11 July 1967

| | | | |
|---|---|---|---|
| Sworn of the Privy Council | 22 Apr. | 1963 | |
| Minister of Citizenship and Immigration | 22 Apr. | 1963 – | 2 Feb. 1964 |
| Minister of Justice and Attorney General | 3 Feb. | 1964 – | 29 June 1965 |
| President of the Privy Council | 7 July | 1965 – | 3 Apr. 1967 |
| Registrar General of Canada | 1 Oct. | 1966 – | 3 Apr. 1967 |

## FERGUSON, Hon. Donald
7 Mar. 1839 – 4 Sept. 1909

| | | | |
|---|---|---|---|
| Member of the Senate | 4 Sept. | 1893 – | 4 Sept. 1909 |
| Sworn of the Privy Council | 2 Jan. | 1895 | |
| Minister without Portfolio   *Ministry Resigned* | 2 Jan. | 1895 – | 10 July 1896 |
| Acting Minister of Agriculture | 6 Jan. | 1896 – | 14 Jan. 1896 |

## FIELDING, Rt. Hon. William Stevens
24 Nov. 1848 – 23 June 1929

| | | | |
|---|---|---|---|
| Sworn of the Privy Council | 20 July | 1896 | |
| Minister of Finance and Receiver General   *Ministry Resigned* | 20 July | 1896 – | 9 Oct. 1911 |
| Acting Minister of Railways and Canals | 21 July | 1903 – | 14 Jan. 1904 |
| | 9 Apr. | 1907 – | 29 Aug. 1907 |
| Member of the United Kingdom Privy Council | 3 June | 1923 | |
| Minister of Finance and Receiver General | 29 Dec. | 1921 – | 4 Sept. 1925 |

## FISHER, Hon. Sydney Arthur
12 June 1850 – 9 Apr. 1921

| | | | |
|---|---|---|---|
| Sworn of the Privy Council | 13 July | 1896 | |
| Minister of Agriculture   *Ministry Resigned* | 13 July | 1896 – | 9 Oct. 1911 |

## FITZPATRICK, Rt. Hon. Sir Charles
19 Dec. 1853 – 17 June 1942

| | | | |
|---|---|---|---|
| Solicitor General of Canada | 13 July | 1896 – | 9 Feb. 1902 |
| Sworn of the Privy Council | 11 Feb. | 1902 | |
| Minister of Justice and Attorney General | 11 Feb. | 1902 – | 3 June 1906 |
| Member of the United Kingdom Privy Council | 4 July | 1908 | |

## FLEMING, Hon. Donald Methuen
23 May 1905 –

| | | |
|---|---|---|
| Sworn of the Privy Council | 21 June 1957 | |
| Minister of Finance and Receiver General | 21 June 1957 – | 8 Aug. 1962 |
| Minister of Justice and Attorney General  *Ministry Resigned* | 9 Aug. 1962 – | 21 Apr. 1963 |

## FLEMING, Hon. James Sydney Clark
30 Oct. 1939 –

| | | |
|---|---|---|
| Parliamentary Secretary – Communications | 10 Oct. 1975 – | 30 Sept. 1976 |
| Parliamentary Secretary – Environment | 1 Oct. 1976 – | 30 Sept. 1977 |
| Sworn of the Privy Council | 3 Mar. 1980 | |
| Minister of State (Multiculturalism) | 3 Mar. 1980 – | |

## FLEMMING, Hon. Hugh John
5 Jan. 1899 –

| | | |
|---|---|---|
| Sworn of the Privy Council | 11 Oct. 1960 | |
| Minister of Forestry | 11 Oct. 1960 – | 17 Mar. 1963 |
| Acting Minister of Mines and Technical Surveys | 18 July 1962 – | 8 Aug. 1962 |
| Minister of National Revenue  *Ministry Resigned* | 9 Aug. 1962 – | 21 Apr. 1963 |

## FLYNN, Hon. Jacques
22 Aug. 1915 –

| | | |
|---|---|---|
| Sworn of the Privy Council | 28 Dec. 1961 | |
| Minister of Mines and Technical Surveys | 28 Dec. 1961 – | 12 July 1962 |
| Member of the Senate | 9 Nov. 1962 – | |
| Minister of Justice and Attorney General  *Ministry Resigned* | 4 June 1979 – | 2 Mar. 1980 |
| Leader of the Government in the Senate  *Ministry Resigned* | 4 June 1979 – | 2 Mar. 1980 |

## FORKE, Hon. Robert
2 June 1860 – 2 Feb. 1934

| | | |
|---|---|---|
| Sworn of the Privy Council | 25 Sept. 1926 | |
| Minister of Immigration and Colonization | 25 Sept. 1926 – | 29 Dec. 1929 |
| Member of the Senate | 30 Dec. 1929 – | 2 Feb. 1934 |

## FOSTER, Rt. Hon. Sir George Eulas
3 Sept. 1847 – 30 Dec. 1931

| | | |
|---|---|---|
| Sworn of the Privy Council | 10 Dec. 1885 | |
| Minister of Marine and Fisheries | 10 Dec. 1885 – | 28 May 1888 |
| Minister of Finance and Receiver General | 29 May 1888 – | 5 Jan. 1896 |
| Minister of Finance and Receiver General  *Ministry Resigned* | 15 Jan. 1896 – | 10 July 1896 |
| Minister of Trade and Commerce | 10 Oct. 1911 – | 20 Sept. 1921 |
| Member of the United Kingdom Privy Council | 27 June 1916 | |
| Member of the Senate | 22 Sept. 1921 – | 30 Dec. 1931 |

## FOSTER, Hon. Walter Edward
9 Apr. 1873 – 14 Nov. 1947

| | | |
|---|---|---|
| Sworn of the Privy Council | 26 Sept. 1925 | |
| Secretary of State of Canada | 26 Sept. 1925 – | 12 Nov. 1925 |
| Member of the Senate | 6 Dec. 1928 – | 14 Nov. 1947 |

## FOURNIER, Hon. Alphonse
24 Mar. 1893 – 8 Oct. 1961

| | | |
|---|---|---|
| Sworn of the Privy Council | 7 Oct. 1942 | |
| Minister of Public Works | 7 Oct. 1942 – | 11 June 1953 |

## FOURNIER, Hon. Télesphore
5 Aug. 1824 – 10 May 1896

| | | |
|---|---|---|
| Sworn of the Privy Council | 7 Nov. 1873 | |
| Minister of Inland Revenue | 7 Nov. 1873 – | 7 July 1874 |
| Minister of Justice and Attorney General | 8 July 1874 – | 18 May 1875 |
| Postmaster General | 19 May 1875 – | 7 Oct. 1875 |

## FOX, Hon. Francis
2 Dec. 1939 –

| | | |
|---|---|---|
| Parliamentary Secretary – Justice | 10 Oct. 1975 – | 14 Sept. 1976 |
| Sworn of the Privy Council | 14 Sept. 1976 | |
| Solicitor General of Canada | 14 Sept. 1976 – | 27 Jan. 1978 |
| Secretary of State for Canada | 3 Mar. 1980 – | 21 Sept. 1981 |
| Minister of Communications | 3 Mar. 1980 – | |

**FRASER, Hon. John Allen**
15 Dec. 1931 –

| | | | |
|---|---|---|---|
| Sworn of the Privy Council | 4 June 1979 | | |
| Minister of the Environment   *Ministry Resigned* | 4 June 1979 – | 2 Mar. | 1980 |
| Postmaster General   *Ministry Resigned* | 4 June 1979 – | 2 Mar. | 1980 |

**FULTON, Hon. Edmund Davie**
10 Mar. 1916 –

| | | | |
|---|---|---|---|
| Sworn of the Privy Council | 21 June 1957 | | |
| Minister of Justice and Attorney General | 21 June 1957 – | 8 Aug. | 1962 |
| Acting Minister of Citizenship and Immigration | 21 June 1957 – | 11 May | 1958 |
| Minister of Public Works   *Ministry Resigned* | 9 Aug. 1962 – | 21 Apr. | 1963 |

**GAGNON, Hon. Onésime**
23 Oct. 1888 – 30 Sept. 1961

| | | | |
|---|---|---|---|
| Sworn of the Privy Council | 30 Aug. 1935 | | |
| Minister without Portfolio   *Ministry Resigned* | 30 Aug. 1935 – | 22 Oct. | 1935 |

**GALT, Hon. Sir Alexander Tilloch**
6 Sept. 1817 – 19 Sept. 1893

| | | | |
|---|---|---|---|
| Sworn of the Privy Council | 1 July  1867 | | |
| Minister of Finance | 1 July  1867 – | 7 Nov. | 1867 |

**GARDINER, Rt. Hon. James Garfield**
30 Nov. 1883 – 12 Jan. 1962

| | | | |
|---|---|---|---|
| Sworn of the Privy Council | 4 Nov.  1935 | | |
| Minister of Agriculture   *Ministry Resigned* | 4 Nov.  1935 – | 20 June 1957 | |
| Minister of National War Services | 12 July 1940 – | 10 June 1941 | |
| Member of the United Kingdom Privy Council | 1 Jan.  1947 | | |

**GARLAND, Hon. John Richard**
1 Jan. 1918 – 14 Mar. 1964

| | | | |
|---|---|---|---|
| Sworn of the Privy Council | 22 Apr.  1963 | | |
| Minister of National Revenue | 22 Apr.  1963 – | 14 Mar. 1964 | |

**GARSON, Hon. Stuart Sinclair**
1 Dec. 1898 –

| | | |
|---|---|---|
| Sworn of the Privy Council | 15 Nov. 1948 | |
| Minister of Justice and Attorney General *Ministry Resigned* | 15 Nov. 1948 – | 20 June 1957 |
| Solicitor General of Canada | 7 Aug. 1950 – | 14 Oct. 1952 |

**GEARY, Hon. George Reginald**
12 Aug. 1873 – 30 Apr. 1954

| | | |
|---|---|---|
| Sworn of the Privy Council | 14 Aug. 1935 | |
| Minister of Justice and Attorney General *Ministry Resigned* | 14 Aug. 1935 – | 22 Oct. 1935 |

**GENDRON, Hon. Lucien Henri**
28 Aug. 1890 – 5 Apr. 1959

| | | |
|---|---|---|
| Sworn of the Privy Council | 30 Aug. 1935 | |
| Minister of Marine   *Ministry Resigned* | 30 Aug. 1935 – | 22 Oct. 1935 |

**GEOFFRION, Hon. Christophe Alphonse**
23 Nov. 1843 – 18 July 1899

| | | |
|---|---|---|
| Sworn of the Privy Council | 21 Aug. 1896 | |
| Minister without Portfolio | 21 Aug. 1896 – | 18 July 1899 |

**GEOFFRION, Hon. Félix**
4 Oct. 1832 – 7 Aug. 1894

| | | |
|---|---|---|
| Sworn of the Privy Council | 8 July 1874 | |
| Minister of Inland Revenue | 8 July 1874 – | 8 Nov. 1876 |

**GIBBS, Hon. Thomas Nicholson**
11 Mar. 1821 – 7 Apr. 1883

| | | |
|---|---|---|
| Sworn of the Privy Council | 14 June 1873 | |
| Superintendent-General of Indian Affairs | 14 June 1873 – | 30 June 1873 |
| Secretary of State for the Provinces | 14 June 1873 – | 30 June 1873 |
| Minister of Inland Revenue   *Ministry Resigned* | 1 July 1873 – | 6 Nov. 1873 |
| Member of the Senate | 3 Apr. 1880 – | 7 Apr. 1883 |

## GIBSON, Hon. Colin William George
16 Feb. 1891 – 3 July 1974

| | | | |
|---|---|---|---|
| Sworn of the Privy Council | 8 July | 1940 | |
| Minister of National Revenue | 8 July | 1940 – | 7 Mar. 1945 |
| Acting Minister of National Defence for Air | 11 Jan. | 1945 – | 7 Mar. 1945 |
| Minister of National Defence for Air | 8 Mar. | 1945 – | 11 Dec. 1946 |
| Secretary of State of Canada | 12 Dec. | 1946 – | 31 Mar. 1949 |
| Minister of Mines and Resources | 1 Apr. | 1949 – | 17 Jan. 1950 |

## GILLESPIE, Hon. Alastair William
1 May 1922 –

| | | | |
|---|---|---|---|
| Parliamentary Secretary – Treasury Board | 1 Oct. | 1970 – | 11 Aug. 1971 |
| Sworn of the Privy Council | 12 Aug. | 1971 | |
| Minister of State for Science and Technology | 12 Aug. | 1971 – | 26 Nov. 1972 |
| Minister of Industry, Trade and Commerce | 27 Nov. | 1972 – | 25 Sept. 1975 |
| Minister of Energy, Mines and Resources | 26 Sept. | 1975 – | 3 June 1979 |
| Minister of State for Science and Technology | | | |
|    *Ministry Resigned* | 24 Nov. | 1978 – | 3 June 1979 |

## GLEN, Hon. James Allison
18 Dec. 1877 – 28 June 1950

| | | | |
|---|---|---|---|
| Sworn of the Privy Council | 18 Apr. | 1945 | |
| Minister of Mines and Resources | 18 Apr. | 1945 – | 10 June 1948 |

## GOBEIL, Hon. Samuel
17 Aug. 1875 – 1 Jan. 1961

| | | | |
|---|---|---|---|
| Sworn of the Privy Council | 14 Aug. | 1935 | |
| Postmaster General   *Ministry Resigned* | 16 Aug. | 1935 – | 22 Oct. 1935 |

## GORDON, Hon. George Newcombe
15 Apr. 1879 – 21 Mar. 1949

| | | | |
|---|---|---|---|
| Sworn of the Privy Council | 7 Sept. | 1925 | |
| Minister of Immigration and Colonization | 7 Sept. | 1925 – | 12 Nov. 1925 |

**GORDON, Hon. Walter Lockhart**
27 Jan. 1906 –

| | | |
|---|---|---|
| Sworn of the Privy Council | 22 Apr. 1963 | |
| Minister of Finance and Receiver General | 22 Apr. 1963 – | 10 Nov. 1965 |
| Minister without Portfolio | 9 Jan. 1967 – | 3 Apr. 1967 |
| President of the Privy Council | 4 Apr. 1967 – | 10 Mar. 1968 |

**GORDON, Hon. Wesley Ashton**
11 Feb. 1884 – 9 Feb. 1943

| | | |
|---|---|---|
| Sworn of the Privy Council | 7 Aug. 1930 | |
| Minister of Immigration and Colonization | 7 Aug. 1930 – | 2 Feb. 1932 |
| Minister of Mines  *Ministry Resigned* | 7 Aug. 1930 – | 22 Oct. 1935 |
| Minister of Labour  *Ministry Resigned* | 3 Feb. 1932 – | 22 Oct. 1935 |
| Acting Minister of Immigration and Colonization  *Ministry Resigned* | 3 Feb. 1932 – | 22 Oct. 1935 |

**GOUIN, Hon. Sir Jean Lomer**
19 Mar. 1861 – 29 Mar. 1929

| | | |
|---|---|---|
| Sworn of the Privy Council | 29 Dec. 1921 | |
| Minister of Justice and Attorney General | 29 Dec. 1921 – | 3 Jan. 1924 |

**GOYER, Hon. Jean-Pierre**
17 Jan. 1932 –

| | | |
|---|---|---|
| Parliamentary Secretary – External Affairs | 30 Aug. 1968 – | 30 Sept. 1970 |
| Sworn of the Privy Council | 22 Dec. 1970 | |
| Solicitor General of Canada | 22 Dec. 1970 – | 26 Nov. 1972 |
| Minister of Supply and Services | 27 Nov. 1972 – | 23 Nov. 1978 |

**GRAFFTEY, Hon. William Heward**
5 Aug. 1928 –

| | | |
|---|---|---|
| Sworn of the Privy Council | 4 June 1979 | |
| Minister of State for Social Programs | 4 June 1979 – | 7 Oct. 1979 |
| Minister of State for Science and Technology  *Ministry Resigned* | 8 Oct. 1979 – | 2 Mar. 1980 |

## GRAHAM, Rt. Hon. George Perry
31 Mar. 1859 – 1 Jan. 1943

| | | |
|---|---|---|
| Sworn of the Privy Council | 30 Aug. 1907 | |
| Minister of Railways and Canals   *Ministry Resigned* | 30 Aug. 1907 – | 9 Oct. 1911 |
| Minister of Militia and Defence | 29 Dec. 1921 – | 31 Dec. 1922 |
| Minister of the Naval Service | 29 Dec. 1921 – | 31 Dec. 1922 |
| Minister of National Defence | 1 Jan. 1923 – | 27 Apr. 1923 |
| Minister of Railways and Canals | 28 Apr. 1923 – | 19 Feb. 1926 |
| Minister without Portfolio | 20 Feb. 1926 – | 6 Apr. 1926 |
| Member of the United Kingdom Privy Council | 26 July 1926 | |
| Member of the Senate | 20 Dec. 1926 – | 1 Jan. 1943 |

## GRANGER, Hon. Charles Ronald McKay
12 Aug. 1912 –

| | | |
|---|---|---|
| Parliamentary Secretary – Fisheries | 7 Jan. 1966 – | 31 July 1966 |
| Sworn of the Privy Council | 25 Sept. 1967 | |
| Minister without Portfolio | 25 Sept. 1967 – | 5 July 1968 |

## GRAY, Hon. Herbert Eser
25 May 1931 –

| | | |
|---|---|---|
| Parliamentary Secretary – Finance | 30 Aug. 1968 – | 19 Oct. 1969 |
| Sworn of the Privy Council | 20 Oct. 1969 | |
| Minister without Portfolio | 20 Oct. 1969 – | 23 Sept. 1970 |
| Minister of National Revenue | 24 Sept. 1970 – | 26 Nov. 1972 |
| Minister of Consumer and Corporate Affairs | 27 Nov. 1972 – | 7 Aug. 1974 |
| Minister of Industry, Trade and Commerce | 3 Mar. 1980 – | |
| Minister of Regional Economic Expansion | 12 Jan. 1982 – | |

## GREEN, Hon. Howard Charles
5 Nov. 1895 –

| | | |
|---|---|---|
| Sworn of the Privy Council | 21 June 1957 | |
| Minister of Public Works | 21 June 1957 – | 19 Aug. 1959 |
| Acting Minister of Defence Production | 21 June 1957 – | 11 May 1958 |
| Secretary of State for External Affairs   *Ministry Resigned* | 4 June 1959 – | 21 Apr. 1963 |
| Acting Minister of Public Works | 18 July 1962 – | 8 Aug. 1962 |

## GREENE, Hon. John James
24 June 1920 – 23 Oct. 1978

| | |
|---|---|
| Sworn of the Privy Council | 18 Dec. 1965 |
| Minister of Agriculture | 18 Dec. 1965 – 5 July 1968 |
| Minister of Energy, Mines and Resources | 6 July 1968 – 27 Jan. 1972 |
| Member of the Senate | 1 Sept. 1972 – 23 Oct. 1978 |

## GREGG, Hon. Milton Fowler
10 Apr. 1892 –

| | |
|---|---|
| Sworn of the Privy Council | 2 Sept. 1947 |
| Minister of Fisheries | 2 Sept. 1947 – 18 Jan. 1948 |
| Minister of Veterans Affairs | 19 Jan. 1948 – 6 Aug. 1950 |
| Minister of Labour  *Ministry Resigned* | 7 Aug. 1950 – 20 June 1957 |

## GUAY, Hon. Joseph-Philippe
4 Oct. 1915 –

| | |
|---|---|
| Parliamentary Secretary – Transport | 22 Dec. 1972 – 9 May 1974 |
| Parliamentary Secretary – Regional Economic Expansion | 15 Sept. 1974 – 14 Sept. 1975 |
| Sworn of the Privy Council | 3 Nov. 1976 |
| Minister without Portfolio | 3 Nov. 1976 – 20 Apr. 1977 |
| Minister of State (Multiculturalism) | 21 Apr. 1977 – 15 Sept. 1977 |
| Minister of National Revenue | 16 Sept. 1977 – 23 Nov. 1978 |
| Member of the Senate | 23 Nov. 1978 – |

## GUTHRIE, Hon. Hugh
13 Aug. 1866 – 3 Nov. 1939

| | |
|---|---|
| Solicitor General of Canada | 4 Oct. 1917 – 23 Jan. 1920 |
| Sworn of the Privy Council | 5 July 1919 |
| Minister of Militia and Defence  *Ministry Resigned* | 24 Jan. 1920 – 28 Dec. 1921 |
| Acting Solicitor General of Canada | 24 Jan. 1920 – 30 Sept. 1921 |
| Acting Minister of Justice and Attorney General | 29 June 1926 – 12 July 1926 |
| Acting Minister of National Defence | 29 June 1926 – 12 July 1926 |
| Minister of National Defence  *Ministry Resigned* | 13 July 1926 – 24 Sept. 1926 |
| Minister of Justice and Attorney General | 7 Aug. 1930 – 11 Aug. 1935 |

## HAGGART, Hon. John Graham
14 Nov. 1836 – 13 Mar. 1913

| | | |
|---|---|---|
| Sworn of the Privy Council | 6 Aug. 1888 | |
| Postmaster General | 6 Aug. 1888 – | 10 Jan. 1892 |
| Minister of Railways and Canals | 11 Jan. 1892 – | 5 Jan. 1896 |
| Minister of Railways and Canals   *Ministry Resigned* | 15 Jan. 1896 – | 10 July 1896 |

## HAIDASZ, Hon. Stanley
4 Mar. 1923 –

| | | |
|---|---|---|
| Parliamentary Secretary – National Health and Welfare | 14 May 1963 – | 19 Feb. 1964 |
| | 20 Oct. 1969 – | 30 Sept. 1970 |
| Parliamentary Secretary – External Affairs | 20 Feb. 1964 – | 8 Sept. 1965 |
| Parliamentary Secretary – Northern Affairs and National Resources | 7 Jan. 1966 – | 30 Sept. 1966 |
| Parliamentary Secretary – Indian Affairs and Northern Development | 1 Oct. 1966 – | 23 Apr. 1968 |
| Parliamentary Secretary – Consumer and Corporate Affairs | 30 Aug. 1968 – | 19 Oct. 1969 |
| Sworn of the Privy Council | 27 Nov. 1972 | |
| Minister of State | 27 Nov. 1972 – | 7 Aug. 1974 |
| Member of the Senate | 23 Mar. 1978 – | |

## HAIG, Hon. John Thomas
15 Dec. 1877 – 22 Oct. 1962

| | | |
|---|---|---|
| Member of the Senate | 14 Aug. 1935 – | 17 Jan. 1961 |
| Sworn of the Privy Council | 9 Oct. 1957 | |
| Minister without Portfolio | 9 Oct. 1957 – | 11 May 1958 |
| Leader of the Government in the Senate | 9 Oct. 1957 – | 11 May 1958 |

## HALPENNY, Hon. George Ernest
14 June 1903 – 10 May 1974

| | | |
|---|---|---|
| Parliamentary Assistant – National Health and Welfare | 7 Aug. 1957 – | 1 Feb. 1958 |
| Sworn of the Privy Council | 11 Oct. 1960 | |
| Minister without Portfolio | 11 Oct. 1960 – | 8 Aug. 1962 |
| Secretary of State of Canada   *Ministry Resigned* | 9 Aug. 1962 – | 21 Apr. 1963 |

259

## HAMILTON, Hon. Francis Alvin George
30 Mar. 1912 –

| | | |
|---|---|---|
| Sworn of the Privy Council | 22 Aug. 1957 | |
| Minister of Northern Affairs and National Resources | 22 Aug. 1957 – | 10 Oct. 1960 |
| Minister of Agriculture   *Ministry Resigned* | 11 Oct. 1960 – | 21 Apr. 1963 |

## HAMILTON, Hon. William McLean
23 Feb. 1919 –

| | | |
|---|---|---|
| Sworn of the Privy Council | 21 June 1957 | |
| Postmaster General | 21 June 1957 – | 12 July 1962 |

## HANSON, Hon. Richard Burpee
20 Mar. 1879 – 14 July 1948

| | | |
|---|---|---|
| Sworn of the Privy Council | 17 Nov. 1934 | |
| Minister of Trade and Commerce   *Ministry Resigned* | 17 Nov. 1934 – | 22 Oct. 1935 |

## HARKNESS, Hon. Douglas Scott
29 Mar. 1903 –

| | | |
|---|---|---|
| Sworn of the Privy Council | 21 June 1957 | |
| Minister of Northern Affairs and National Resources | 21 June 1957 – | 18 Aug. 1957 |
| Acting Minister of Agriculture | 21 June 1957 – | 6 Aug. 1957 |
| Minister of Agriculture | 7 Aug. 1957 – | 10 Oct. 1960 |
| Minister of National Defence | 11 Oct. 1960 – | 3 Feb. 1963 |

## HARRIS, Hon. Walter Edward
14 Jan. 1904 –

| | | |
|---|---|---|
| Parliamentary Assistant – External Affairs | 30 Oct. 1947 – | 14 Nov. 1948 |
| Parliamentary Assistant – Prime Minister | 15 Nov. 1948 – | 30 Apr. 1949 |
| | 18 July 1949 – | 17 Jan. 1950 |
| Sworn of the Privy Council | 18 Jan. 1950 | |
| Minister of Citizenship and Immigration | 18 Jan. 1950 – | 30 June 1954 |
| Acting Minister of Public Works | 12 June 1953 – | 16 Sept. 1953 |
| Minister of Finance and Receiver General   *Ministry Resigned*  1 July 1954 – | | 20 June 1957 |

## HAYS, Hon. Harry William
25 Dec. 1909 –

| | | | | |
|---|---|---|---|---|
| Sworn of the Privy Council | 22 Apr. | 1963 | | |
| Minister of Agriculture | 22 Apr. | 1963 | – 17 Dec. | 1965 |
| Member of the Senate | 24 Feb. | 1966 | | |

## HAZEN, Hon. Sir John Douglas
5 June 1860 – 27 Dec. 1937

| | | | | |
|---|---|---|---|---|
| Sworn of the Privy Council | 10 Oct. | 1911 | | |
| Minister of Marine and Fisheries   *Ministry Resigned* | 10 Oct. | 1911 | – 11 Oct. | 1917 |
| Minister of the Naval Service   *Ministry Resigned* | 10 Oct. | 1911 | – 11 Oct. | 1917 |

## HEENAN, Hon. Peter
19 Feb. 1875 – 12 May 1948

| | | | | |
|---|---|---|---|---|
| Sworn of the Privy Council | 25 Sept. | 1926 | | |
| Minister of Labour   *Ministry Resigned* | 25 Sept. | 1926 | –  6 Aug. | 1930 |

## HEES, Hon. George Harris
17 June 1910 –

| | | | | |
|---|---|---|---|---|
| Sworn of the Privy Council | 21 June | 1957 | | |
| Minister of Transport | 21 June | 1957 | – 10 Oct. | 1960 |
| Minister of Trade and Commerce | 11 Oct. | 1960 | –  8 Feb. | 1963 |

## HELLYER, Hon. Paul Theodore
6 Aug. 1923 –

| | | | | |
|---|---|---|---|---|
| Parliamentary Assistant – National Defence | 9 Feb. | 1956 | – 12 Apr. | 1957 |
| Sworn of the Privy Council | 26 Apr. | 1957 | | |
| Associate Minister of National Defence   *Ministry Resigned* | 26 Apr. | 1957 | – 20 June | 1957 |
| Minister of National Defence | 22 Apr. | 1963 | – 18 Sept. | 1967 |
| Minister of Transport | 19 Sept. | 1967 | – 29 Apr. | 1969 |

## HINCKS, Hon. Sir Francis
14 Dec. 1807 – 18 Aug. 1885

| | | | | |
|---|---|---|---|---|
| Sworn of the Privy Council | 9 Oct. | 1869 | | |
| Minister of Finance | 9 Oct. | 1869 | – 21 Feb. | 1873 |

## HNATYSHYN, Hon. Ramon John
16 Mar. 1934 –

| | | |
|---|---|---|
| Sworn of the Privy Council | 4 June 1979 | |
| Minister of State for Science and Technology | 4 June 1979 – | 7 Oct. 1979 |
| Minister of Energy, Mines and Resources  *Ministry Resigned* | 4 June 1979 – | 2 Mar. 1980 |

## HORNER, Hon. John Henry
20 July 1927 –

| | | |
|---|---|---|
| Sworn of the Privy Council | 21 Apr. 1977 | |
| Minister without Portfolio | 21 Apr. 1977 – | 15 Sept. 1977 |
| Minister of Industry, Trade and Commerce  *Ministry Resigned* | 16 Sept. 1977 – | 3 June 1979 |

## HOWE, Rt. Hon. Clarence Decatur
15 Jan. 1886 – 31 Dec. 1960

| | | |
|---|---|---|
| Sworn of the Privy Council | 23 Oct. 1935 | |
| Minister of Marine | 23 Oct. 1935 – | 1 Nov. 1936 |
| Minister of Railways and Canals | 23 Oct. 1935 – | 1 Nov. 1936 |
| Minister of Transport | 2 Nov. 1936 – | 7 July 1940 |
| Minister of Munitions and Supply | 9 Apr. 1940 – | 31 Dec. 1945 |
| Acting Minister of Transport | 13 May 1942 – | 5 Oct. 1942 |
| Minister of Reconstruction | 13 Oct. 1944 – | 31 Dec. 1945 |
| Minister of Reconstruction and Supply  *Ministry Resigned* | 1 Jan. 1946 – | 14 Nov. 1948 |
| Member of the United Kingdom Privy Council | 13 June 1946 | |
| Minister of Trade and Commerce  *Ministry Resigned* | 15 Nov. 1948 – | 20 June 1957 |
| Minister of Defence Production | 1 Apr. 1951 – | 20 June 1957 |

## HOWE, Hon. Joseph
13 Dec. 1804 – 1 June 1873

| | | |
|---|---|---|
| Sworn of the Privy Council | 30 Jan. 1869 | |
| President of the Privy Council | 30 Jan. 1869 – | 15 Nov. 1869 |
| Secretary of State for the Provinces | 16 Nov. 1869 – | 6 May 1873 |
| Superintendent-General of Indian Affairs | 8 Dec. 1869 – | 6 May 1873 |

## HOWIE, Hon. J. Robert
2 Oct. 1929 –

| | | |
|---|---|---|
| Sworn of the Privy Council | 4 June 1979 | |
| Minister of State (Transport)  *Ministry Resigned* | 4 June 1979 – | 2 Mar. 1980 |

**HOWLAND, Hon. Sir William Pearce**
29 May 1811 – 1 Jan. 1907

| | | | |
|---|---|---|---|
| Sworn of the Privy Council | 1 July | 1867 | |
| Minister of Inland Revenue | 1 July | 1867 – | 14 July 1868 |

**HUGHES, Hon. Sir Samuel**
8 Jan. 1853 – 24 Aug. 1921

| | | | |
|---|---|---|---|
| Sworn of the Privy Council | 10 Oct. | 1911 | |
| Minister of Militia and Defence | 10 Oct. | 1911 – | 12 Oct. 1916 |

**HUNTINGTON, Hon. Lucius Seth**
26 May 1827 – 19 May 1886

| | | | |
|---|---|---|---|
| Sworn of the Privy Council | 20 Jan. | 1874 | |
| President of the Privy Council | 20 Jan. | 1874 – | 8 Oct. 1875 |
| Postmaster General  *Ministry Resigned* | 9 Oct. | 1875 – | 16 Oct. 1878 |

**HUNTINGTON, Hon. Ronald**
13 Feb. 1921 –

| | | | |
|---|---|---|---|
| Sworn of the Privy Council | 4 June 1979 | | |
| Minister of State (Small Businesses and Industry) *Ministry Resigned* | 4 June 1979 – | 2 Mar. 1980 | |

**HYMAN, Hon. Charles Smith**
31 Aug. 1854 – 8 Oct. 1926

| | | | |
|---|---|---|---|
| Sworn of the Privy Council | 5 Feb. | 1904 | |
| Minister without Portfolio | 5 Feb. | 1904 – | 21 May 1905 |
| Minister of Public Works | 22 May | 1905 – | 29 Aug. 1907 |

**ILSLEY, Rt. Hon. James Lorimer**
3 Jan. 1894 – 14 Jan. 1967

| | | | |
|---|---|---|---|
| Sworn of the Privy Council | 23 Oct. | 1935 | |
| Minister of National Revenue | 23 Oct. | 1935 – | 7 July 1940 |
| Acting Postmaster General | 23 May | 1940 – | 7 July 1940 |
| Minister of Finance and Receiver General | 8 July | 1940 – | 9 Dec. 1946 |
| Member of the United Kingdom Privy Council | 1 Jan. | 1946 | |
| Minister of Justice and Attorney General | 10 Dec. | 1946 – | 30 June 1948 |

## IVES, Hon. William Bullock
17 Nov. 1841 – 25 July 1899

| | | |
|---|---|---|
| Sworn of the Privy Council | 7 Dec. 1892 | |
| President of the Privy Council   *Ministry Dissolved* | 7 Dec. 1892 – | 20 Dec. 1894 |
| Minister of Trade and Commerce | 21 Dec. 1894 – | 5 Jan. 1896 |
| Minister of Trade and Commerce   *Ministry Resigned* | 15 Jan. 1896 – | 10 July 1896 |

## JAMIESON, Hon. Donald Campbell
30 Apr. 1921 –

| | | |
|---|---|---|
| Sworn of the Privy Council | 6 July 1968 | |
| Minister of Defence Production | 6 July 1968 – | 31 Mar. 1969 |
| Minister of Supply and Services | 1 Apr. 1969 – | 4 May 1969 |
| Minister of Transport | 5 May 1969 – | 26 Nov. 1972 |
| Minister of Regional Economic Expansion | 27 Nov. 1972 – | 25 Sept. 1975 |
| Minister of Industry, Trade and Commerce | 26 Sept. 1975 – | 13 Sept. 1976 |
| Secretary of State for External Affairs   *Ministry Resigned* | 14 Sept. 1976 – | 3 June 1979 |

## JARVIS, Hon. William
15 Aug. 1930 –

| | | |
|---|---|---|
| Sworn of the Privy Council | 4 June 1979 | |
| Minister of State (Federal-Provincial Relations)   *Ministry Resigned* | 4 June 1979 – | 2 Mar. 1980 |

## JEAN, Hon. Joseph
7 Feb. 1890 – 18 July 1973

| | | |
|---|---|---|
| Parliamentary Assistant – Justice | 6 May 1943 – | 30 Nov. 1944 |
| Sworn of the Privy Council | 18 Apr. 1945 | |
| Solicitor General of Canada | 18 Apr. 1945 – | 23 Aug. 1949 |

## JOHNSTON, Hon. Donald
26 June 1936 –

| | | |
|---|---|---|
| Sworn of the Privy Council | 3 Mar. 1980 | |
| President of the Treasury Board | 3 Mar. 1980 – | |

## JOLY DE LOTBINIÈRE, Hon. Sir Henri Gustave
5 Dec. 1829 – 15 Nov. 1908

| | | |
|---|---|---|
| Controller of Inland Revenue | 13 July 1896 – | 29 June 1897 |
| Sworn of the Privy Council | 30 June 1897 | |
| Minister of Inland Revenue | 30 June 1897 – | 21 June 1900 |

**JONES, Hon. Alfred Gilpin**
28 Sept. 1824 – 15 Mar. 1906

| | | |
|---|---|---|
| Sworn of the Privy Council | 21 Jan. 1878 | |
| Minister of Militia and Defence   *Ministry Resigned* | 21 Jan. 1878 – 16 Oct. 1878 | |

**JONES, Hon. George Burpee**
9 Jan. 1866 – 27 Apr. 1950

| | | |
|---|---|---|
| Sworn of the Privy Council | 13 July 1926 | |
| Minister of Labour   *Ministry Resigned* | 13 July 1926 – 24 Sept. 1926 | |
| Member of the Senate | 20 July 1935 – 27 Apr. 1950 | |

**JOYAL, Hon. Serge**
1 Feb. 1945 –

| | | |
|---|---|---|
| Parliamentary Secretary – Treasury Board | 1 Oct. 1980 – 21 Sept. 1981 | |
| Sworn of the Privy Council | 22 Sept. 1981 | |
| Minister of State | 22 Sept. 1981 – | |

**JUNEAU, Hon. Pierre**
17 Oct. 1922 –

| | | |
|---|---|---|
| Sworn of the Privy Council | 29 Aug. 1975 | |
| Minister of Communications | 29 Aug. 1975 – 24 Oct. 1975 | |

**KAPLAN, Hon. Robert Phillip**
27 Dec. 1936 –

| | | |
|---|---|---|
| Parliamentary Secretary – National Health and Welfare | 10 Oct. 1975 – 30 Sept. 1976 | |
| Parliamentary Secretary – Finance | 1 Oct. 1976 – 30 Sept. 1977 | |
| Sworn of the Privy Council | 3 Mar. 1980 | |
| Solicitor General of Canada | 3 Mar. 1980 – | |

**KAY, Hon. William Frederic**
18 May 1876 – 8 May 1948

| | | |
|---|---|---|
| Sworn of the Privy Council | 17 June 1930 | |
| Minister without Portfolio   *Ministry Resigned* | 17 June 1930 – 6 Aug. 1930 | |

**KEEFER, Francis Henry**
24 July 1860 – 4 Dec. 1928

| | | |
|---|---|---|
| Parliamentary Under Secretary of State for External Affairs | 7 Nov. 1918 – 1 July 1920 | |

**KEMP, Hon. Sir Albert Edward**
11 Aug. 1858 – 12 Aug. 1929

| | |
|---|---|
| Sworn of the Privy Council | 10 Oct. 1911 |
| Minister without Portfolio | 10 Oct. 1911 – 22 Nov. 1916 |
| Minister of Militia and Defence   *Ministry Resigned* | 23 Nov. 1916 – 11 Oct. 1917 |
| Minister of the Overseas Military Forces | 12 Oct. 1917 – 1 July 1920 |
| Minister without Portfolio   *Ministry Resigned* | 13 July 1920 – 28 Dec. 1921 |
| Member of the Senate | 4 Nov. 1921 – 12 Aug. 1929 |

**KENNEDY, Hon. William Costello**
27 Aug. 1868 – 17 Jan. 1923

| | |
|---|---|
| Sworn of the Privy Council | 29 Dec. 1921 |
| Minister of Railways and Canals | 29 Dec. 1921 – 18 Jan. 1923 |

**KENNY, Hon. Sir Edward**
July 1800 – 16 May 1891

| | |
|---|---|
| Sworn of the Privy Council | 4 July 1867 |
| Receiver General | 4 July 1867 – 15 Nov. 1869 |
| Member of the Senate* | 23 Oct. 1867 – 11 Apr. 1876 |
| President of the Privy Council | 16 Nov. 1869 – 20 June 1870 |

**KIERANS, Hon. Eric William**
2 Feb. 1914 –

| | |
|---|---|
| Sworn of the Privy Council | 6 July 1968 |
| Postmaster General | 6 July 1968 – 28 Apr. 1971 |
| Minister of Communications | 1 Apr. 1969 – 28 Apr. 1971 |

**KING, Hon. James Horace**
18 Jan. 1873 – 14 July 1955

| | |
|---|---|
| Sworn of the Privy Council | 3 Feb. 1922 |
| Minister of Public Works   *Ministry Resigned* | 3 Feb. 1922 – 28 June 1926 |
| Acting Minister of Labour | 13 Nov. 1925 – 7 Mar. 1926 |
| Minister of Soldiers' Civil Re-establishment | 25 Sept. 1926 – 10 June 1928 |
| Minister of Pensions and National Health | 11 June 1928 – 18 June 1930 |
| Member of the Senate | 7 June 1930 – 14 July 1955 |
| Minister without Portfolio | 26 May 1942 – 23 Aug. 1945 |
| Leader of the Government in the Senate | 1942 – 1945 |

*Seat declared vacant because of absence for two consecutive sessions.*

## KING, Rt. Hon. William Lyon Mackenzie
17 Dec. 1874 – 22 July 1950

| | | | |
|---|---|---|---|
| Sworn of the Privy Council | 2 June 1909 | | |
| Minister of Labour   *Ministry Resigned* | 2 June 1909 | – | 9 Oct.  1911 |
| Prime Minister | 29 Dec. 1921 | – | 27 June 1926 |
| Secretary of State for External Affairs   *Ministry Resigned* | 29 Dec. 1921 | – | 28 June 1926 |
| President of the Privy Council   *Ministry Resigned* | 29 Dec. 1921 | – | 28 June 1928 |
| Member of the United Kingdom Privy Council | 20 June 1922 | | |
| Prime Minister   *Ministry Resigned* | 25 Sept. 1926 | – | 6 Aug.  1930 |
| Secretary of State for External Affairs   *Ministry Resigned* | 25 Sept. 1926 | – | 6 Aug.  1930 |
| President of the Privy Council   *Ministry Resigned* | 25 Sept. 1926 | – | 6 Aug.  1930 |
| Prime Minister   *Ministry Resigned* | 23 Oct.  1935 | – | 14 Nov. 1948 |
| Secretary of State for External Affairs | 23 Oct.  1935 | – | 3 Sept. 1946 |
| President of the Privy Council   *Ministry Resigned* | 23 Oct.  1935 | – | 14 Nov. 1948 |

## LAFLAMME, Hon. Toussaint Antoine Rodolphe
15 May 1827 – 7 Dec. 1893

| | | | |
|---|---|---|---|
| Sworn of the Privy Council | 9 Nov.  1876 | | |
| Minister of Inland Revenue | 9 Nov.  1876 | – | 7 June 1877 |
| Minister of Justice and Attorney General   *Ministry Resigned* | 8 June 1877 | – | 16 Oct.  1878 |

## LAFLÈCHE, Hon. Léo Richer
16 Apr. 1888 – 7 Mar. 1956

| | | | |
|---|---|---|---|
| Sworn of the Privy Council | 7 Oct.  1942 | | |
| Minister of National War Services | 7 Oct.  1942 | – | 17 Apr.  1945 |

## LAING, Hon. Arthur
9 Sept. 1904 – 13 Feb. 1975

| | | | |
|---|---|---|---|
| Sworn of the Privy Council | 22 Apr.  1963 | | |
| Minister of Northern Affairs and National Resources | 22 Apr.  1963 | – | 30 Sept. 1966 |
| Minister of Indian Affairs and Northern Development | 1 Oct.  1966 | – | 5 July  1968 |
| Minister of Public Works | 6 July  1968 | – | 27 Jan.  1972 |
| Minister of Veterans Affairs | 28 Jan.  1972 | – | 26 Nov. 1972 |
| Member of the Senate | 1 Sept. 1972 | – | 13 Feb. 1975 |

**LAIRD, Hon. David**
12 Mar. 1833 – 12 Jan. 1914

| | | |
|---|---|---|
| Sworn of the Privy Council | 7 Nov. 1873 | |
| Superintendent-General of Indian Affairs | 7 Nov. 1873 – | 6 Oct. 1876 |
| Minister of the Interior | 7 Nov. 1873 – | 6 Oct. 1876 |

**LALONDE, Hon. Marc**
26 July 1929 –

| | | |
|---|---|---|
| Sworn of the Privy Council | 27 Nov. 1972 | |
| Minister of National Health and Welfare | 27 Nov. 1972 – | 15 Sept. 1977 |
| Minister of State for Federal-Provincial Relations | 16 Sept. 1977 – | 23 Nov. 1978 |
| Minister of Justice and Attorney General   *Ministry Resigned* | 24 Nov. 1978 – | 3 June 1979 |
| Minister of Energy, Mines and Resources | 3 Mar. 1980 – | |

**LAMARSH, Hon. Julia Verlyn**
20 Dec. 1924 – 27 Oct. 1980

| | | |
|---|---|---|
| Sworn of the Privy Council | 22 Apr. 1963 | |
| Minister of National Health and Welfare | 22 Apr. 1963 – | 17 Dec. 1965 |
| Secretary of State of Canada | 18 Dec. 1965 – | 9 Apr. 1968 |

**LAMBERT, Hon. Marcel Joseph Aimé**
21 Aug. 1919 –

| | | |
|---|---|---|
| Parliamentary Assistant – National Defence | 7 Aug. 1957 – | 1 Feb. 1958 |
| Parliamentary Assistant – National Revenue | 18 Nov. 1959 – | 17 Nov. 1961 |
| | 18 Jan. 1962 – | 19 Apr. 1962 |
| Sworn of the Privy Council | 12 Feb. 1963 | |
| Minister of Veterans Affairs   *Ministry Resigned* | 12 Feb. 1963 – | 21 Apr. 1963 |

**LAMONTAGNE, Hon. Gilles**
17 Apr. 1919 –

| | | |
|---|---|---|
| Parliamentary Secretary – Energy, Mines and Resources | 1 Oct. 1977 – | 18 Jan. 1978 |
| Sworn of the Privy Council | 19 Jan. 1978 | |
| Minister without Portfolio | 19 Jan. 1978 – | 1 Feb. 1978 |
| Postmaster General   *Ministry Resigned* | 2 Feb. 1978 – | 3 June 1979 |
| Minister of National Defence | 3 Mar. 1980 – | |
| Acting Minister of Veterans Affairs | 1 Oct. 1980 – | 21 Sept. 1981 |

**LAMONTAGNE, Hon. Maurice**

7 Sept. 1917 –

| | | |
|---|---|---|
| Sworn of the Privy Council | 22 Apr. 1963 | |
| President of the Privy Council | 22 Apr. 1963 – | 2 Feb. 1964 |
| Secretary of State of Canada | 3 Feb. 1964 – | 17 Dec. 1965 |
| Member of the Senate | 6 Apr. 1967 – | |

**LANG, Hon. Otto Emil**

14 May 1932 –

| | | |
|---|---|---|
| Sworn of the Privy Council | 6 July 1968 | |
| Minister without Portfolio | 6 July 1968 – | 23 Sept. 1970 |
| Minister of Manpower and Immigration | 24 Sept. 1970 – | 27 Jan. 1972 |
| Minister of Justice and Attorney General | 28 Jan. 1972 – | 25 Sept. 1975 |
| Minister of Transport  *Ministry Resigned* | 26 Sept. 1975 – | 3 June 1979 |
| Acting Minister of Communications | 25 Oct. 1975 – | 4 Dec. 1975 |
| Acting Minister of Justice and Attorney General | 3 Aug. 1978 – | 8 Aug. 1978 |
| Minister of Justice and Attorney General | 9 Aug. 1978 – | 23 Nov. 1978 |

**LANGEVIN, Hon. Sir Hector Louis**

26 Aug. 1826 – 11 June 1906

| | | |
|---|---|---|
| Sworn of the Privy Council | 1 July 1867 | |
| Secretary of State of Canada | 1 July 1867 – | 7 Dec. 1869 |
| Superintendent-General of Indian Affairs | 22 May 1868 – | 7 Dec. 1869 |
| Acting Minister of Public Works | 29 Sept. 1869 – | 7 Dec. 1869 |
| Minister of Public Works  *Ministry Resigned* | 8 Dec. 1869 – | 6 Nov. 1873 |
| Acting Minister of Militia and Defence | 21 May 1873 – | 30 June 1873 |
| Postmaster General | 19 Oct. 1878 – | 19 May 1879 |
| Minister of Public Works | 20 May 1879 – | 11 Aug. 1891 |

**LAPOINTE, Hon. Charles**

17 July 1944 –

| | | |
|---|---|---|
| Parliamentary Secretary – Transport | 1 Oct. 1977 – | 30 Sept. 1978 |
| | 1 Oct. 1978 – | 26 Mar. 1979 |
| Minister of State (Small Businesses) | 3 Mar. 1980 – | 23 Feb. 1981 |
| Minister of State (Small Businesses and Tourism) | 24 Feb. 1981 – | |

## LAPOINTE, Rt. Hon. Ernest
6 Oct. 1876 – 26 Nov. 1941

| | | |
|---|---|---|
| Sworn of the Privy Council | 29 Dec. 1921 | |
| Minister of Marine and Fisheries | 29 Dec. 1921 – | 29 Jan. 1924 |
| Acting Minister of Justice and Attorney General | 4 Jan. 1924 – | 29 Jan. 1924 |
| Minister of Justice and Attorney General *Ministry Resigned* | 30 Jan. 1924 – | 28 June 1926 |
| Secretary of State of Canada *Ministry Resigned* | 24 Mar. 1926 – | 28 June 1926 |
| Minister of Justice and Attorney General *Ministry Resigned* | 25 Sept. 1926 – | 6 Aug. 1930 |
| Minister of Justice and Attorney General | 23 Oct. 1935 – | 26 Nov. 1941 |
| Member of the United Kingdom Privy Council | 28 May 1937 | |
| Acting Secretary of State of Canada | 26 July 1939 – | 8 May 1940 |

## LAPOINTE, Hon. Hugues
3 Mar. 1911 –

| | | |
|---|---|---|
| Parliamentary Assistant – National Defence | 25 Sept. 1945 – | 18 Jan. 1949 |
| Parliamentary Assistant – External Affairs | 19 Jan. 1949 – | 30 Apr. 1949 |
| | 12 July 1949 – | 23 Aug. 1949 |
| Sworn of the Privy Council | 25 Aug. 1949 | |
| Solicitor General of Canada | 25 Aug. 1949 – | 6 Aug. 1950 |
| Minister of Veterans Affairs *Ministry Resigned* | 7 Aug. 1950 – | 20 June 1957 |
| Postmaster General *Ministry Resigned* | 3 Nov. 1955 – | 20 June 1957 |

## LASALLE, Hon. Roch
6 Aug. 1929 –

| | | |
|---|---|---|
| Sworn of the Privy Council | 4 June 1979 | |
| Minister of Supply and Services *Ministry Resigned* | 4 June 1979 – | 2 Mar. 1980 |

## LAURIER, Rt. Hon. Sir Wilfrid
20 Nov. 1841 – 17 Feb. 1919

| | | |
|---|---|---|
| Sworn of the Privy Council | 8 Oct. 1877 | |
| Minister of Inland Revenue *Ministry Resigned* | 8 Oct. 1877 – | 16 Oct. 1878 |
| Prime Minister | 11 July 1896 – | 5 Oct. 1911 |
| President of the Privy Council *Ministry Resigned* | 11 July 1896 – | 9 Oct. 1911 |
| Member of the United Kingdom Privy Council | 7 July 1897 | |
| Acting Superintendent-General of Indian Affairs | 13 Mar. 1905 – | 7 Apr. 1905 |
| Acting Minister of the Interior | 13 Mar. 1905 – | 7 Apr. 1905 |
| Acting Minister of Marine and Fisheries | 6 Jan. 1906 – | 5 Feb. 1906 |

**LAWRENCE, Hon. Allan Frederick**
8 Nov. 1925 –

| | | |
|---|---|---|
| Sworn of the Privy Council | 4 June 1979 – | |
| Minister of Consumer and Corporate Affairs | | |
| *Ministry Resigned* | 4 June 1979 – | 2 Mar. 1980 |
| Solicitor General of Canada   *Ministry Resigned* | 4 June 1979 – | 2 Mar. 1980 |

**LAWSON, Hon. James Earl**
21 Oct. 1891 – 13 May 1950

| | | |
|---|---|---|
| Sworn of the Privy Council | 14 Aug. 1935 | |
| Minister of National Revenue   *Ministry Resigned* | 14 Aug. 1935 – | 22 Oct.  1935 |

**LEBLANC, Hon. Roméo**
18 Dec. 1927 –

| | | |
|---|---|---|
| Sworn of the Privy Council | 8 Aug. 1974 | |
| Minister of State (Fisheries) | 8 Aug. 1974 – | 13 Sept. 1976 |
| Acting Minister of the Environment | 5 Dec. 1975 – | 21 Jan.  1976 |
| | 1 July  1976 – | 13 Sept. 1976 |
| Minister of Fisheries and the Environment | 14 Sept. 1976 – | 1 Apr.  1979 |
| Minister of Fisheries and Oceans   *Ministry Resigned* | 2 Apr.  1979 – | 3 June 1979 |
| Minister of Fisheries and Oceans | 3 Mar.  1980 – | |

**LEMIEUX, Hon. Rodolphe**
1 Nov. 1866 – 28 Sept. 1937

| | | |
|---|---|---|
| Solicitor General of Canada | 29 Jan.  1904 – | 3 June 1906 |
| Sworn of the Privy Council | 4 June 1906 | |
| Postmaster General | 4 June 1906 – | 10 Aug.  1911 |
| Minister of Marine and Fisheries   *Ministry Resigned* | 11 Aug.  1911 – | 9 Oct.  1911 |
| Minister of the Naval Service   *Ministry Resigned* | 11 Aug.  1911 – | 9 Oct.  1911 |
| Member of the Senate | 3 June 1930 – | 28 Sept. 1937 |

**LESAGE, Hon. Jean**
10 June 1912 – 12 Dec. 1980

| | | |
|---|---|---|
| Parliamentary Assistant – External Affairs | 24 Jan.  1951 – | 31 Dec.  1952 |
| Parliamentary Assistant – Finance | 1 Jan.  1953 – | 13 June 1953 |
| | 24 Aug.  1953 – | 16 Sept. 1953 |
| Sworn of the Privy Council | 17 Sept. 1953 | |
| Minister of Resources and Development | 17 Sept. 1953 – | 15 Dec.  1953 |
| Minister of Northern Affairs and National Resources | | |
| *Ministry Resigned* | 16 Dec.  1953 – | 20 June 1957 |

**LESSARD, Hon. Marcel**

14 Aug. 1926 –

| | | |
|---|---|---|
| Parliamentary Secretary – Agriculture | 1 Oct. 1970 – | 1 Sept. 1972 |
| Sworn of the Privy Council | 26 Sept. 1975 | |
| Minister of Regional Economic Expansion *Ministry Resigned* | 26 Sept. 1975 – | 3 June 1979 |

**LETELLIER DE ST-JUST, Hon. Luc**

12 May 1820 – 28 Jan. 1881

| | | |
|---|---|---|
| Member of the Senate | 23 Oct. 1867 – | 14 Dec. 1876 |
| Sworn of the Privy Council | 7 Nov. 1873 | |
| Minister of Agriculture | 7 Nov. 1873 – | 14 Dec. 1876 |
| Leader of the Government in the Senate | 1873 – | 1874 |

**LOUGHEED, Hon. Sir James Alexander**

1 Sept. 1854 – 2 Nov. 1925

| | | |
|---|---|---|
| Member of the Senate | 10 Dec. 1889 – | 2 Nov. 1925 |
| Sworn of the Privy Council | 10 Oct. 1911 | |
| Minister without Portfolio | 10 Oct. 1911 – | 20 Feb. 1918 |
| Leader of the Government in the Senate *Ministry Resigned* | 10 Oct. 1911 – | 28 Dec. 1921 |
| Minister of Soldiers' Civil Re-establishment *Ministry Resigned* | 21 Feb. 1818 – | 9 July 1920 |
| Superintendent-General of Indian Affairs *Ministry Resigned* | 10 July 1920 – | 28 Dec. 1921 |
| Minister of the Interior *Ministry Resigned* | 10 July 1920 – | 28 Dec. 1921 |
| Minister of Mines *Ministry Resigned* | 10 July 1920 – | 28 Dec. 1921 |
| Acting Minister of Soldiers' Civil Re-establishment | 19 July 1920 – | 21 Sept. 1921 |

**LOW, Hon. Thomas Andrew**

12 Mar. 1871 – 9 Feb. 1931

| | | |
|---|---|---|
| Sworn of the Privy Council | 29 Dec. 1921 | |
| Minister without Portfolio | 29 Dec. 1921 – | 16 Aug. 1923 |
| Minister of Trade and Commerce | 17 Aug. 1923 – | 12 Nov. 1925 |

**LUMLEY, Hon. Edward**

27 Oct. 1939 –

| | | |
|---|---|---|
| Parliamentary Secretary – Regional Economic Expansion | 1 Oct. 1976 – | 30 Sept. 1977 |
| Parliamentary Secretary – Finance | 1 Oct. 1977 – | 30 Sept. 1978 |
| Sworn of the Privy Council | 3 Mar. 1980 | |
| Minister of State (Trade) | 3 Mar. 1980 – | 11 Jan. 1982 |
| Minister of State (International Trade) | 12 Jan. 1982 | |

**MACDONALD, Hon. Angus Lewis**
10 Aug. 1890 – 13 Apr. 1954

| | |
|---|---|
| Sworn of the Privy Council | 12 July 1940 |
| Minister of National Defence for Naval Services | 12 July 1940 – 17 Apr. 1945 |
| Acting Minister of National Defence for Air | 30 Nov. 1944 – 10 Jan. 1945 |

**MACDONALD, Hon. Daniel Joseph**
23 July 1918 – 30 Sept. 1980

| | |
|---|---|
| Sworn of the Privy Council | 27 Nov. 1972 |
| Minister of Veterans Affairs   *Ministry Resigned* | 27 Nov. 1972 – 3 June 1979 |
| Minister of Veterans Affairs | 3 Mar. 1980 – 30 Sept. 1980 |

**MACDONALD, Hon. David S.H.**
20 Aug. 1936 –

| | |
|---|---|
| Sworn of the Privy Council | 4 June 1979 |
| Minister of Communications   *Ministry Resigned* | 4 June 1979 – 2 Mar. 1980 |
| Secretary of State of Canada   *Ministry Resigned* | 4 June 1979 – 2 Mar. 1980 |

**MACDONALD, Hon. Donald Alexander**
17 Feb. 1817 – 10 June 1896

| | |
|---|---|
| Sworn of the Privy Council | 7 Nov. 1873 |
| Postmaster General | 7 Nov. 1873 – 17 May 1875 |

**MACDONALD, Hon. Donald Stovel**
1 Mar. 1932 –

| | |
|---|---|
| Parliamentary Secretary – Justice | 14 May 1963 – 15 July 1965 |
| Parliamentary Secretary – Finance | 16 July 1965 – 8 Sept. 1965 |
| Parliamentary Secretary – External Affairs | 7 Jan. 1966 – 6 Jan. 1968 |
| Parliamentary Secretary – Industry | 7 Jan. 1968 – 19 Apr. 1968 |
| Sworn of the Privy Council | 20 Apr. 1968 |
| Minister without Portfolio | 20 Apr. 1968 – 5 July 1968 |
| President of the Privy Council | 6 July 1968 – 23 Sept. 1970 |
| Minister of National Defence | 24 Sept. 1970 – 27 Jan. 1972 |
| Minister of Energy, Mines and Resources | 28 Jan. 1972 – 25 Sept. 1975 |
| Minister of Finance | 26 Sept. 1975 – 15 Sept. 1977 |

## MACDONALD, Hon. Edward Mortimer
16 Aug. 1865 – 25 May 1940

| | | |
|---|---|---|
| Sworn of the Privy Council | 12 Apr. 1923 | |
| Minister without Portfolio | 12 Apr. 1923 – | 16 Aug. 1923 |
| Acting Minister of National Defence | 28 Apr. 1923 – | 16 Aug. 1923 |
| Minister of National Defence *Ministry Resigned* | 17 Aug. 1923 – | 28 June 1926 |

## MACDONALD, Hon. Flora Isabel
3 June 1926 –

| | | |
|---|---|---|
| Sworn of the Privy Council | 4 June 1979 | |
| Secretary of State for External Affairs *Ministry Resigned* | 4 June 1979 – | 2 Mar. 1980 |

## MACDONALD, Hon. Sir Hugh John
13 Mar. 1850 – 29 Mar. 1929

| | | |
|---|---|---|
| Sworn of the Privy Council | 1 May 1896 | |
| Superintendent-General of Indian Affairs *Ministry Resigned* | 1 May 1896 – | 10 July 1896 |
| Minister of the Interior *Ministry Resigned* | 1 May 1896 – | 10 July 1896 |

## MACDONALD, Rt. Hon. Sir John Alexander
11 Jan. 1815 – 6 June 1891

| | | |
|---|---|---|
| Sworn of the Privy Council | 1 July 1867 | |
| Prime Minister *Ministry Dissolved* | 1 July 1867 – | 4 Nov. 1873 |
| Minister of Justice and Attorney General *Ministry Resigned* | 1 July 1867 – | 6 Nov. 1873 |
| Prime Minister *Ministry Dissolved* | 17 Oct. 1878 – | 5 June 1891 |
| Superintendent-General of Indian Affairs | 17 Oct. 1878 – | 2 Oct. 1887 |
| Minister of the Interior | 17 Oct. 1878 – | 16 Oct. 1883 |
| Member of the United Kingdom Privy Council | 14 Aug. 1879 | |
| President of the Privy Council | 17 Oct. 1883 – | 27 Nov. 1889 |
| Acting Superintendent-General of Indian Affairs | 8 May 1888 – | 24 Sept. 1888 |
| Acting Minister of the Interior | 8 May 1888 – | 24 Sept. 1888 |
| Acting Minister of Railways and Canals | 10 Apr. 1889 – | 27 Nov. 1889 |
| Minister of Railways and Canals *Ministry Dissolved* | 28 Nov. 1889 – | 5 June 1891 |

**MACDONALD, Hon. John Alexander**
12 Apr. 1874 – 15 Nov. 1948

| | | |
|---|---|---|
| Sworn of the Privy Council | 13 July 1926 | |
| Minister without Portfolio  *Ministry Resigned* | 13 July 1926 – | 24 Sept. 1926 |
| Minister without Portfolio | 7 Aug. 1930 – | 13 Aug. 1935 |
| Member of the Senate | 20 July 1935 – | 15 Nov. 1948 |

**MACDONALD, Hon. William Ross**
25 Dec. 1891 – 28 May 1976

| | | |
|---|---|---|
| Sworn of the Privy Council | 12 May 1953 | |
| Member of the Senate | 12 June 1953 – | 22 Dec. 1967 |
| Leader of the Government in the Senate | 1953 – | 1957 |
| Minister without Portfolio | 14 Oct. 1953 – | 11 Jan. 1954 |
| Solicitor General of Canada  *Ministry Resigned* | 12 Jan. 1954 – | 20 June 1957 |
| Minister without Portfolio | 22 Apr. 1963 – | 2 Feb. 1964 |
| Leader of the Government in the Senate | 22 Apr. 1963 – | 2 Feb. 1964 |

**MACDONNELL, Hon. James MacKerras**
15 Dec. 1884 – 27 July 1973

| | | |
|---|---|---|
| Sworn of the Privy Council | 21 June 1957 | |
| Minister without Portfolio | 21 June 1957 – | 19 Aug. 1959 |

**MACEACHEN, Hon. Allan Joseph**
6 July 1921 –

| | | |
|---|---|---|
| Sworn of the Privy Council | 22 Apr. 1963 | |
| Minister of Labour | 22 Apr. 1963 – | 17 Dec. 1965 |
| Minister of National Health and Welfare | 18 Dec. 1965 – | 5 July 1968 |
| Acting President of the Privy Council | 2 May 1968 – | 5 July 1968 |
| Minister of Manpower and Immigration | 6 July 1968 – | 23 Sept. 1970 |
| President of the Privy Council | 24 Sept. 1970 – | 7 Aug. 1974 |
| Secretary of State for External Affairs | 8 Aug. 1974 – | 13 Sept. 1976 |
| President of the Privy Council  *Ministry Resigned* | 14 Sept. 1976 – | 3 June 1979 |
| Minister of Finance | 3 Mar. 1980 – | |

**MACGUIGAN, Hon. Mark**
17 Feb. 1931 –

| | | | |
|---|---|---|---|
| Parliamentary Secretary – Manpower and Immigration | 22 Dec. 1972 – | 21 Dec. 1973 |
| | 1 Jan. 1974 – | 9 May 1974 |
| Parliamentary Secretary – Labour | 15 Sept. 1974 – | 14 Sept. 1975 |
| Sworn of the Privy Council | 3 Mar. 1980 | |
| Secretary of State for External Affairs | 3 Mar. 1980 | |

**MACKASEY, Hon. Bryce Stuart**
25 Aug. 1921 –

| | | | |
|---|---|---|---|
| Parliamentary Secretary – National Health and Welfare | 16 July 1965 – | 8 Sept. 1965 |
| Parliamentary Secretary – Labour | 7 Jan. 1966 – | 8 Feb. 1968 |
| Sworn of the Privy Council | 9 Feb. 1968 | |
| Minister without Portfolio | 9 Feb. 1968 – | 5 July 1968 |
| Minister of Labour | 6 July 1968 – | 27 Jan. 1972 |
| Minister of Manpower and Immigration | 28 Jan. 1972 – | 26 Nov. 1972 |
| Minister of State | 3 June 1974 – | 7 Aug. 1974 |
| Postmaster General | 8 Aug. 1974 – | 13 Sept. 1976 |
| Acting Minister of Consumer and Corporate Affairs | 16 Mar. 1976 – | 7 Apr. 1976 |
| Minister of Consumer and Corporate Affairs | 8 Apr. 1976 – | 13 Sept. 1976 |

**MACKAY, Hon. Elmer MacIntosh**
5 Oct. 1936 –

| | | | |
|---|---|---|---|
| Sworn of the Privy Council | 4 June 1979 | |
| Minister of Regional Economic Expansion *Ministry Resigned* | 4 June 1979 – | 2 Mar. 1980 |

**MACKENZIE, Hon. Alexander**
28 Jan. 1822 – 17 Apr. 1892

| | | | |
|---|---|---|---|
| Sworn of the Privy Council | 7 Nov. 1873 | |
| Prime Minister | 7 Nov. 1873 – | 7 Oct. 1878 |
| Minister of Public Works *Ministry Resigned* | 7 Nov. 1873 – | 16 Oct. 1878 |

**MACKENZIE, Rt. Hon. Ian Alistair**
27 July 1890 – 2 Sept. 1949

| | | |
|---|---|---|
| Sworn of the Privy Council | 27 June 1930 | |
| Minister of Immigration and Colonization | 27 June 1930 – | 7 Aug. 1930 |
| Superintendent-General of Indian Affairs | 27 June 1930 – | 7 Aug. 1930 |
| Minister of National Defence | 23 Oct. 1935 – | 18 Sept. 1939 |
| Minister of Pensions and National Health | 19 Sept. 1939 – | 17 Oct. 1944 |
| Minister of Veterans Affairs | 18 Oct. 1944 – | 18 Jan. 1948 |
| Member of the United Kingdom Privy Council | 1 Jan. 1947 | |
| Member of the Senate | 19 Jan. 1948 – | 2 Sept. 1949 |

**MACKINNON, Hon. James Angus**
4 Oct. 1881 – 18 Apr. 1958

| | | |
|---|---|---|
| Sworn of the Privy Council | 23 Jan. 1939 | |
| Minister without Portfolio | 23 Jan. 1939 – | 8 May 1940 |
| Minister of Trade and Commerce | 9 May 1940 – | 18 Jan. 1948 |
| Acting Minister of National Revenue | 8 Mar. 1945 – | 18 Apr. 1945 |
| | 30 July 1945 – | 28 Aug. 1945 |
| Minister of Fisheries | 19 Jan. 1948 – | 10 June 1948 |
| Minister of Mines and Resources | 11 June 1948 – | 31 Mar. 1949 |
| Minister without Portfolio | 1 Apr. 1949 – | 13 Dec. 1950 |
| Member of the Senate | 9 May 1949 – | 18 Apr. 1958 |

**MACLAREN, Hon. David Laurence**
27 Oct. 1893 – 7 Sept. 1960

| | | |
|---|---|---|
| Sworn of the Privy Council | 19 Apr. 1945 | |
| Minister of National Revenue | 19 Apr. 1945 – | 29 July 1945 |

**MACLAREN, Hon. Murray**
30 Apr. 1861 – 24 Dec. 1942

| | | |
|---|---|---|
| Sworn of the Privy Council | 7 Aug. 1930 | |
| Minister of Pensions and National Health | 7 Aug. 1930 – | 16 Nov. 1934 |

**MACLEAN, Hon. Alexander Kenneth**
18 Oct. 1869 – 31 July 1942

| | | |
|---|---|---|
| Sworn of the Privy Council | 23 Oct. 1917 | |
| Minister without Portfolio | 23 Oct. 1917 – | 24 Feb. 1920 |

**MACLEAN, Hon. John Angus**

15 May 1914 –

| | | |
|---|---|---|
| Sworn of the Privy Council | 21 June 1957 | |
| Minister of Fisheries   *Ministry Resigned* | 21 June 1957 – | 21 Apr.  1963 |
| Acting Postmaster General | 18 July  1962 – |  8 Aug. 1962 |

**MACMILLAN, Hon. Cyrus**

12 Sept. 1882 – 29 June 1953

| | | |
|---|---|---|
| Sworn of the Privy Council | 17 June 1930 | |
| Minister of Fisheries   *Ministry Resigned* | 17 June 1930 – |  6 Aug. 1930 |
| Parliamentary Assistant – National Defence for Air | 1 Apr.  1943 – |  6 June 1946 |

**MACNAUGHT, Hon. John Watson**

19 June 1904 –

| | | |
|---|---|---|
| Parliamentary Assistant – Fisheries | 11 June 1948 – | 30 Apr.  1949 |
| | 11 July  1949 – | 13 June 1953 |
| | 24 Aug.  1953 – | 12 Apr.  1957 |
| Sworn of the Privy Council | 22 Apr.  1963 | |
| Minister without Portfolio | 22 Apr.  1963 – |  6 July  1965 |
| Solicitor General of Canada | 22 Apr.  1963 – |  6 July  1965 |
| Minister of Mines and Technical Surveys |  7 July  1965 – | 17 Dec.  1965 |

**MACPHERSON, Hon. Sir David Lewis**

12 Sept. 1818 – 16 Aug. 1896

| | | |
|---|---|---|
| Member of the Senate | 23 Oct.  1867 – | 16 Aug.  1896 |
| Sworn of the Privy Council | 11 Feb.  1880 | |
| Minister without Portfolio | 11 Feb.  1880 – | 16 Oct.  1883 |
| Minister of the Interior | 17 Oct.  1883 – |  4 Aug.  1885 |

**MAHONEY, Hon. Patrick Morgan**

20 Jan. 1929 –

| | | |
|---|---|---|
| Parliamentary Secretary – Finance |  1 Oct.  1970 – | 27 Jan.  1972 |
| Sworn of the Privy Council | 28 Jan.  1972 | |
| Minister of State | 28 Jan.  1972 – | 26 Nov.  1972 |

**MALCOLM, Hon. James**

14 July 1880 – 6 Dec. 1935

| | | |
|---|---|---|
| Sworn of the Privy Council | 25 Sept. 1926 | |
| Minister of Trade and Commerce   *Ministry Resigned* | 25 Sept. 1926 – |  6 Aug. 1930 |

**MANION, Hon. Robert James**
19 Nov. 1881 – 2 July 1943

| | |
|---|---|
| Sworn of the Privy Council | 22 Sept. 1921 |
| Minister of Soldiers' Civil Re-establishment | |
|    *Ministry Resigned* | 22 Sept. 1921 – 28 Dec. 1921 |
| Acting Minister of Immigration and Colonization | 29 June 1926 – 12 July 1926 |
| Acting Minister of Labour | 29 June 1926 – 12 July 1926 |
| Acting Postmaster General | 29 June 1926 – 12 July 1926 |
| Acting Minister of Soldiers' Civil Re-establishment | 29 June 1926 – 12 July 1926 |
| Postmaster General   *Ministry Resigned* | 13 July 1926 – 24 Sept. 1926 |
| Minister of Railways and Canals   *Ministry Resigned* | 7 Aug. 1930 – 22 Oct. 1935 |

**MARCHAND, Hon. Jean**
20 Dec. 1918 –

| | |
|---|---|
| Sworn of the Privy Council | 18 Dec. 1965 |
| Minister of Citizenship and Immigration | 18 Dec. 1965 – 30 Sept. 1966 |
| Minister of Manpower and Immigration | 1 Oct. 1966 – 5 July 1968 |
| Secretary of State of Canada | 20 Apr. 1968 – 5 July 1968 |
| Minister of Forestry and Rural Development | 6 July 1968 – 31 Mar. 1969 |
| Minister of Regional Economic Expansion | 1 Apr. 1969 – 26 Nov. 1972 |
| Minister of Transport | 27 Nov. 1972 – 25 Sept. 1975 |
| Minister without Portfolio | 26 Sept. 1975 – 21 Jan. 1976 |
| Minister of the Environment | 22 Jan. 1976 – 30 June 1976 |
| Member of the Senate | 9 Dec. 1976 – |

**MARCHAND, Hon. Leonard Stephen**
16 Nov. 1933 –

| | |
|---|---|
| Parliamentary Secretary – Indian Affairs and Northern Development | 22 Dec. 1972 – 21 Dec. 1973 |
| | 1 Jan. 1974 – 9 May 1974 |
| Parliamentary Secretary – Environment | 15 Sept. 1974 – 14 Sept. 1975 |
| Sworn of the Privy Council | 14 Sept. 1976 |
| Minister of State (Small Businesses) | 14 Sept. 1976 – 15 Sept. 1977 |
| Minister of State (Environment) | 16 Sept. 1977 – 1 Apr. 1979 |
| Minister of the Environment   *Ministry Resigned* | 2 Apr. 1979 – 3 June 1979 |

**MARLER, Hon. George Carlyle**
14 Sept. 1901 – 10 April 1981

| | | |
|---|---|---|
| Sworn of the Privy Council | 1 July 1954 | |
| Minister of Transport   *Ministry Resigned* | 1 July 1954 – 20 June 1957 | |

**MARLER, Hon. Sir Herbert Meredith**
7 Mar. 1876 – 31 Jan. 1940

| | | |
|---|---|---|
| Sworn of the Privy Council | 9 Sept. 1925 | |
| Minister without Portfolio | 9 Sept. 1925 – 6 Jan. 1926 | |

**MARTIN, Hon. Paul Joseph James**
23 June 1903 –

| | | |
|---|---|---|
| Parliamentary Assistant – Labour | 7 May 1943 – 16 Apr. 1945 | |
| Sworn of the Privy Council | 18 Apr. 1945 | |
| Secretary of State of Canada | 18 Apr. 1945 – 11 Dec. 1946 | |
| Minister of National Health and Welfare | | |
|    *Ministry Resigned* | 12 Dec. 1946 – 20 June 1957 | |
| Acting Minister of Labour | 3 Aug. 1950 – 6 Aug. 1950 | |
| Secretary of State for External Affairs | | |
|    *Ministry Resigned* | 22 Apr. 1963 – 19 Apr. 1968 | |
| Member of the Senate | 20 Apr. 1968 – 30 Oct. 1974 | |
| Minister without Portfolio | 20 Apr. 1968 – 31 Mar. 1969 | |
| Leader of the Government in the Senate | 20 Apr. 1968 – 7 Aug. 1974 | |

**MARTINEAU, Hon. Paul**
10 Apr. 1921 –

| | | |
|---|---|---|
| Parlimentary Secretary – Prime Minister | 18 Nov. 1959 – 17 Nov. 1961 | |
| Sworn of the Privy Council | 9 Aug. 1962 | |
| Minister of Mines and Technical Surveys   *Ministry Resigned* | 9 Aug. 1962 – 21 Apr. 1963 | |

**MASSEY, Rt. Hon. Charles Vincent**
20 Feb. 1887 – 30 Dec. 1967

| | | |
|---|---|---|
| Sworn of the Privy Council | 16 Sept. 1925 | |
| Minister without Portfolio | 16 Sept. 1925 – 12 Nov. 1925 | |
| Member of the United Kingdom Privy Council | 26 June 1941 | |

**MASSON, Hon. Louis François Rodrigue**
7 Nov. 1833 – 8 Nov. 1903

| | | |
|---|---|---|
| Sworn of the Privy Council | 19 Oct. 1878 | |
| Minister of Militia and Defence | 19 Oct. 1878 – | 15 Jan. 1880 |
| President of the Privy Council | 16 Jan. 1880 – | 31 July 1880 |
| Member of the Senate* | 29 Sept. 1882 – | 6 Nov. 1884 |
| Member of the Senate** | 3 Feb. 1890 – | 11 June 1903 |

**MATTHEWS, Hon. Robert Charles**
14 June 1871 – 19 Sept. 1952

| | | |
|---|---|---|
| Sworn of the Privy Council | 6 Dec. 1933 | |
| Minister of National Revenue | 6 Dec. 1933 – | 13 Aug. 1935 |

**MAYHEW, Hon. Robert Wellington**
13 Oct. 1880 – 28 July 1971

| | | |
|---|---|---|
| Parliamentary Assistant – Finance | 25 Sept. 1945 – | 10 June 1948 |
| Sworn of the Privy Council | 11 June 1948 | |
| Minister of Fisheries | 11 June 1948 – | 14 Oct. 1952 |

**MAZANKOWSKI, Hon. Donald F.**
27 July 1935 –

| | | |
|---|---|---|
| Sworn of the Privy Council | 4 June 1979 | |
| Minister of Transport   *Ministry Resigned* | 4 June 1979 – | 2 Mar. 1980 |

**MCCANN, Hon. James Joseph**
29 Mar. 1887 – 11 Apr. 1961

| | | |
|---|---|---|
| Sworn of the Privy Council | 18 Apr. 1945 | |
| Minister of National War Services | 18 Apr. 1945 – | 18 Jan. 1948 |
| Minister of National Revenue   *Ministry Resigned* | 29 Aug. 1945 – | 20 June 1957 |
| Minister of Mines and Technical Surveys | 18 Jan. 1950 – | 12 Dec. 1950 |

**MCCURDY, Hon. Fleming Blanchard**
17 Feb. 1875 – 29 Aug. 1952

| | | |
|---|---|---|
| Parliamentary Secretary of Militia and Defence | 19 July 1916 – | 22 Feb. 1918 |
| Parliamentary Secretary of Soldiers' Civil Re-establishment | 23 Feb. 1918 – | 6 Nov. 1918 |
| Sworn of the Privy Council | 13 July 1920 | |
| Minister of Public Works   *Ministry Resigned* | 13 July 1920 – | 28 Dec. 1921 |

*Masson served as Lieutenant-Governor of Quebec from 7 Nov. 1884 to 28 Oct. 1887, but did not formally resign from the Senate until 1 Feb. 1887.*
**Seat declared vacant because of absence for two consecutive sessions.*

**MCCUTCHEON, Hon. Malcolm Wallace**
18 May 1906 – 23 Jan. 1969

| | |
|---|---|
| Member of the Senate | 9 Aug. 1962 – 13 May 1968 |
| Sworn of the Privy Council | 9 Aug. 1962 |
| Minister without Portfolio | 9 Aug. 1962 – 11 Feb. 1963 |
| Minister of Trade and Commerce *Ministry Resigned* | 12 Feb. 1963 – 21 Apr. 1963 |

**MCDONALD, Hon. Hugh**
4 May 1827 – 28 Feb. 1899

| | |
|---|---|
| Sworn of the Privy Council | 13 Aug. 1873 |
| President of the Privy Council* | 14 June 1873 – 30 June 1873 |
| Minister of Militia and Defence | 1 July 1873 – 4 Nov. 1873 |

**MCDONALD, Hon. James**
1 July 1828 – 3 Oct. 1912

| | |
|---|---|
| Sworn of the Privy Council | 17 Oct. 1878 |
| Minister of Justice and Attorney General | 17 Oct. 1878 – 19 May 1881 |

**MCDOUGALL, Hon. William**
25 Jan. 1822 – 29 May 1905

| | |
|---|---|
| Sworn of the Privy Council | 1 July 1867 |
| Minister of Public Works | 1 July 1867 – 27 Sept. 1869 |

**MCGEE, Hon. Frank Charles**
3 Mar. 1926 –

| | |
|---|---|
| Parliamentary Secretary – Citizenship and Immigration | 17 Aug. 1962 – 6 Feb. 1963 |
| Sworn of the Privy Council | 18 Mar. 1963 |
| Minister without Portfolio *Ministry Resigned* | 18 Mar. 1963 – 21 Apr. 1963 |

**MCGIVERN, Hon. Harold Buchanan**
4 Aug. 1870 – 4 Feb. 1931

| | |
|---|---|
| Sworn of the Privy Council | 20 Sept. 1924 |
| Minister without Portfolio | 20 Sept. 1924 – 29 Oct. 1925 |

**MCGRATH, Hon. James Aloysius**
11 Jan. 1932 –

| | |
|---|---|
| Sworn of the Privy Council | 4 June 1979 |
| Minister of Fisheries and Oceans *Ministry Resigned* | 4 June 1979 – 2 Mar. 1980 |

*McDonald was appointed and served as President of the Privy Council and began his term as Minister of Militia and Defence before being sworn as a Privy Councillor.*

**MCILRAITH, Hon. George James**

29 July 1908 –

| | |
|---|---|
| Parliamentary Assistant – Reconstruction | 28 Sept. 1945 – 31 Dec. 1945 |
| Parliamentary Assistant – Reconstruction and Supply | 1 Jan. 1946 – 14 Nov. 1948 |
| Parliamentary Assistant – Trade and Commerce | 3 Feb. 1948 – 30 Apr. 1949 |
| | 11 July 1949 – 13 June 1953 |
| Parliamentary Assistant – Defence Production | 1 Apr. 1951 – 4 Feb. 1952 |
| Sworn of the Privy Council | 22 Apr. 1963 |
| Minister of Transport | 22 Apr. 1963 – 2 Feb. 1964 |
| President of the Privy Council | 3 Feb. 1964 – 6 July 1965 |
| Acting Minister of National Revenue | 19 Mar. 1964 – 28 June 1964 |
| Acting Minister of Justice and Attorney General | 30 June 1965 – 6 July 1965 |
| Minister of Public Works | 7 July 1965 – 5 July 1968 |
| Solicitor General of Canada | 6 July 1968 – 21 Dec. 1970 |
| Member of the Senate | 27 Apr. 1972 – |

**MCKENZIE, Hon. Daniel Duncan**

8 Jan. 1859 – 8 June 1927

| | |
|---|---|
| Sworn of the Privy Council | 29 Dec. 1921 |
| Solicitor General of Canada | 29 Dec. 1921 – 10 Apr. 1923 |

**MCKINNON, Hon. Allan Bruce**

11 Jan. 1917 –

| | |
|---|---|
| Sworn of the Privy Council | 4 June 1979 |
| Minister of National Defence | 4 June 1979 – 2 Mar. 1980 |
| Minister of Veterans Affairs   *Ministry Resigned* | 4 June 1979 – 2 Mar. 1980 |

**MCLARTY, Hon. Norman Alexander**

18 Feb. 1889 – 16 Sept. 1945

| | |
|---|---|
| Sworn of the Privy Council | 23 Jan. 1939 |
| Postmaster General | 23 Jan. 1939 – 18 Sept. 1939 |
| Minister of Labour | 19 Sept. 1939 – 14 Dec. 1941 |
| Secretary of State of Canada | 15 Dec. 1941 – 17 Apr. 1945 |

**MCLELAN, Hon. Archibald Woodbury**
24 Dec. 1824 – 26 June 1890

| | |
|---|---|
| Member of the Senate | 21 June 1869 – 20 May 1881 |
| Sworn of the Privy Council | 20 May 1881 |
| President of the Privy Council | 20 May 1881 – 9 July 1882 |
| Minister of Marine and Fisheries | 10 July 1882 – 9 Dec. 1885 |
| Minister of Finance and Receiver General | 10 Dec. 1885 – 26 Jan. 1887 |
| Postmaster General | 27 Jan. 1887 – 9 July 1888 |

**MCMURRAY, Hon. Edward James**
4 June 1878 –

| | |
|---|---|
| Sworn of the Privy Council | 14 Nov. 1923 |
| Solicitor General of Canada | 14 Nov. 1923 – 22 May 1925 |

**MCNAUGHTON, Hon. Andrew George Latta**
25 Feb. 1887 – 11 July 1966

| | |
|---|---|
| Sworn of the Privy Council | 2 Nov. 1944 |
| Minister of National Defence | 2 Nov. 1944 – 20 Aug. 1945 |

**MEIGHEN, Rt. Hon. Arthur**
16 June 1874 – 5 Aug. 1960

| | |
|---|---|
| Solicitor General of Canada | 26 June 1913 – 24 Aug. 1917 |
| Sworn of the Privy Council | 2 Oct. 1915 |
| Minister of Mines   *Ministry Resigned* | 25 Aug. 1917 – 11 Oct. 1917 |
| Secretary of State of Canada   *Ministry Resigned* | 25 Aug. 1917 – 11 Oct. 1917 |
| Acting Solicitor General of Canada | 31 Aug. 1917 – 3 Oct. 1917 |
| Superintendent-General of Indian Affairs | 12 Oct. 1917 – 9 July 1921 |
| Minister of the Interior | 12 Oct. 1917 – 9 July 1921 |
| Minister of Mines   *Ministry Resigned* | 31 Dec. 1919 – 9 July 1921 |
| Prime Minister   *Ministry Resigned* | 10 July 1920 – 28 Dec. 1921 |
| Secretary of State for External Affairs   *Ministry Resigned* | 10 July 1920 – 28 Dec. 1921 |
| Member of the United Kingdom Privy Council | 27 June 1921 |
| Prime Minister   *Ministry Resigned* | 29 June 1926 – 24 Sept. 1926 |
| Secretary of State for External Affairs   *Ministry Resigned* | 29 June 1926 – 24 Sept. 1926 |
| President of the Privy Council   *Ministry Resigned* | 29 June 1926 – 24 Sept. 1926 |
| Minister without Portfolio   *Ministry Resigned* | 3 Feb. 1932 – 22 Oct. 1935 |
| Member of the Senate | 3 Feb. 1932 – 16 Jan. 1942 |
| Leader of the Government in the Senate | 1932 – 1935 |

## MEWBURN, Hon. Sydney Chilton
4 Dec. 1863 – 11 Aug. 1956

| | | |
|---|---|---|
| Sworn of the Privy Council | 12 Oct. 1917 | |
| Minister of Militia and Defence | 12 Oct. 1917 – | 15 Jan. 1920 |

## MICHAUD, Hon. Joseph-Enoil
26 Sept. 1888 – 23 May 1967

| | | |
|---|---|---|
| Sworn of the Privy Council | 23 Oct. 1935 | |
| Minister of Fisheries | 23 Oct. 1935 – | 5 Oct. 1942 |
| Acting Minister of Justice and Attorney General | 27 Nov. 1941 – | 9 Dec. 1941 |
| Acting Minister of Public Works | 13 May 1942 – | 6 Oct. 1942 |
| Minister of Transport | 6 Oct. 1942 – | 17 Apr. 1945 |

## MILLS, Hon. David
18 Mar. 1831 – 8 May 1903

| | | |
|---|---|---|
| Sworn of the Privy Council | 24 Oct. 1876 | |
| Superintendent-General of Indian Affairs  *Ministry Resigned* | 24 Oct. 1876 – | 16 Oct. 1878 |
| Minister of the Interior  *Ministry Resigned* | 24 Oct. 1876 – | 16 Oct. 1878 |
| Member of the Senate | 13 Nov. 1896 – | 7 Feb. 1902 |
| Minister of Justice and Attorney General | 18 Nov. 1897 – | 7 Feb. 1902 |
| Leader of the Government in the Senate | 1897 – | 1902 |

## MITCHELL, Hon. Humphrey
9 Sept. 1894 – 2 Aug. 1950

| | | |
|---|---|---|
| Sworn of the Privy Council | 15 Dec. 1941 | |
| Minister of Labour | 15 Dec. 1941 – | 2 Aug. 1950 |

## MITCHELL, Hon. Peter
4 Jan. 1824 – 25 Oct. 1899

| | | |
|---|---|---|
| Sworn of the Privy Council | 1 July 1867 | |
| Minister of Marine and Fisheries  *Ministry Resigned* | 1 July 1867 – | 6 Nov. 1873 |
| Member of the Senate | 23 Oct. 1867 – | 13 July 1872 |

## MONK, Hon. Frederick Debartzch
6 Apr. 1856 – 15 May 1914

| | | |
|---|---|---|
| Sworn of the Privy Council | 10 Oct. 1911 | |
| Minister of Public Works | 10 Oct. 1911 – | 28 Oct. 1912 |

**MONTAGUE, Hon. Walter Humphries**

21 Nov. 1858 – 14 Nov. 1915

| | | |
|---|---|---|
| Sworn of the Privy Council | 21 Dec. 1894 | |
| Minister without Portfolio | 21 Dec. 1894 – | 25 Mar. 1895 |
| Secretary of State of Canada | 26 Mar. 1895 – | 20 Dec. 1895 |
| Minister of Agriculture | 21 Dec. 1895 – | 5 Jan. 1896 |
| Minister of Agriculture   *Ministry Resigned* | 15 Jan. 1896 – | 10 July 1896 |

**MONTEITH, Hon. Jay Waldo**

24 June 1903 – 19 Dec. 1981

| | | |
|---|---|---|
| Sworn of the Privy Council | 22 Aug. 1957 | |
| Minister of National Health and Welfare   *Ministry Resigned* | 22 Aug. 1957 – | 21 Apr. 1963 |

**MONTY, Hon. Rodolphe**

30 Nov. 1874 – 1 Dec. 1928

| | | |
|---|---|---|
| Sworn of the Privy Council | 21 Sept. 1921 | |
| Secretary of State of Canada   *Ministry Resigned* | 21 Sept. 1921 – | 28 Dec. 1921 |

**MORAND, Hon. Raymond Ducharme**

30 Jan. 1887 – 3 Feb. 1952

| | | |
|---|---|---|
| Sworn of the Privy Council | 13 July 1926 | |
| Minister without Portfolio   *Ministry Resigned* | 13 July 1926 – | 24 Sept. 1926 |
| Acting Minister of Soldiers' Civil Re-establishment | 13 July 1926 – | 22 Aug. 1926 |

**MORRIS, Hon. Alexander**

17 Mar. 1826 – 28 Oct. 1889

| | | |
|---|---|---|
| Sworn of the Privy Council | 16 Nov. 1869 | |
| Minister of Inland Revenue | 16 Nov. 1869 – | 1 July 1872 |

**MOTHERWELL, Hon. William Richard**

6 Jan. 1860 – 24 May 1943

| | | |
|---|---|---|
| Sworn of the Privy Council | 29 Dec. 1921 | |
| Minister of Agriculture   *Ministry Resigned* | 29 Dec. 1921 – | 28 June 1926 |
| Minister of Agriculture   *Ministry Resigned* | 25 Sept. 1926 – | 6 Aug. 1930 |

**MOUSSEAU, Hon. Joseph-Alfred**

18 July 1838 – 30 Mar. 1886

| | | |
|---|---|---|
| Sworn of the Privy Council | 8 Nov. 1880 | |
| President of the Privy Council | 8 Nov. 1880 – | 19 May 1881 |
| Secretary of State of Canada | 20 May 1881 – | 28 July 1882 |

## MOWAT, Hon. Sir Oliver
22 July 1820 – 19 Apr. 1903

| | | | |
|---|---|---|---|
| Sworn of the Privy Council | 13 July | 1896 | |
| Minister of Justice and Attorney General | 13 July | 1896 – | 17 Nov. 1897 |
| Member of the Senate | 15 July | 1896 – | 17 Nov. 1897 |
| Leader of the Government in the Senate | | 1896 – | 1897 |

## MULOCK, Rt. Hon. Sir William
19 Jan. 1844 – 1 Oct. 1944

| | | | |
|---|---|---|---|
| Sworn of the Privy Council | 13 July | 1896 | |
| Postmaster General | 13 July | 1896 – | 15 Oct. 1905 |
| Member of the United Kingdom Privy Council | 22 June | 1925 | |

## MULOCK, Hon. William Pate
8 July 1897 – 25 Aug. 1954

| | | | |
|---|---|---|---|
| Sworn of the Privy Council | 8 July | 1940 | |
| Postmaster General | 8 July | 1940 – | 8 June 1945 |

## MUNRO, Hon. John Carr
16 Mar. 1931 –

| | | | |
|---|---|---|---|
| Parliamentary Secretary – Citizenship and Immigration | 14 May | 1963 – | 19 Feb. 1964 |
| Parliamentary Secretary – National Health and Welfare | 20 Feb. | 1964 – | 15 July 1965 |
| Parliamentary Secretary – Trade and Commerce | 16 July | 1965 – | 8 Sept. 1965 |
| Parliamentary Secretary – Citizenship and Immigration | 7 Jan. | 1966 – | 30 Sept. 1966 |
| Parliamentary Secretary – Manpower and Immigration | 1 Oct. | 1966 – | 19 Apr. 1968 |
| Sworn of the Privy Council | 20 Apr. | 1968 | |
| Minister without Portfolio | 20 Apr. | 1968 – | 5 July 1968 |
| Minister of National Health and Welfare | 6 July | 1968 – | 26 Nov. 1972 |
| Minister of Labour | 27 Nov. | 1972 – | 7 Sept. 1978 |
| Minister of Indian Affairs and Northern Development | 3 Mar. | 1980 – | |

## MURDOCK, Hon. James
15 Aug. 1871 – 15 May 1949

| | | | |
|---|---|---|---|
| Sworn of the Privy Council | 29 Dec. | 1921 | |
| Minister of Labour | 29 Dec. | 1921 – | 12 Nov. 1925 |
| Member of the Senate | 20 Mar. | 1930 – | 15 May 1949 |

**MURPHY, Hon. Charles**

8 Dec. 1862 – 24 Nov. 1935

| | | |
|---|---|---|
| Sworn of the Privy Council | 5 Oct. 1908 | |
| Secretary of State of Canada   *Ministry Resigned* | 9 Oct. 1908 – | 9 Oct. 1911 |
| Postmaster General   *Ministry Resigned* | 29 Dec. 1921 – | 28 June 1926 |
| Member of the Senate | 5 Sept. 1925 – | 24 Nov. 1935 |
| Acting Secretary of State of Canada | 13 Nov. 1925 – | 23 Mar. 1926 |

**MURPHY, Hon. Thomas Gerow**

29 Oct. 1883 –

| | | |
|---|---|---|
| Sworn of the Privy Council | 7 Aug. 1930 | |
| Superintendent-General of Indian Affairs   *Ministry Resigned* | 7 Aug. 1930 – | 23 Oct. 1935 |
| Minister of the Interior   *Ministry Resigned* | 7 Aug. 1930 – | 23 Oct. 1935 |

**NANTEL, Hon. Wilfrid Bruno**

8 Nov. 1857 – 22 May 1940

| | | |
|---|---|---|
| Sworn of the Privy Council | 10 Oct. 1911 | |
| Minister of Mines | 10 Oct. 1911 – | 29 Mar. 1912 |
| Minister of Inland Revenue | 10 Oct. 1911 – | 19 Oct. 1914 |

**NICHOLSON, Hon. John Robert**

1 Dec. 1901 –

| | | |
|---|---|---|
| Sworn of the Privy Council | 22 Apr. 1963 | |
| Minister of Forestry | 22 Apr. 1963 – | 2 Feb. 1964 |
| Postmaster General | 3 Feb. 1964 – | 14 Feb. 1965 |
| Minister of Citizenship and Immigration | 15 Feb. 1965 – | 17 Dec. 1965 |
| Minister of Labour   *Ministry Resigned* | 18 Dec. 1965 – | 19 Apr. 1968 |

**NIELSEN, Hon. Erik H.**

24 Feb. 1924 –

| | | |
|---|---|---|
| Sworn of the Privy Council | 4 June 1979 | |
| Minister of Public Works   *Ministry Resigned* | 4 June 1979 – | 2 Mar. 1980 |

**NORMAND, Hon. Louis-Philippe**

21 Sept. 1863 – 27 June 1928

| | | |
|---|---|---|
| Sworn of the Privy Council | 21 Sept. 1921 | |
| President of the Privy Council   *Ministry Resigned* | 21 Sept. 1921 – | 28 Dec. 1921 |

### NOWLAN, Hon. George Clyde
14 Aug. 1898 – 31 May 1965

| | | |
|---|---|---|
| Sworn of the Privy Council | 21 June 1957 | |
| Minister of National Revenue | 21 June 1957 – | 8 Aug. 1962 |
| Minister of Finance and Receiver General *Ministry Resigned* | 9 Aug. 1962 – | 21 Apr. 1963 |

### O'CONNELL, Hon. Martin Patrick
1 Aug. 1916 –

| | | |
|---|---|---|
| Parliamentary Secretary – Regional Economic Expansion | 20 Oct. 1969 – | 11 Aug. 1971 |
| Sworn of the Privy Council | 12 Aug. 1971 | |
| Minister of State | 12 Aug. 1971 – | 27 Jan. 1972 |
| Minister of Labour | 28 Jan. 1972 – | 26 Nov. 1972 |
| Minister of Labour *Ministry Resigned* | 24 Nov. 1978 – | 3 June 1979 |

### O'CONNOR, Hon. John
Jan. 1824 – 3 Nov. 1887

| | | |
|---|---|---|
| Sworn of the Privy Council | 2 July 1872 | |
| President of the Privy Council | 2 July 1872 – | 3 Mar. 1873 |
| Minister of Inland Revenue | 4 Mar. 1873 – | 30 June 1873 |
| Postmaster General *Ministry Resigned* | 1 July 1873 – | 6 Nov. 1873 |
| President of the Privy Council | 17 Oct. 1878 – | 15 Jan. 1880 |
| Postmaster General | 16 Jan. 1880 – | 7 Nov. 1880 |
| Secretary of State of Canada | 8 Nov. 1880 – | 19 May 1881 |
| Postmaster General | 20 May 1881 – | 22 May 1882 |

### O'HURLEY, Hon. Raymond Joseph Michael
1 Oct. 1909 – 27 Mar. 1970

| | | |
|---|---|---|
| Parliamentary Assistant – Mines and Technical Surveys | 7 Aug. 1957 – | 1 Feb. 1958 |
| Sworn of the Privy Council | 12 May 1958 | |
| Minister of Defence Production *Ministry Resigned* | 12 May 1958 – | 21 Apr. 1963 |

### OLIVER, Hon. Frank
14 Sept. 1853 – 31 Mar. 1933

| | | |
|---|---|---|
| Sworn of the Privy Council | 8 Apr. 1905 | |
| Superintendent-General of Indian Affairs *Ministry Resigned* | 8 Apr. 1905 – | 9 Oct. 1911 |
| Minister of the Interior *Ministry Resigned* | 8 Apr. 1905 – | 9 Oct. 1911 |

**OLSON, Hon. Horace Andrew**
6 Oct. 1925 –

| | | |
|---|---|---|
| Sworn of the Privy Council | 6 July 1968 | |
| Minister of Agriculture | 6 July 1968 – | 26 Nov. 1972 |
| Member of the Senate | 5 Apr. 1977 – | |
| Minister of State for Economic Development | 3 Mar. 1980 – | |

**OUELLET, Hon. André**
6 Apr. 1939 –

| | | |
|---|---|---|
| Parliamentary Secretary – External Affairs | 1 Oct. 1970 – | 12 Aug. 1971 |
| Parliamentary Secretary – National Health and Welfare | 13 Aug. 1971 – | 1 Sept. 1972 |
| Sworn of the Privy Council | 27 Nov. 1972 | |
| Postmaster General | 27 Nov. 1972 – | 7 Aug. 1974 |
| Minister of Consumer and Corporate Affairs | 8 Aug. 1974 – | 15 Mar. 1976 |
| Minister of State for Urban Affairs | 3 Nov. 1976 – | 31 Mar. 1979 |
| Acting Minister of Labour | 8 Sept. 1978 – | 23 Nov. 1978 |
| Minister of Public Works   *Ministry Resigned* | 24 Nov. 1978 – | 3 June 1979 |
| Postmaster General | 3 Mar. 1980 – | 15 Oct. 1980 |
| Minister of Consumer and Corporate Affairs | 3 Mar. 1980 – | |

**OUIMET, Hon. Joseph Aldéric**
20 May 1848 – 12 May 1916

| | | |
|---|---|---|
| Sworn of the Privy Council | 20 May 1891 | |
| Minister of Public Works   *Ministry Resigned* | 11 Jan. 1892 – | 30 Apr. 1896 |
| Acting Minister of Agriculture | 13 July 1895 – | 20 Dec. 1895 |
| Acting Minister of Railways and Canals | 6 Jan. 1896 – | 14 Jan. 1896 |
| Acting Secretary of State of Canada | 29 Dec. 1895 – | 5 Jan. 1896 |

**PACAUD, Lucien-Turcotte**
21 Sept. 1879 – 5 Mar. 1960

| | | |
|---|---|---|
| Parliamentary Under Secretary of State for External Affairs | 29 Dec. 1921 – | 26 Oct. 1922 |

## PAPROSKI, Hon. Steven Eugene

23 Sept. 1928 –

| | | |
|---|---|---|
| Sworn of the Privy Council | 4 June 1979 | |
| Minister of State (Fitness, Amateur Sport and Multiculturalism) | | |
| *Ministry Resigned* | 4 June 1979 – | 2 Mar. 1980 |

## PAQUET, Hon. Eugène

23 Oct. 1867 – 8 May 1951

| | | |
|---|---|---|
| Sworn of the Privy Council | 23 Aug. 1926 | |
| Minister of Soldiers' Civil Re-establishment | | |
| *Ministry Resigned* | 23 Aug. 1926 – | 24 Sept. 1926 |
| Member of the Senate | 14 Aug. 1935 – | 8 May 1951 |

## PATENAUDE, Hon. Esioff-Léon

12 Feb. 1875 – 7 Feb. 1963

| | | |
|---|---|---|
| Sworn of the Privy Council | 6 Oct. 1915 | |
| Minister of Inland Revenue | 6 Oct. 1915 – | 7 Jan. 1917 |
| Minister of Mines | 8 Jan. 1917 – | 12 June 1917 |
| Secretary of State of Canada | 8 Jan. 1917 – | 12 June 1917 |
| Minister of Justice and Attorney General   *Ministry Resigned* | 13 July 1926 – | 24 Sept. 1926 |
| Acting Minister of Marine and Fisheries   *Ministry Resigned* | 13 July 1926 – | 24 Sept. 1926 |

## PATERSON, Hon. William

19 Sept. 1839 – 18 Mar. 1914

| | | |
|---|---|---|
| Controller of Customs | 13 July 1896 – | 29 June 1897 |
| Sworn of the Privy Council | 30 June 1897 | |
| Minister of Customs   *Ministry Resigned* | 30 June 1897 – | 9 Oct. 1911 |

## PATTERSON, Hon. James Colebrooke

1839 – 17 Feb. 1929

| | | |
|---|---|---|
| Sworn of the Privy Council | 25 Jan. 1892 | |
| Secretary of State of Canada   *Ministry Resigned* | 25 Jan. 1892 – | 4 Dec. 1892 |
| Minister of Militia and Defence | 5 Dec. 1892 – | 25 Mar. 1895 |
| Minister without Portfolio | 26 Mar. 1895 – | 1 Sept. 1895 |

**PEARKES, Hon. George Randolph**
26 Feb. 1888 –

| | | |
|---|---|---|
| Sworn of the Privy Council | 21 June 1957 | |
| Minister of National Defence | 21 June 1957 – | 10 Oct. 1960 |

**PEARSON, Rt. Hon. Lester Bowles**
23 Apr. 1897 – 27 Dec. 1972

| | | |
|---|---|---|
| Sworn of the Privy Council | 10 Sept. 1948 | |
| Secretary of State for External Affairs   *Ministry Resigned* | 10 Sept. 1948 – | 20 June 1957 |
| Prime Minister   *Ministry Resigned* | 22 Apr. 1963 – | 19 Apr. 1968 |
| Member of the United Kingdom Privy Council | 13 May 1963 | |

**PELLETIER, Hon. Sir Charles Alphonse Pantaléon**
22 Jan. 1837 – 29 Apr. 1911

| | | |
|---|---|---|
| Sworn of the Privy Council | 26 Jan. 1877 | |
| Minister of Agriculture   *Ministry Resigned* | 26 Jan. 1877 – | 16 Oct. 1878 |
| Member of the Senate | 2 Feb. 1877 – | Sept. 1904 |

**PELLETIER, Hon. Gérard**
21 June 1919 –

| | | |
|---|---|---|
| Parliamentary Secretary – External Affairs | 20 Apr. 1967 – | 19 Apr. 1968 |
| Sworn of the Privy Council | 20 Apr. 1968 | |
| Minister without Portfolio | 20 Apr. 1968 – | 5 July 1968 |
| Secretary of State of Canada | 6 July 1968 – | 26 Nov. 1972 |
| Acting Minister of Communications | 11 May 1971 – | 11 Aug. 1971 |
| Minister of Communications | 27 Nov. 1972 – | 28 Aug. 1975 |

**PELLETIER, Hon. Louis-Philippe**
2 Feb. 1857 – 8 Feb. 1921

| | | |
|---|---|---|
| Sworn of the Privy Council | 10 Oct. 1911 | |
| Postmaster General | 10 Oct. 1911 – | 19 Oct. 1914 |

**PENNELL, Hon. Lawrence**
11 Mar. 1915 –

| | | |
|---|---|---|
| Parliamentary Secretary – Finance | 30 June 1964 – | 6 July 1965 |
| Sworn of the Privy Council | 7 July 1965 | |
| Minister without Portfolio | 7 July 1965 – | 30 Sept. 1966 |
| Solicitor General of Canada | 7 July 1965 – | 19 Apr. 1968 |

**PEPIN, Hon. Jean-Luc**
1 Nov. 1924 –

| | | |
|---|---|---|
| Parliamentary Secretary – Trade and Commerce | 14 May 1963 – | 6 July 1965 |
| Sworn of the Privy Council | 7 July 1965 | |
| Minister without Portfolio | 7 July 1965 – | 17 Dec. 1965 |
| Minister of Mines and Technical Surveys | 18 Dec. 1965 – | 30 Sept. 1966 |
| Minister of Energy, Mines and Resources | 1 Oct. 1966 – | 5 July 1968 |
| Acting Minister of Trade and Commerce | 30 Mar. 1968 – | 19 Apr. 1968 |
| Minister of Labour | 20 Apr. 1968 – | 5 July 1968 |
| Minister of Industry | 6 July 1968 – | 31 Mar. 1969 |
| Minister of Trade and Commerce | 6 July 1968 – | 31 Mar. 1969 |
| Minister of Industry, Trade and Commerce | 1 Apr. 1969 – | 26 Nov. 1972 |
| Minister of Transport | 3 Mar. 1980 – | |

**PERLEY, Rt. Hon. Sir George Halsey**
12 Sept. 1857 – 4 Jan. 1938

| | | |
|---|---|---|
| Sworn of the Privy Council | 10 Oct. 1911 | |
| Minister without Portfolio | 10 Oct. 1911 – | 30 Oct. 1916 |
| Minister of the Overseas Military Forces  *Ministry Resigned* | 31 Oct. 1916 – | 11 Oct. 1917 |
| Acting Minister of Public Works | 29 June 1926 – | 12 July 1926 |
| Acting Secretary of State of Canada | 29 June 1926 – | 12 July 1926 |
| Secretary of State of Canada  *Ministry Resigned* | 13 July 1926 – | 24 Sept. 1926 |
| Minister without Portfolio | 7 Aug. 1930 – | 22 Oct. 1935 |
| Member of the United Kingdom Privy Council | 12 Feb. 1931 – | |

**PERRAULT, Hon. Raymond Joseph**
6 Feb. 1926 –

| | | |
|---|---|---|
| Parliamentary Secretary – Labour | 1 Oct. 1970 – | 2 Feb. 1972 |
| Parliamentary Secretary – Manpower and Immigration | 3 Feb. 1972 – | 1 Sept. 1972 |
| Member of the Senate | 1 Oct. 1973 – | |
| Sworn of the Privy Council | 8 Aug. 1974 | |
| Leader of the Government in the Senate   *Ministry Resigned* | 8 Aug. 1974 – | 3 June 1979 |
| Leader of the Government in the Senate | 3 Mar. 1980 – | |

**PICKERSGILL, Hon. John Whitney**
23 June 1905 –

| | | |
|---|---|---|
| Sworn of the Privy Council | 12 June 1953 | |
| Secretary of State of Canada | 12 June 1953 – | 30 June 1954 |
| Minister of Citizenship and Immigration   *Ministry Resigned* | 1 July 1954 – | 20 June 1957 |
| Secretary of State of Canada | 22 Apr. 1963 – | 2 Feb. 1964 |
| Minister of Transport | 3 Feb. 1964 – | 18 Sept. 1967 |

**PINARD, Hon. Roch**
26 July 1910 – 23 Apr. 1974

| | | |
|---|---|---|
| Parliamentary Assistant – External Affairs | 14 Oct. 1953 – | 30 June 1954 |
| Sworn of the Privy Council | 1 July 1954 | |
| Secretary of State of Canada   *Ministry Resigned* | 1 July 1954 – | 20 June 1957 |
| Acting Postmaster General | 16 Aug. 1955 – | 2 Nov. 1955 |

**PINARD, Hon. Yvon**
10 Oct. 1940 –

| | | |
|---|---|---|
| Parliamentary Secretary – Privy Council | 1 Oct. 1977 – | 30 Sept. 1978 |
| | 1 Oct. 1978 – | 26 Mar. 1979 |
| Sworn of the Privy Council | 3 Mar. 1980 | |
| President of the Privy Council | 3 Mar. 1980 – | |

**POPE, Hon. James Colledge**
11 June 1826 – 18 May 1885

| | | |
|---|---|---|
| Sworn of the Privy Council | 19 Oct. 1878 | |
| Minister of Marine and Fisheries | 19 Oct. 1878 – | 9 July 1882 |

## POPE, Hon. John Henry
19 Dec. 1824 – 1 Apr. 1889

| | |
|---|---|
| Sworn of the Privy Council | 25 Oct. 1871 |
| Minister of Agriculture   *Ministry Resigned* | 25 Oct. 1871 – 6 Nov. 1873 |
| Minister of Agriculture | 17 Oct. 1878 – 24 Sept. 1885 |
| Acting Minister of Railways and Canals | 29 May 1884 – 24 Sept. 1885 |
| Minister of Railways and Canals | 25 Sept. 1885 – 1 Apr. 1889 |

## POWER, Hon. Charles Gavan
18 Jan. 1888 – 30 May 1968

| | |
|---|---|
| Sworn of the Privy Council | 23 Oct. 1935 |
| Minister of Pensions and National Health | 23 Oct. 1935 – 18 Sept. 1939 |
| Postmaster General | 19 Sept. 1939 – 22 May 1940 |
| Minister of National Defence for Air | 23 May 1940 – 26 Nov. 1944 |
| Acting Minister of National Defence | 11 June 1940 – 4 July 1940 |
| Associate Minister of National Defence | 12 July 1940 – 26 Nov. 1944 |
| Member of the Senate | 28 July 1955 – 30 May 1968 |

## PRÉFONTAINE, Hon. Joseph Raymond Fournier
16 Sept. 1850 – 25 Dec. 1905

| | |
|---|---|
| Sworn of the Privy Council | 11 Nov. 1902 |
| Minister of Marine and Fisheries | 11 Nov. 1902 – 25 Dec. 1905 |

## PRIOR, Hon. Edward Gawler
21 May 1853 – 12 Dec. 1920

| | |
|---|---|
| Controller of Inland Revenue   *Ministry Resigned* | 17 Dec. 1895 – 10 July 1896 |
| Sworn of the Privy Council | 15 Jan. 1896 |

## PRUDHAM, Hon. George
27 Feb. 1904 – 28 Aug. 1974

| | |
|---|---|
| Parliamentary Assistant – Resources and Development | 1 Feb. 1950 – 12 Dec. 1950 |
| Sworn of the Privy Council | 13 Dec. 1950 |
| Minister of Mines and Technical Surveys   *Ministry Resigned* | 13 Dec. 1950 – 20 June 1957 |

**PUGSLEY, Hon. William**
27 Sept. 1850 – 3 Mar. 1925

| | |
|---|---|
| Sworn of the Privy Council | 30 Aug. 1907 |
| Minister of Public Works *Ministry Resigned* | 30 Aug. 1907 – 9 Oct. 1911 |

**RALSTON, Hon. James Layton**
27 Sept. 1881 – 22 May 1948

| | |
|---|---|
| Sworn of the Privy Council | 8 Oct. 1926 |
| Minister of National Defence *Ministry Resigned* | 8 Oct. 1926 – 6 Aug. 1930 |
| Acting Minister of Pensions and National Health | 19 June 1930 – 6 Aug. 1930 |
| Minister of Finance and Receiver General | 6 Sept. 1939 – 4 July 1940 |
| Minister of National Defence | 5 July 1940 – 1 Nov. 1944 |

**REGAN, Hon. Gerald**
13 Feb. 1929 –

| | |
|---|---|
| Sworn of the Privy Council | 3 Mar. 1980 |
| Minister of State (Sports) | 3 Mar. 1980 – 5 Mar. 1980 |
| Minister of Labour | 3 Mar. 1980 – 21 Sept. 1981 |
| Secretary of State of Canada | 22 Sept. 1981 – |

**REID, Hon. John Dowsley**
1 Jan. 1859 – 26 Aug. 1929

| | |
|---|---|
| Sworn of the Privy Council | 10 Oct. 1911 |
| Minister of Customs *Ministry Resigned* | 10 Oct. 1911 – 11 Oct. 1917 |
| Minister of Railways and Canals | 12 Oct. 1917 – 20 Sept. 1921 |
| Acting Minister of Public Works | 6 Aug. 1919 – 2 Sept. 1919 |
| Acting Minister of Customs and Inland Revenue | 2 Sept. 1919 – 30 Dec. 1919 |
| Acting Minister of Public Works | 31 Dec. 1919 – 12 July 1920 |
| Member of the Senate | 22 Sept. 1921 – 26 Aug. 1929 |

**REID, Hon. John M.**
8 Feb. 1937 –

| | |
|---|---|
| Parliamentary Secretary – Privy Council | 22 Dec. 1972 – 21 Dec. 1973 |
| | 1 Jan. 1974 – 9 May 1974 |
| | 15 Sept. 1974 – 14 Sept. 1975 |
| Sworn of the Privy Council | 24 Nov. 1978 |
| Minister of State (Federal-Provincial Relations) *Ministry Resigned* | 24 Nov. 1978 – 3 June 1979 |

## RHODES, Hon. Edgar Nelson
5 Jan. 1876 – 15 Mar. 1942

| | | | | |
|---|---|---|---|---|
| Sworn of the Privy Council | | 22 Feb. 1921 | | |
| Minister of Fisheries | | 7 Aug. 1930 – | 2 Feb. 1932 |
| Minister of Finance and Receiver General  *Ministry Resigned* | 3 Feb. 1932 – | 22 Oct. 1935 |
| Member of the Senate | | 20 July 1935 – | 15 Mar. 1942 |

## RICARD, Hon. Théogène
30 Apr. 1909 –

| | | |
|---|---|---|
| Parliamentary Secretary – Prime Minister | 18 Jan. 1962 – | 19 Apr. 1962 |
| | 17 Aug. 1962 – | 6 Feb. 1963 |
| Sworn of the Privy Council | 18 Mar. 1963 | |
| Minister without Portfolio  *Ministry Resigned* | 18 Mar. 1963 – | 21 Apr. 1963 |

## RICHARDSON, Hon. James Armstrong
28 Mar. 1922 –

| | | |
|---|---|---|
| Sworn of the Privy Council | 6 July 1968 | |
| Minister without Portfolio | 6 July 1968 – | 4 May 1969 |
| Acting Minister of Transport | 30 Apr. 1969 – | 4 May 1969 |
| Minister of Supply and Services | 5 May 1969 – | 26 Nov. 1972 |
| Minister of National Defence | 27 Nov. 1972 – | 12 Oct. 1976 |

## RINFRET, Hon. Fernand
28 Feb. 1883 – 12 July 1939

| | | |
|---|---|---|
| Sworn of the Privy Council | 25 Sept. 1926 | |
| Secretary of State of Canada  *Ministry Resigned* | 25 Sept. 1926 – | 6 Aug. 1930 |
| Secretary of State of Canada | 23 Oct. 1935 – | 12 July 1939 |

## RINFRET, Hon. Gabriel Édouard
12 May 1905 –

| | | |
|---|---|---|
| Sworn of the Privy Council | 25 Aug. 1949 | |
| Postmaster General | 25 Aug. 1949 – | 12 Feb. 1952 |

## ROBB, Hon. James Alexander
10 Aug. 1859 – 11 Nov. 1929

| | | |
|---|---|---|
| Sworn of the Privy Council | 29 Dec. 1921 | |
| Minister of Trade and Commerce | 29 Dec. 1921 – | 16 Aug. 1923 |
| Minister of Immigration and Colonization | 17 Aug. 1923 – | 4 Sept. 1925 |
| Minister of Finance and Receiver General   *Ministry Resigned* | 5 Sept. 1925 – | 28 June 1926 |
| Acting Minister of Trade and Commerce | 13 Nov. 1925 – | 28 June 1926 |
| Minister of Finance and Receiver General | 25 Sept. 1925 – | 11 Nov. 1929 |
| Acting Minister of National Defence | 1 Oct. 1926 – | 7 Oct. 1926 |

## ROBERTS, Hon. John
28 Nov. 1933 –

| | | |
|---|---|---|
| Parliamentary Secretary – Regional Economic Expansion | 1 Oct. 1971 – | 1 Sept. 1972 |
| Sworn of the Privy Council | 14 Sept. 1976 | |
| Secretary of State of Canada   *Ministry Resigned* | 14 Sept. 1976 – | 3 June 1979 |
| Minister of the Environment | 3 Mar. 1980 – | |
| Minister of State for Science and Technology | 3 Mar. 1980 – | |

## ROBERTSON, Hon. Gideon Decker
26 Aug. 1874 – 25 Aug. 1933

| | | |
|---|---|---|
| Member of the Senate | 20 Jan. 1917 – | 25 Aug. 1933 |
| Sworn of the Privy Council | 23 Oct. 1917 | |
| Minister without Portfolio | 23 Oct. 1917 – | 7 Nov. 1918 |
| Minister of Labour   *Ministry Resigned* | 8 Nov. 1918 – | 28 Dec. 1921 |
| Minister of Labour | 7 Aug. 1930 – | 2 Feb. 1932 |

## ROBERTSON, Hon. Wishart McLea
15 Feb. 1891 – 16 Aug. 1967

| | | |
|---|---|---|
| Member of the Senate | 19 Feb. 1943 – | 24 Dec. 1965 |
| Sworn of the Privy Council | 4 Sept. 1945 | |
| Minister without Portfolio | 4 Sept. 1945 – | 13 Oct. 1953 |
| Leader of the Government in the Senate | 1945 – | 1953 |

## ROBICHAUD, Hon. Hédard
2 Nov. 1911 –

| | | |
|---|---|---|
| Sworn of the Privy Council | 22 Apr. 1963 | |
| Minister of Fisheries | 22 Apr. 1963 – | 5 July 1968 |

**ROBITAILLE, Hon. Théodore**
29 Jan. 1834 – 17 Aug. 1897

| | | |
|---|---|---|
| Sworn of the Privy Council | 30 Jan. 1873 | |
| Receiver General  *Ministry Resigned* | 30 Jan. 1873 – | 6 Nov. 1873 |
| Member of the Senate | 29 Jan. 1885 – | 17 Aug. 1897 |

**ROCHE, Hon. William James**
30 Nov. 1859 – 30 Sept. 1937

| | | |
|---|---|---|
| Sworn of the Privy Council | 10 Oct. 1911 | |
| Secretary of State of Canada | 10 Oct. 1911 – | 28 Oct. 1912 |
| Superintendent-General of Indian Affairs  *Ministry Resigned* | 29 Oct. 1912 – | 11 Oct. 1917 |
| Minister of the Interior  *Ministry Resigned* | 29 Oct. 1912 – | 11 Oct. 1917 |
| Minister of Mines | 29 Oct. 1912 – | 9 Feb. 1913 |

**ROGERS, Hon. Norman McLeod**
25 July 1894 – 10 June 1940

| | | |
|---|---|---|
| Sworn of the Privy Council | 23 Oct. 1935 | |
| Minister of Labour | 23 Oct. 1935 – | 18 Sept. 1939 |
| Minister of National Defence | 19 Sept. 1939 – | 10 June 1940 |

**ROGERS, Hon. Robert**
2 Mar. 1864 – 21 July 1936

| | | |
|---|---|---|
| Sworn of the Privy Council | 10 Oct. 1911 | |
| Superintendent-General of Indian Affairs | 10 Oct. 1911 – | 28 Oct. 1912 |
| Minister of the Interior | 10 Oct. 1911 – | 28 Oct. 1912 |
| Minister of Mines | 30 Mar. 1912 – | 28 Oct. 1912 |
| Minister of Public Works | 29 Oct. 1912 – | 22 Aug. 1917 |

**ROMPKEY, Hon. William**
13 May 1936 –

| | | |
|---|---|---|
| Parliamentary Secretary – Environment | 22 Dec. 1972 – | 21 Dec. 1973 |
| | 1 Jan. 1974 – | 9 May 1974 |
| Parliamentary Secretary – Manpower and Immigration | 15 Sept. 1974 – | 14 Sept. 1975 |
| Sworn of the Privy Council | 3 Mar. 1980 | |
| Minister of National Revenue | 3 Mar. 1980 – | |

## ROSE, Rt. Hon. Sir John
2 Aug. 1820 – 24 Aug. 1888

| | | |
|---|---|---|
| Sworn of the Privy Council | 18 Nov. 1867 | |
| Minister of Finance | 18 Nov. 1867 – | 30 Sept. 1869 |
| Member of the United Kingdom Privy Council | June 1886 | |

## ROSS, Hon. John Jones
16 Aug. 1832 – 4 May 1901

| | | |
|---|---|---|
| Member of the Senate | 12 Apr. 1887 – | 4 May 1901 |
| Sworn of the Privy Council | 1 May 1896 | |
| Minister without Portfolio *Ministry Resigned* | 1 May 1896 – | 10 July 1896 |

## ROSS, Hon. William
20 Dec. 1824 – 17 Mar. 1912

| | | |
|---|---|---|
| Sworn of the Privy Council | 7 Nov. 1873 | |
| Minister of Militia and Defence | 7 Nov. 1873 – | 29 Sept. 1874 |
| Member of the Senate | 18 May 1905 – | 17 Mar. 1912 |

## ROWE, Hon. William Earl
13 May 1894 –

| | | |
|---|---|---|
| Sworn of the Privy Council | 30 Aug. 1935 | |
| Minister without Portfolio *Ministry Resigned* | 30 Aug. 1935 – | 22 Oct. 1935 |

## ROWELL, Hon. Newton Wesley
1 Nov. 1867 – 22 Nov. 1941

| | | |
|---|---|---|
| Sworn of the Privy Council | 12 Oct. 1917 | |
| President of the Privy Council *Ministry Resigned* | 12 Oct. 1917 – | 9 July 1920 |

## RYCKMAN, Hon. Edmond Baird
15 Apr. 1866 – 11 Jan. 1934

| | | |
|---|---|---|
| Sworn of the Privy Council | 13 July 1926 | |
| Minister of Public Works *Ministry Resigned* | 13 July 1926 – | 24 Sept. 1926 |
| Minister of National Revenue | 7 Aug. 1930 – | 1 Dec. 1933 |

## SAUVÉ, Hon. Arthur
1 Oct. 1875 – 6 Feb. 1944

| | | |
|---|---|---|
| Sworn of the Privy Council | 7 Aug. 1930 | |
| Postmaster General | 7 Aug. 1930 – | 13 Aug. 1935 |
| Member of the Senate | 20 July 1935 – | 6 Feb. 1944 |

**SAUVÉ, Hon. Jeanne**
26 Apr. 1922 –

| | | |
|---|---|---|
| Sworn of the Privy Council | 27 Nov. 1972 | |
| Minister of State for Science and Technology | 27 Nov. 1972 – | 7 Aug. 1974 |
| Minister of the Environment | 8 Aug. 1974 – | 4 Dec. 1975 |
| Minister of Communications  *Ministry Resigned* | 5 Dec. 1975 – | 3 June 1979 |

**SAUVÉ, Hon. Maurice**
20 Sept. 1923 –

| | | |
|---|---|---|
| Sworn of the Privy Council | 3 Feb. 1964 | |
| Minister of Forestry | 3 Feb. 1964 – | 30 Sept. 1966 |
| Minister of Forestry and Rural Development | 1 Oct. 1966 – | 5 July 1968 |

**SCOTT, Hon. Sir Richard William**
24 Feb. 1825 – 23 Apr. 1913

| | | |
|---|---|---|
| Sworn of the Privy Council | 7 Nov. 1873 | |
| Minister without Portfolio | 7 Nov. 1873 – | 8 Jan. 1874 |
| Secretary of State of Canada | 9 Jan. 1874 – | 16 Oct. 1878 |
| Member of the Senate | 13 Mar. 1874 – | 23 Apr. 1913 |
| Leader of the Government in the Senate | 1874 – | 1878 |
| Acting Superintendent-General of Indian Affairs | 7 Oct. 1876 – | 23 Oct. 1876 |
| Acting Minister of the Interior | 7 Oct. 1876 – | 23 Oct. 1876 |
| Secretary of State of Canada | 13 July 1896 – | 8 Oct. 1908 |
| Acting Superintendent-General of Indian Affairs | 17 July 1896 – | 16 Nov. 1896 |
| Acting Minister of the Interior | 17 July 1896 – | 16 Nov. 1896 |
| Leader of the Government in the Senate | 1902 – | 1908 |

**SÉVIGNY, Hon. Albert**
31 Dec. 1881 – 14 May 1961

| | | |
|---|---|---|
| Sworn of the Privy Council | 8 Jan. 1917 | |
| Minister of Inland Revenue | 8 Jan. 1917 – | 1 Apr. 1918 |
| Acting Secretary of State of Canada | 13 June 1917 – | 24 Aug. 1917 |
| Acting Minister of Mines | 13 June 1917 – | 24 Aug. 1917 |

**SÉVIGNY, Hon. Joseph Pierre Albert**
17 Sept. 1917 –

| | | |
|---|---|---|
| Sworn of the Privy Council | 20 Aug. 1959 | |
| Associate Minister of National Defence | 20 Aug. 1959 – | 8 Feb. 1963 |

**SHARP, Hon. Mitchell William**
11 May 1911 –

| | | |
|---|---|---|
| Sworn of the Privy Council | 22 Apr. 1963 | |
| Minister of Trade and Commerce | 22 Apr. 1963 – | 3 Jan. 1966 |
| Acting Minister of Finance and Receiver General | 11 Nov. 1965 – | 17 Dec. 1965 |
| Minister of Finance and Receiver General   *Ministry Resigned* | 18 Dec. 1965 – | 19 Apr. 1968 |
| Secretary of State for External Affairs | 20 Apr. 1968 – | 7 Aug. 1974 |
| President of the Privy Council | 8 Aug. 1974 – | 13 Sept. 1976 |

**SIFTON, Rt. Hon. Arthur Lewis**
26 Oct. 1859 – 21 Jan. 1921

| | | |
|---|---|---|
| Sworn of the Privy Council | 12 Oct. 1917 | |
| Minister of Customs | 12 Oct. 1917 – | 17 May 1918 |
| Minister of Inland Revenue | 14 May 1918 – | 17 May 1918 |
| Minister of Customs and Inland Revenue | 18 May 1918 – | 1 Sept. 1919 |
| Minister of Public Works | 3 Sept. 1919 – | 30 Dec. 1919 |
| Secretary of State of Canada | 31 Dec. 1919 – | 21 Jan. 1921 |
| Member of the United Kingdom Privy Council | 22 Jan. 1920 – | |

**SIFTON, Hon. Sir Clifford**
10 Mar. 1861 – 17 Apr. 1929

| | | |
|---|---|---|
| Sworn of the Privy Council | 17 Nov. 1896 | |
| Superintendent-General of Indian Affairs | 17 Nov. 1896 – | 28 Feb. 1905 |
| Minister of the Interior | 17 Nov. 1896 – | 28 Feb. 1905 |

**SINCLAIR, Hon. James**
26 May 1908 –

| | | |
|---|---|---|
| Parliamentary Assistant – Finance | 19 Jan. 1949 – | 30 Apr. 1949 |
| | 11 July 1949 – | 14 Oct. 1952 |
| Sworn of the Privy Council | 15 Oct. 1952 | |
| Minister of Fisheries   *Ministry Resigned* | 15 Oct. 1952 – | 20 June 1957 |

**SINCLAIR, Hon. John Ewen**
24 Dec. 1879 – 23 Dec. 1949

| | | |
|---|---|---|
| Sworn of the Privy Council | 30 Dec. 1921 | |
| Minister without Portfolio | 30 Dec. 1921 – | 29 Oct. 1925 |
| Member of the Senate | 7 June 1930 – | 23 Dec. 1949 |

**SMITH, Hon. Sir Albert James**
12 Mar. 1822 – 30 June 1883

| | |
|---|---|
| Sworn of the Privy Council | 7 Nov. 1873 |
| Minister of Marine and Fisheries   *Ministry Resigned* | 7 Nov. 1873 – 16 Oct. 1878 |
| Acting Minister of Justice and Attorney General | 1 June 1874 – 7 July 1874 |

**SMITH, Hon. Sir Frank**
13 Mar. 1822 – 17 Jan. 1901

| | |
|---|---|
| Member of the Senate | 2 Feb. 1871 – 17 Jan. 1901 |
| Sworn of the Privy Council | 2 Aug. 1882 |
| Minister without Portfolio | 2 Aug. 1882 – 13 Aug. 1891 |
| Minister of Public Works | 14 Aug. 1891 – 10 Jan. 1892 |
| Minister without Portfolio   *Ministry Resigned* | 11 Jan. 1892 – 10 July 1896 |
| Acting Controller of Customs | 6 Jan. 1896 – 14 Jan. 1896 |

**SMITH, Hon. Sidney Earle**
9 Mar. 1897 – 17 Mar. 1959

| | |
|---|---|
| Sworn of the Privy Council | 13 Sept. 1957 |
| Secretary of State for External Affairs | 13 Sept. 1957 – 17 Mar. 1959 |

**SPINNEY, Hon. Edgar Keith**
26 Jan. 1851 – 12 May 1926

| | |
|---|---|
| Sworn of the Privy Council | 13 July 1920 |
| Minister without Portfolio   *Ministry Resigned* | 13 July 1920 – 28 Dec. 1921 |

**STANBURY, Hon. Robert Douglas George**
26 Oct. 1929 –

| | |
|---|---|
| Parliamentary Secretary – Secretary of State of Canada | 30 Aug. 1968 – 19 Oct. 1969 |
| Sworn of the Privy Council | 20 Oct. 1969 |
| Minister without Portfolio | 20 Oct. 1969 – 11 Aug. 1971 |
| Minister of Communications | 12 Aug. 1971 – 26 Nov. 1972 |
| Minister of National Revenue | 27 Nov. 1972 – 7 Aug. 1974 |

**STARR, Hon. Michael**
14 Nov. 1910 –

| | |
|---|---|
| Sworn of the Privy Council | 21 June 1957 |
| Minister of Labour   *Ministry Resigned* | 21 June 1957 – 21 Apr. 1963 |

## STEVENS, Hon. Henry Herbert
8 Dec. 1878 – 14 June 1973

| | | |
|---|---|---|
| Sworn of the Privy Council | 21 Sept. 1921 | |
| Minister of Trade and Commerce   *Ministry Resigned* | 21 Sept. 1921 – | 28 Dec. 1921 |
| Acting Minister of Agriculture | 29 June 1926 – | 12 July 1926 |
| Acting Minister of Customs and Excise | 29 June 1926 – | 12 July 1926 |
| Acting Superintendent-General of Indian Affairs | 29 June 1926 – | 12 July 1926 |
| Acting Minister of the Interior | 29 June 1926 – | 12 July 1926 |
| Acting Minister of Mines | 29 June 1926 – | 12 July 1926 |
| Acting Minister of Trade and Commerce | 29 June 1926 – | 12 July 1926 |
| Minister of Customs and Excise   *Ministry Resigned* | 13 July 1926 – | 24 Sept. 1926 |
| Minister of Trade and Commerce | 7 Aug. 1930 – | 26 Oct. 1934 |

## STEVENS, Hon. Sinclair McKnight
11 Feb. 1927 –

| | | |
|---|---|---|
| Sworn of the Privy Council | 4 June 1979 | |
| President of the Treasury Board   *Ministry Resigned* | 4 June 1979 – | 2 Mar. 1980 |

## STEWART, Hon. Charles
26 Aug. 1868 – 6 Dec. 1946

| | | |
|---|---|---|
| Sworn of the Privy Council | 29 Dec. 1921 | |
| Superintendent-General of Indian Affairs   *Ministry Resigned* | 29 Dec. 1921 – | 28 June 1926 |
| Minister of the Interior   *Ministry Resigned* | 29 Dec. 1921 – | 28 June 1926 |
| Minister of Mines   *Ministry Resigned* | 29 Dec. 1921 – | 28 June 1926 |
| Acting Minister of Immigration and Colonization | 20 Feb. 1922 – | 16 Aug. 1923 |
| Acting Minister of Immigration and Colonization | 13 Nov. 1925 – | 28 June 1926 |
| Superintendent-General of Indian Affairs | 25 Sept. 1926 – | 18 June 1930 |
| Minister of the Interior   *Ministry Resigned* | 25 Sept. 1926 – | 6 Aug. 1930 |
| Minister of Mines   *Ministry Resigned* | 25 Sept. 1926 – | 6 Aug. 1930 |
| Acting Minister of Immigration and Colonization | 30 Dec. 1929 – | 26 June 1930 |
| Acting Superintendent-General of Indian Affairs | 19 June 1930 – | 26 June 1930 |

## STEWART, Hon. Hugh Alexander
29 Sept. 1871 – 4 Sept. 1956

| | | |
|---|---|---|
| Sworn of the Privy Council | 7 Aug. 1930 | |
| Minister of Public Works   *Ministry Resigned* | 7 Aug. 1930 – | 22 Oct. 1935 |

**STEWART, Hon. John Alexander**
1867 – 7 Oct. 1922

| | | |
|---|---|---|
| Sworn of the Privy Council | 21 Sept. 1921 | |
| Minister of Railways and Canals   *Ministry Resigned* | 21 Sept. 1921 – 28 Dec. 1921 | |

**STIRLING, Hon. Grote**
31 July 1875 – 18 Jan. 1953

| | | |
|---|---|---|
| Sworn of the Privy Council | 17 Nov. 1934 | |
| Minister of National Defence   *Ministry Resigned* | 17 Nov. 1934 – 22 Oct. 1935 | |
| Acting Minister of Fisheries | 17 Nov. 1934 – 13 Aug. 1935 | |

**ST-LAURENT, Rt. Hon. Louis Stephen**
1 Feb. 1882 – 25 July 1973

| | | |
|---|---|---|
| Sworn of the Privy Council | 10 Dec. 1941 | |
| Minister of Justice and Attorney General | 10 Dec. 1941 – 9 Dec. 1946 | |
| Member of the United Kingdom Privy Council | 1 Jan. 1946 | |
| Secretary of State for External Affairs | 4 Sept. 1946 – 9 Sept. 1948 | |
| Acting Minister of Justice and Attorney General | 1 July 1948 – 9 Sept. 1948 | |
| Minister of Justice and Attorney General   *Ministry Resigned* | 10 Sept. 1948 – 14 Nov. 1948 | |
| Prime Minister   *Ministry Resigned* | 15 Nov. 1948 – 20 June 1957 | |
| President of the Privy Council | 15 Nov. 1948 – 24 Apr. 1957 | |

**SUTHERLAND, Hon. Donald**
8 Apr. 1863 – 1 Jan. 1949

| | | |
|---|---|---|
| Sworn of the Privy Council | 13 July 1926 | |
| Minister without Portfolio   *Ministry Resigned* | 13 July 1926 – 24 Sept. 1926 | |
| Member of the Senate | 20 July 1935 – 1 Jan. 1949 | |

**SUTHERLAND, Hon. Donald Matheson**
3 Dec. 1879 – 5 June 1970

| | | |
|---|---|---|
| Sworn of the Privy Council | 7 Aug. 1930 | |
| Minister of National Defence | 7 Aug. 1930 – 16 Nov. 1934 | |
| Minister of Pensions and National Health   *Ministry Resigned* | 17 Nov. 1934 – 22 Oct. 1935 | |

**SUTHERLAND, Hon. James**
17 July 1849 – 3 May 1905

| | | |
|---|---|---|
| Sworn of the Privy Council | 30 Sept. 1899 | |
| Minister without Portfolio | 30 Sept. 1899 – 14 Jan. 1902 | |
| Minister of Marine and Fisheries | 15 Jan. 1902 – 10 Nov. 1902 | |
| Minister of Public Works | 11 Nov. 1902 – 3 May 1905 | |

**TAILLON, Hon. Sir Louis-Olivier**
26 Sept. 1840 – 25 Apr. 1923

| | | | |
|---|---|---|---|
| Sworn of the Privy Council | 1 May 1896 | | |
| Postmaster General *Ministry Resigned* | 1 May 1896 – | 10 July 1896 |

**TARTE, Hon. Joseph Israël**
11 Jan. 1848 – 18 Dec. 1907

| | | | |
|---|---|---|---|
| Sworn of the Privy Council | 13 July 1896 | | |
| Minister of Public Works | 13 July 1896 – | 21 Oct. 1902 |

**TEILLET, Hon. Roger Joseph**
21 Aug. 1912 –

| | | | |
|---|---|---|---|
| Sworn of the Privy Council | 22 Apr. 1963 | | |
| Minister of Veterans Affairs | 22 Apr. 1963 – | 5 July 1968 |

**TEMPLEMAN, Hon. William**
28 Sept. 1842 – 15 Nov. 1914

| | | | |
|---|---|---|---|
| Member of the Senate | 18 Nov. 1897 – | 16 Feb. 1906 |
| Sworn of the Privy Council | 25 Feb. 1902 | | |
| Minister without Portfolio | 25 Feb. 1902 – | 5 Feb. 1906 |
| Minister of Inland Revenue *Ministry Resigned* | 6 Feb. 1906 – | 9 Oct. 1911 |
| Minister of Mines *Ministry Resigned* | 3 May 1907 – | 9 Oct. 1911 |

**THOMPSON, Rt. Hon. Sir John Sparrow David**
10 Nov. 1844 – 12 Dec. 1894

| | | | |
|---|---|---|---|
| Sworn of the Privy Council | 26 Sept. 1885 | | |
| Minister of Justice and Attorney General *Ministry Dissolved* | 26 Sept. 1885 – | 11 Dec. 1894 |
| Prime Minister *Ministry Dissolved* | 5 Dec. 1892 – | 11 Dec. 1894 |
| Member of the United Kingdom Privy Council | 12 Dec. 1894 | | |

**THORSON, Hon. Joseph Thorarinn**
15 Mar. 1889 –

| | | | |
|---|---|---|---|
| Sworn of the Privy Council | 11 June 1941 | | |
| Minister of National War Services | 11 June 1941 – | 5 Oct. 1942 |

## TILLEY, Hon. Sir Samuel Leonard
8 May 1818 – 25 June 1896

| | |
|---|---|
| Sworn of the Privy Council | 1 July 1867 |
| Minister of Customs | 1 July 1867 – 21 Feb. 1873 |
| Minister of Finance   *Ministry Resigned* | 22 Feb. 1873 – 6 Nov. 1873 |
| Minister of Finance | 17 Oct. 1878 – 19 May 1879 |
| Minister of Finance and Receiver General | 20 May 1879 – 10 Nov. 1885 |

## TISDALE, Hon. David
8 Sept. 1835 – 31 Mar. 1911

| | |
|---|---|
| Sworn of the Privy Council | 2 May 1896 |
| Minister of Militia and Defence   *Ministry Resigned* | 2 May 1896 – 10 July 1896 |

## TOLMIE, Hon. Simon Fraser
25 Jan. 1867 – 13 Oct. 1937

| | |
|---|---|
| Sworn of the Privy Council | 12 Aug. 1919 |
| Minister of Agriculture   *Ministry Resigned* | 12 Aug. 1919 – 28 Dec. 1921 |
| Minister of Agriculture   *Ministry Resigned* | 13 July 1926 – 24 Sept. 1926 |

## TREMBLAY, Hon. René
12 Nov. 1922 – 22 Jan. 1968

| | |
|---|---|
| Sworn of the Privy Council | 22 Apr. 1963 |
| Minister without Portfolio | 22 Apr. 1963 – 2 Feb. 1964 |
| Minister of Citizenship and Immigration | 3 Feb. 1964 – 14 Feb. 1965 |
| Postmaster General | 15 Feb. 1965 – 17 Dec. 1965 |

## TRUDEAU, Rt. Hon. Pierre Elliott
18 Oct. 1919 –

| | |
|---|---|
| Parliamentary Secretary – Prime Minister | 7 Jan. 1966 – 3 Apr. 1967 |
| Sworn of the Privy Council | 4 Apr. 1967 |
| Minister of Justice and Attorney General | 4 Apr. 1967 – 5 July 1968 |
| Acting President of the Privy Council | 11 Mar. 1968 – 1 May 1968 |
| Prime Minister   *Ministry Resigned* | 20 Apr. 1968 – 3 June 1979 |
| Prime Minister | 3 Mar. 1980 – |

**TUPPER, Rt. Hon. Sir Charles**

2 July 1821 – 30 Oct. 1915

| | | | | |
|---|---|---|---|---|
| Sworn of the Privy Council | 21 June 1870 | | | |
| President of the Privy Council | 21 June 1870 | – | 1 July | 1872 |
| Minister of Inland Revenue | 2 July 1872 | – | 3 Mar. | 1873 |
| Minister of Customs *Ministry Resigned* | 22 Feb. 1873 | – | 6 Nov. | 1873 |
| Minister of Public Works | 17 Oct. 1878 | – | 19 May | 1879 |
| Minister of Railways and Canals | 20 May 1879 | – | 28 May | 1884 |
| Minister of Finance and Receiver General | 27 Jan. 1887 | – | 22 May | 1888 |
| Secretary of State of Canada *Ministry Resigned* | 15 Jan. 1896 | – | 10 July | 1896 |
| Prime Minister | 1 May 1896 | – | 7 July | 1896 |
| Member of the United Kingdom Privy Council | 19 Oct. 1908 | | | |

**TUPPER, Hon. Sir Charles Hibbert**

3 Aug. 1855 – 30 Mar. 1927

| | | | | |
|---|---|---|---|---|
| Sworn of the Privy Council | 1 June 1888 | | | |
| Minister of Marine and Fisheries *Ministry Dissolved* | 1 June 1888 | – | 20 Dec. | 1894 |
| Minister of Justice and Attorney General | 21 Dec. 1894 | – | 5 Jan. | 1896 |
| Solicitor General of Canada *Ministry Resigned* | 1 May 1896 | – | 10 July | 1896 |

**TURNER, Hon. John Napier**

7 June 1929 –

| | | | | |
|---|---|---|---|---|
| Parliamentary Secretary – Northern Affairs and National Resources | 14 May 1963 | – | 8 Sept. | 1965 |
| Sworn of the Privy Council | 18 Dec. 1965 | | | |
| Minister without Portfolio | 18 Dec. 1965 | – | 3 Apr. | 1967 |
| Registrar General of Canada | 4 Apr. 1967 | – | 20 Dec. | 1967 |
| Minister of Consumer and Corporate Affairs | 21 Dec. 1967 | – | 5 July | 1968 |
| Solicitor General of Canada | 20 Apr. 1968 | – | 5 July | 1968 |
| Minister of Justice and Attorney General | 6 July 1968 | – | 27 Jan. | 1972 |
| Minister of Finance | 28 Jan. 1972 | – | 9 Sept. | 1975 |

**VAIL, Hon. William Berrian**

29 Dec. 1823 – 10 Apr. 1904

| | | | | |
|---|---|---|---|---|
| Sworn of the Privy Council | 30 Sept. 1874 | | | |
| Minister of Militia and Defence | 30 Sept. 1874 | – | 20 Jan. | 1878 |

**VENIOT, Hon. Peter John**
4 Oct. 1863 – 6 July 1936

| | | |
|---|---|---|
| Sworn of the Privy Council | 25 Sept. 1926 | |
| Postmaster General   *Ministry Resigned* | 25 Sept. 1926 – | 1 Aug.  1930 |

**WALKER, Hon. David James**
10 May 1905 –

| | | |
|---|---|---|
| Parliamentary Assistant – Justice | 19 Aug.  1957 – | 1 Feb.  1958 |
| Sworn of the Privy Council | 20 Aug.  1959 | |
| Minister of Public Works | 20 Aug.  1959 – | 12 July  1962 |

**WALLACE, Hon. Nathaniel Clarke**
21 May 1844 – 8 Oct. 1901

| | | |
|---|---|---|
| Controller of Customs | 5 Dec.  1892 – | 13 Dec.  1895 |

**WEIR, Hon. Robert**
5 Dec. 1882 – 7 Mar. 1939

| | | |
|---|---|---|
| Sworn of the Privy Council | 8 Aug.  1930 | |
| Minister of Agriculture   *Ministry Resigned* | 8 Aug.  1930 – | 22 Oct.  1935 |

**WHELAN, Hon. Eugene Francis**
11 July 1924 –

| | | |
|---|---|---|
| Parliamentary Secretary – Fisheries | 30 Aug.  1968 – | 31 Mar.  1969 |
| Parliamentary Secretary – Fisheries and Forestry | 1 Apr.  1969 – | 30 Sept. 1970 |
| Sworn of the Privy Council | 27 Nov.  1972 | |
| Minister of Agriculture   *Ministry Resigned* | 27 Nov.  1972 – | 3 June 1979 |
| Minister of Agriculture | 3 Mar.  1980 – | |

**WHITE, Hon. Thomas**
7 Aug. 1830 – 21 Apr. 1888

| | | |
|---|---|---|
| Sworn of the Privy Council | 5 Apr.  1885 | |
| Minister of the Interior | 5 Aug.  1885 – | 21 Apr.  1888 |
| Superintendent-General of Indian Affairs | 3 Oct.  1887 – | 21 Apr.  1888 |

**WHITE, Rt. Hon. Sir William Thomas**
13 Nov. 1866 – 11 Feb. 1955

| | | |
|---|---|---|
| Sworn of the Privy Council | 10 Oct.  1911 | |
| Minister of Finance and Receiver General | 10 Oct.  1911 – | 1 Aug.  1919 |
| Member of the United Kingdom Privy Council | 22 Jan.  1920 – | |

**WIGMORE, Hon. Rupert Wilson**
10 May 1873 – 3 Apr. 1939

| | | |
|---|---|---|
| Sworn of the Privy Council | 13 July 1920 | |
| Minister of Customs and Inland Revenue | 13 July 1920 – | 3 June 1921 |
| Minister of Customs and Excise | 4 June 1921 – | 20 Sept. 1921 |

**WILMOT, Hon. Robert Duncan**
16 Oct. 1809 – 13 Feb. 1891

| | | |
|---|---|---|
| Member of the Senate | 23 Oct. 1867 – | 10 Feb. 1880 |
| Sworn of the Privy Council | 8 Nov. 1878 | |
| Minister without Portfolio | 8 Nov. 1878 – | 10 Feb. 1880 |

**WILSON, Hon. James Robert**
16 Sept. 1866 – 3 Apr. 1941

| | | |
|---|---|---|
| Sworn of the Privy Council | 26 Sept. 1921 | |
| Minister without Portfolio   *Ministry Resigned* | 26 Sept. 1921 – | 28 Dec. 1921 |

**WILSON, Hon. Michael H.**
4 Nov. 1937 –

| | | |
|---|---|---|
| Sworn of the Privy Council | 4 June 1979 | |
| Minister of State (International Trade)   *Ministry Resigned* | 4 June 1979 – | 2 Mar. 1980 |

**WINTERS, Hon. Robert Henry**
18 Aug. 1910 – 10 Oct. 1969

| | | |
|---|---|---|
| Parliamentary Assistant – National Revenue | 30 Oct. 1947 – | 10 June 1948 |
| Parliamentary Assistant – Transport | 11 June 1948 – | 14 Nov. 1948 |
| Sworn of the Privy Council | 15 Nov. 1948 | |
| Minister of Reconstruction and Supply | 15 Nov. 1948 – | 17 Jan. 1950 |
| Minister of Resources and Development | 18 Jan. 1950 – | 16 Sept. 1953 |
| Minister of Public Works   *Ministry Resigned* | 17 Sept. 1953 – | 20 June 1957 |
| Minister of Trade and Commerce | 4 Jan. 1966 – | 29 Mar. 1968 |

**WISE, Hon. John**
12 Dec. 1935 –

| | | |
|---|---|---|
| Sworn of the Privy Council | 4 June 1979 | |
| Minister of Agriculture   *Ministry Resigned* | 4 June 1979 – | 2 Mar. 1980 |

**WOOD, Hon. John Fisher**
12 Oct. 1852 – 14 Mar. 1899

| | |
|---|---|
| Controller of Inland Revenue | 5 Dec. 1892 – 16 Dec. 1895 |
| Acting Controller of Customs | 14 Dec. 1895 – 16 Dec. 1895 |
| Controller of Customs | 17 Dec. 1895 – 5 Jan. 1896 |
| Sworn of the Privy Council | 24 Dec. 1895 |
| Controller of Customs *Ministry Resigned* | 15 Jan. 1896 – 10 July 1896 |

# Index

Abbott, Anthony Chisholm, 153, 154, 161, 162, 173, 174, 223.
Abbott, Douglas Charles, 95, 99, 100, 101, 102, 105, 107, 109, 223.
Abbott, Sir John Joseph Caldwell, 19, 21, 22, 23, 26, 223.
Aikins, James Cox, ix, 1, 2, 5, 15, 19, 20, 223.
Alexander, Lincoln, 195, 224.
Allmand, William Warren, 153, 157, 158, 165, 166, 224.
Anderson, Hugh, 179.
Andras, Robert Knight, 153, 154, 159, 160, 167, 168, 169, 170, 224.
Andres, William, 191.
Angers, Sir Auguste Réal, 25, 29, 35, 224.
Appolloni, Ursula, 217.
Archibald, Sir Adams George, 5, 224.
Argue, Hazen, 209, 210, 225.
Asselin, Martial, 123, 197, 198, 225.
Atkey, Ronald George, 193, 225.
Austin, Jacob, 211, 225.
Axworthy, Lloyd, 203, 225.
Aylesworth, Sir Allen Bristol, 41, 42, 43, 44, 225.

Baby, Louis François Georges, 15, 226.
Badanai, Hubert, 147, 151.
Baker, George S., 177, 185.
Baker, Loran Ellis, 117.
Baker, Walter David, 195, 196, 226.
Balcer, Léon, 123, 125, 127, 128, 226.
Baldwin, Gerald William, 133.
Ballantyne, Charles Colquhoun, 51, 57, 59, 60, 65, 226.
Basford, Stanley Ronald, 153, 154, 157, 158, 161, 162, 165, 167, 168, 226.
Baxter, John Babington Macaulay, 63, 227.
Beatty, Perrin, 197, 198, 227.
Béchard, Albert, 151, 181, 187.
Beer, Bruce Silas, 147, 175.
Bégin, Monique, 159, 161, 162, 177, 205, 227.
Béland, Henri Sévérin, 43, 73, 227.
Bell, Richard Albert, 121, 129, 131, 227.
Bell, Thomas Miller, 129, 131.
Belley, Louis-de-Gonzague, 65, 227.
Belzile, Gleason, 105, 115.
Benidickson, William Moore, 115, 119, 139, 228.
Bennett, Colin Emerson, 119.
Bennett, Richard Bedford, 65, 77, 79, 81, 82, 89, 90, 91, 96, 228.
Benson, Edgar John, 141, 142, 143, 144, 147, 155, 156, 159, 167, 168, 228.
Bernier, Michel Esdras, 39, 229.
Bertrand, Ernest, 95, 96, 101, 111, 229.
Black, William Anderson, 79, 229.
Blair, Adam Johnston Fergusson, 3, 229.
Blair, Andrew George, 43, 229.
Blais, Jean-Jacques, 161, 162, 165, 185, 207, 229.
Blake, Dominick Edward, 9, 10, 11, 12, 230.
Blaker, Roderick, 189.
Blanchette, Joseph Adéodat, 117.

Blondin, Pierre Édouard, 47, 48, 49, 51, 52, 57, 65, 230.
Blouin, Gustave, 185, 187.
Bockstael, Robert, 219.
Boivin, Georges-Henri, 69, 230.
Borden, Sir Frederick William, 41, 230.
Borden, Sir Robert Laird, vi, ix, 47, 48, 49, 55, 56, 64, 230.
Bosley, John, 201.
Bostock, Hewitt, 69, 71, 231.
Bourget, Maurice, 119.
Bowell, Sir Mackenzie, 13, 21, 22, 23, 27, 29, 30, 31, 36, 231.
Bradley, Frederick Gordon, 113, 231.
Breau, Herb, 177, 181.
Bridges, Hedley Francis Gregory, 95, 231.
Bristol, Edmund James, 67, 231.
Brodeur, Louis-Philippe, 39, 40, 41, 232.
Brooks, Alfred Johnson, 123, 127, 232.
Browne, William Joseph, 127, 128, 232.
Buchanan, J. Judd, 157, 158, 163, 164, 167, 179, 232.
Bujold, Rémi, 213.
Bureau, Jacques, 45, 69, 232.
Burpee, Isaac, 7, 233.
Burrell, Martin, 47, 55, 57, 59, 60, 233.
Bussières, Pierre, 177, 187, 209, 210, 233.
Byrne, James Allen, 149, 151, 189.

Caccia, Charles L., 183, 189, 205, 233.
Cadieux, Léo Alphonse Joseph, 139, 140, 159, 233.
Cafik, Norman A., 173, 174, 175, 183, 234.
Cahan, Charles Hazlitt, 93, 234.
Calder, James Alexander, 55, 57, 63, 64, 65, 66, 234.
Campagnolo, Iona, 171, 172, 179, 234.
Campbell, Sir Alexander, 1, 3, 4, 15, 16, 17, 18, 19, 20, 235.
Campbell, Coline, 183, 187.
Campbell, John, 219.
Campbell, W. Bennett, 207, 235.
Campney, Ralph Osborne, 111, 112, 113, 114, 117, 235.
Cannon, Lucien, 75, 87, 235.
Cantin, Jean-Charles, 149, 151, 181, 189.
Cardiff, Lewis Elston, 131, 133.
Cardin, Louis Joseph Lucien, 115, 139, 140, 141, 142, 236.
Cardin, Pierre Joseph Arthur, 71, 85, 86, 103, 104, 236.
Carling, Sir John, 13, 17, 18, 21, 27, 236.
Caron, Alexis, 149, 151.
Caron, Sir Joseph Philippe René Adolphe, 15, 21, 22, 23, 25, 31, 236.
Caron, Yves, 175.
Carroll, Henry George, 45, 236.
Carter, Chesley William, 151.
Cartier, Sir George Étienne, 3, 237.
Cartwright, Sir Richard John, 7, 43, 237.

Carvell, Frank Broadstreet, 59, 237.
Casgrain, Pierre-François, 103, 237.
Casgrain, Thomas Chase, 49, 237.
Cashin, Richard Joseph, 147, 179.
Casselman, Jean, 133.
Cauchon, Joseph Édouard, 7, 9, 10, 237.
Chambers, Egan, 133.
Chapais, Jean-Charles, 1, 2, 5, 238.
Chapleau, Sir Joseph Adolphe, 19, 21, 23, 24, 238.
Chaplin, James Dew, 81, 238.
Charlton, John Alpheus, 127, 131.
Chénier, Raymond, 215.
Chevrier, Lionel, 103, 105, 111, 113, 114, 139, 238.
Chrétien, Joseph Jacques Jean, 141, 145, 146, 147, 151, 155, 157, 158, 161, 162, 167, 168, 205, 206, 238.
Christie, David, 9, 239.
Churchill, Gordon, 123, 127, 128, 239.
Clark, Charles Joseph, v, 193, 204, 239.
Clark, Hugh, 51, 59, 60, 61, 239.
Claxton, Brooke, 99, 101, 102, 107, 111, 239.
Clermont, Gaston, 181, 189.
Cobbe, Gerald Richard, 185.
Cochrane, Francis, 51, 59, 239.
Coderre, Louis, 49, 51, 240.
Coffin, Thomas, 9, 240.
Colby, Charles Carrol, 17, 240.
Collonette, David, 185, 217.
Comtois, Joseph-Roland, 175, 179, 183.
Comtois, Paul, 123, 240.
Connolly, John Joseph, 143, 145, 240.
Cooper, George, 199.
Copp, Arthur Bliss, 73, 240.
Corbin, Eymard Georges, 177, 179.
Corriveau, Léopold, 175.
Cosgrove, Paul James, 205, 240.
Costigan, John, 15, 21, 27, 31, 35, 241.
Côté, Alcide, 111, 241.
Côté, Florian, 175.
Côté, Joseph Julien Jean-Pierre, 141, 153, 161, 162, 169, 170, 241.
Côté, Paul-Émile, 105, 117.
Courtemanche, Henri, 125, 241.
Crerar, Thomas Alexander, 55, 85, 95, 96, 97, 98, 242.
Crombie, David, 195, 242.
Crosbie, John C., 193, 242.
Crothers, Thomas Wilson, 49, 57, 242.
Cullen, Jack Sydney George, 159, 160, 161, 162, 177, 179, 183, 242.
Curran, John Joseph, 27, 33, 243.
Cyr, Alexandre, 185.

Daly, Thomas Mayne, 21, 25, 29, 31, 243.
Dandurand, Raoul, 73, 87, 105, 243.
Danson, Barnett Jerome, 159, 167, 168, 185, 243.
Daudlin, Robert, 187, 219.
Davies, Sir Louis Henry, 41, 243.
Davis, Jack, 147, 149, 151, 155, 156, 169, 170, 177, 244.
Dawson, Dennis M., 181, 213.
De Bané, Pierre, 165, 175, 177, 191, 205, 206, 211, 212, 244.
de Cotret, Robert R., 195, 196, 244.
Demers, Yves, 185, 217.
Deniger, Pierre, 219.
Denis, Azellus, 141, 244.
Deschatelets, Jean-Paul, 141, 244.
Desjardins, Alphonse, 31, 37, 245.
Desmarais, Louis, 215.
Dewdney, Edgar, 13, 15, 21, 245.
Dickey, Arthur Rupert, 29, 31, 32, 35, 245.
Dickey, John Horace, 115.
Diefenbaker, John George, v, 121, 122, 125, 138, 245.
Dinsdale, Walter Gilbert, 123, 125, 129, 135, 245.
Dionne, Maurice Adrien, 183.
Dobell, Richard Reid, 45, 246.
Doherty, Charles Joseph, 47, 57, 65, 246.
Dorion, Sir Antoine-Aimé, 9, 246.
Dorion, Noël, 125, 126, 246.
Douglas, Crawford, 175.
Drayton, Sir Henry Lumley, 55, 63, 67, 77, 79, 81, 246.
Drury, Charles Mills, 137, 139, 153, 155, 157, 158, 159, 163, 164, 165, 166, 167, 168, 247.
Dubé, Jean-Eudes, 159, 163, 167, 168, 247.
Duclos, Louis, 177, 213.
Dunkin, Christopher, 1, 247.
Dunning, Charles Avery, 73, 83, 85, 86, 95, 247.
Dupont, Raymond, 175, 183, 219.
Dupras, Maurice, 177.
Dupré, Maurice, 93, 247.
Dupuis, Yvon, 145, 151, 248.
Duquet, Gérard, 189.
Duranleau, Alfred, 89, 91, 248.

Edwards, John Wesley, 63, 248.
Elliott, John Campbell, 71, 72, 73, 74, 85, 101, 248.
Emmerson, Henry Robert, 43, 248.
English, Roland Léo, 131.
Epp, Arthur Jacob, 195, 248.
Ernst, William Gordon, 89, 249.
Erola, Judy, 211, 212, 249.
Euler, William Daum, 83, 84, 85, 103, 249.
Evans, John, 215.

Fairclough, Ellen Louks, 121, 122, 125, 126, 249.
Faulkner, James Hugh, 157, 163, 164, 187, 249.

Fauteux, Guillaume André, 67, 81, 249.
Favreau, Guy, 137, 138, 139, 140, 141, 142, 250.
Fennell, Scott, 199.
Ferguson, Donald, 29, 33, 37, 250.
Ferguson, Ralph, 221.
Fielding, William Stevens, 39, 43, 69, 250.
Fisher, Sydney Arthur, 39, 250.
Fitzpatrick, Sir Charles, 41, 45, 46, 250.
Fleming, Donald Methuen, 121, 122, 123, 251.
Fleming, James Sydney Clark, 175, 177, 209, 210, 251.
Flemming, Hugh John, 123, 124, 125, 126, 251.
Flynn, Jacques, 123, 195, 196, 197, 198, 251.
Forest, Yves, 185.
Forke, Robert, 83, 251.
Foster, Sir George Eulas, 13, 15, 16, 21, 25, 29, 35, 51, 59, 67, 252.
Foster, Maurice Brydon, 177, 185.
Foster, Walter Edward, 73, 252.
Fournier, Alphonse, 103, 111, 252.
Fournier, Télesphore, 7, 8, 9, 10, 252.
Fox, Francis, 165, 166, 181, 203, 204, 207, 208, 252.
Francis, Cyril Lloyd, 189, 191.
Fraser, John Allen, 193, 194, 195, 196, 253.
Frith, Doug, 217.
Fulton, Edmund Davie, 121, 123, 124, 125, 253.

Gagnon, Onésime, 93, 253.
Galt, Sir Alexander Tilloch, 1, 253.
Gardiner, James Garfield, 95, 96, 101, 102, 109, 253.
Garland, John Richard, 141, 253.
Garson, Stuart Sinclair, 109, 113, 254.
Gauthier, Jean-Robert, 191.
Geary, George Reginald, 89, 254.
Gendron, Lucien Henri, 91, 254.
Gendron, Rosaire, 183.
Geoffrion, Christophe Alphonse, 45, 254.
Geoffrion, Félix, 7, 254.
Gibbs, Thomas Nicholson, 1, 3, 5, 6, 254.
Gibson, Colin William George, 99, 100, 101, 102, 103, 109, 113, 114, 255.
Gilbault, Jacques, 183.
Gillespie, Alastair William, 155, 157, 158, 163, 164, 189, 255.
Glen, James Allison, 97, 255.
Gobeil, Samuel, 91, 255.
Goodale, Ralph, 185, 189.
Gordon, George Newcombe, 69, 255.
Gordon, Walter Lockhart, 137, 138, 141, 145, 146, 256.
Gordon, Wesley Ashton, 89, 90, 91, 92, 256.
Gouin, Sir Jean Lomer, 71, 256.
Goyer, Jean-Pierre, 165, 166, 177, 256.
Grafftey, William Heward, 131, 195, 197, 198, 256.
Graham, George Perry, 43, 71, 72, 73, 74, 257.

Granger, Charles Ronald McKay, 145, 147, 169, 257.
Gray, Herbert Eser, 153, 161, 162, 169, 170, 179, 205, 206, 257.
Green, Howard Charles, 121, 125, 126, 257.
Greene, John James, 137, 153, 154, 155, 258.
Gregg, Milton Fowler, 95, 96, 105, 109, 113, 114, 258.
Groos, David Walter, 183.
Guay, Joseph-Philippe, 161, 162, 169, 170, 173, 174, 187, 189, 258.
Guay, Raynald J.A., 181, 185.
Guilbault, Jacques, 187.
Gurbin, Gary, 199.
Guthrie, Hugh, 53, 57, 59, 60, 61, 65, 67, 77, 79, 89, 258.

Haggart, John Graham, 17, 23, 24, 27, 31, 37, 259.
Hahn, David George, 149.
Haidasz, Stanley, 147, 149, 171, 175, 179, 183, 259.
Haig, John Thomas, 127, 259.
Hales, Alfred Dryden, 131.
Halpenny, George Ernest, 125, 127, 128, 129, 259.
Hamilton, Francis Alvin George, 121, 125, 126, 260.
Hamilton, John Borden, 127.
Hamilton, William McLean, 125, 260.
Hanson, Richard Burpee, 93, 260.
Hargrave, Herbert Thomas, 199.
Harkness, Douglas Scott, 121, 122, 123, 125, 126, 260.
Harquail, Maurice, 189, 191, 217.
Harris, Walter Edward, 105, 109, 110, 111, 119, 260.
Hays, Harry William, 137, 261.
Hazen, Sir John Douglas, 49, 58, 261.
Heenan, Peter, 85, 261.
Hees, George Harris, 127, 128, 261.
Hellyer, Paul Theodore, 111, 117, 139, 140, 143, 167, 261.
Henderson, George, 215.
Herbert, Harold Thomas, 185, 191.
Hervieux-Payette, Céline, 219.
Hincks, Sir Francis, 1, 261.
Hnatyshyn, Ramon John, 193, 194, 195, 196, 262.
Hodgson, Clayton Wesley, 129, 135.
Hogarth, Douglas Aird, 189.
Holmes, John Robert, 199.
Honey, Russell Clayton, 179, 187.
Hopkins, Leonard, 183.
Horner, John Henry, 157, 169, 170, 262.
Howard, Bruce Andrew Thomas, 181.
Howe, Clarence Decatur, 97, 98, 103, 104, 109, 110, 113, 114, 262.
Howe, Joseph, 1, 3, 4, 5, 262.
Howie, J. Robert, 197, 198, 262.
Howland, Sir William Pearce, 3, 263.
Hughes, Sir Samuel, 49, 263.
Huntington, Lucius Seth, 9, 10, 263.

Huntington, Ronald, 197, 198, 263.
Hyman, Charles Smith, 43, 45, 46, 263.

Ilsley, James Lorimer, 95, 96, 97, 101, 102, 263.
Irwin, Ron, 213, 215, 217.
Isabelle, Gaston Joseph, 177, 183.
Ives, William Bullock, 25, 31, 37, 264.

Jamieson, Donald Campbell, 153, 154, 157, 158, 163, 164, 165, 166, 167, 168, 264.
Janelle, Richard, 201.
Jarvis, Robert, 199.
Jarvis, William, 197, 198, 264.
Jean, Joseph, 103, 105, 113, 264.
Jelinek, Otto John, 201.
Jerome, James Alexander, 185.
Johnston, Donald, 207, 264.
Joly de Lotbinière, Sir Henri Gustave, 39, 45, 46, 264.
Jones, Alfred Gilpin, 9, 265.
Jones, George Burpee, 79, 265.
Jones, Henry Frank, 135.
Jorgenson, Warner Herbert, 131.
Joyal, Serge, 211, 219, 265.
Juneau, Pierre, 153, 265.

Kaplan, Robert Phillip, 179, 183, 207, 265.
Kay, William Frederic, ix, 87, 265.
Keefer, Francis Henry, 59, 265.
Kelly, Norman, 219.
Kemp, Sir Albert Edward, 49, 51, 52, 57, 67, 266.
Kennedy, William Costello, 73, 266.
Kenny, Sir Edward, 3, 5, 6, 266.
Kierans, Eric William, 153, 161, 266.
Kilgour, David, 201.
Killens, Thérèse, 221.
King, James Horace, 71, 85, 87, 88, 105, 266.
King, William Lyon Mackenzie, v, 41, 69, 70, 71, 76, 78, 83, 84, 85, 90, 95, 96, 101, 110, 267.
Kirk, Thomas Andrew Murray, 117.

Lachance, Claude-André, 181, 221.
Laflamme, Ovide, 147, 151, 175.
Laflamme, Toussaint Antoine Rodolphe, 7, 8, 9, 267.
Laflèche, Léo Richer, 101, 267.
Laing, Arthur, 139, 141, 142, 157, 158, 163, 164, 167, 267.
Laird, David, 7, 268.
Lajoie, Claude G., 175, 185.
Lalonde, Marc, 157, 159, 160, 173, 174, 203, 268.
LaMarsh, Julia Verlyn, 141, 142, 143, 268.
Lambert, Marcel Joseph Aimé, 127, 129, 133, 268.
Lamontagne, Gilles, 161, 169, 170, 177, 205, 207, 268.

Lamontagne, Maurice, 141, 142, 143, 269.
Landers, Michael, 181, 191.
Lang, Otto Emil, 153, 157, 158, 159, 160, 167, 168, 169, 170, 269.
Langevin, Sir Hector Louis, 1, 2, 3, 5, 6, 17, 18, 23, 269.
Langlois, Léopold, 117, 119.
Langlois, Paul, 175, 185.
Laniel, Gérald, 215.
Lapierre, Jean, 219.
Lapointe, Charles, 189, 209, 210, 269.
Lapointe, Ernest, 71, 72, 73, 74, 85, 97, 103, 270.
Lapointe, Hugues, 107, 111, 112, 113, 114, 115, 117, 270.
LaSalle, Roch, 197, 270.
Laurier, Sir Wilfrid, 7, 39, 40, 41, 43, 48, 270.
Lawrence, Allan Frederick, 193, 194, 197, 198, 271.
Lawson, James Earl, 91, 271.
Leblanc, Fernand E., 177, 181.
LeBlanc, Roméo, 155, 156, 157, 171, 172, 203, 271.
Lee, Arthur John, 175, 189.
Lefebvre, Thomas-Henri, 189.
Lemieux, Rodolphe, 41, 42, 43, 44, 45, 46, 271.
Lesage, Jean, 111, 113, 114, 115, 271.
Lessard, Marcel, 163, 175, 272.
Letellier de St-Just, Luc, 7, 272.
Lewis, Douglas, 201.
Loiselle, Bernard, 181, 215.
Loiselle, Gérard, 183, 189.
Lougheed, Sir James Alexander, 51, 59, 60, 63, 65, 67, 272.
Low, Thomas Andrew, 73, 74, 272.
Lumley, Edward, 179, 187, 209, 210, 272.

Macdonald, Angus Lewis, 99, 101, 273.
Macdonald, Angus Ronald, 129.
MacDonald, Daniel Joseph, 167, 207, 208, 273.
MacDonald, David S.H., 193, 194, 197, 198, 273.
Macdonald, Donald Alexander, 9, 273.
Macdonald, Donald Stovel, 147, 149, 155, 156, 159, 160, 161, 162, 169, 170, 273.
MacDonald, Edward Mortimer, 71, 73, 74, 274.
MacDonald, Flora Isabel, 193, 274.
Macdonald, Sir Hugh John, 35, 274.
Macdonald, Sir John Alexander, ix, 1, 2, 3, 8, 13, 14, 15, 17, 22, 274.
Macdonald, John Alexander, 81, 93, 275.
Macdonald, William Chisholm, 107.
Macdonald, William Ross, 113, 115, 116, 145, 275.
Macdonnell, James MacKerras, 127, 275.
MacEachen, Allan Joseph, 139, 140, 141, 155, 156, 159, 160, 161, 162, 203, 204, 275.
MacFarlane, Gus, 191.
MacGuigan, Mark, 181, 183, 203, 276.
Mackasey, Bryce Stuart, 145, 149, 153, 154, 159, 160, 161, 162, 169, 170, 171, 172, 276.

MacKay, Elmer MacIntosh, 195, 276.
Mackenzie, Alexander, 7, 8, 9, 14, 276.
Mackenzie, Ian Alistair, 83, 99, 100, 101, 102, 105, 277.
MacKinnon, James Angus, 95, 96, 97, 101, 103, 104, 105, 106, 109, 110, 115, 277.
MacLaren, David Laurence, 101, 277.
MacLaren, Murray, 91, 277.
MacLaren, Roy, 213.
Maclean, Alexander Kenneth, 59, 277.
MacLean, John Angus, 121, 125, 278.
MacLellan, Russell, 217, 221.
Macmillan, Cyrus, 83, 107, 278.
MacNaught, John Watson, 105, 115, 139, 143, 144, 145, 278.
Macpherson, Sir David Lewis, 15, 19, 20, 278.
Macquarrie, Heath Nelson, 131.
Mahoney, Patrick Morgan, 171, 179, 278.
Maine, Frank, 175, 185, 187.
Malcolm, James, 87, 278.
Maloney, Arthur, 129.
Manion, Robert James, 67, 77, 79, 91, 279.
Marceau, Gilles, 181, 187.
Marchand, Jean, 137, 138, 139, 155, 156, 157, 158, 159, 160, 163, 164, 167, 168, 169, 170, 279.
Marchand, Leonard Stephen, 155, 171, 172, 177, 179, 279.
Marler, George Carlyle, 113, 280.
Marler, Sir Herbert Meredith, 73, 280.
Martin, Alan A., 175, 179.
Martin, Paul Joseph James, 101, 103, 104, 105, 109, 111, 137, 165, 169, 170, 280.
Martineau, Paul, 123, 133, 280.
Martini, Quinto Antonio, 135.
Massey, Charles Vincent, 73, 280.
Masson, Louis François Rodrigue, 15, 16, 17, 281.
Masters, Jack, 213, 221.
Matheson, John Ross, 151, 185.
Matthews, Robert Charles, 91, 281.
Maybank, Ralph, 107, 117, 119.
Mayhew, Robert Wellington, 95, 105, 109, 281.
Mazankowski, Donald F., 197, 281.
McBain, James Alexander, 135.
McCann, James Joseph, 101, 102, 111, 112, 281.
McCauley, Gary, 213, 217.
McCleave, Robert Jardine, 133.
McCrossan, Paul, 199.
McCubbin, Robert, 105, 115.
McCurdy, Fleming Blanchard, 53, 61, 62, 65, 281.
McCusker, Emmet Andrew, 117.
McCutcheon, Malcolm Wallace, 127, 128, 282.
McDonald, Hugh, ix, 3, 4, 282.
McDonald, James, 15, 282.
McDougall, William, 5, 282.
McGee, Frank Charles, 127, 131, 282.
McGiverin, Harold Buchanan, 73, 282.
McGrath, James Aloysius, 133, 193, 282.

McIlraith, George James, 107, 115, 119, 139, 141, 142, 143, 144, 163, 164, 165, 283.
McIsaac, Joseph Clifford, 187, 189.
McKenzie, A. Daniel, 201.
McKenzie, Daniel Duncan, 73, 283.
McKinnon, Allan Bruce, 195, 196, 197, 198, 283.
McLarty, Norman Alexander, 97, 98, 101, 102, 103, 283.
McLelan, Archibald Woodbury, 13, 14, 15, 16, 17, 18, 284.
McMurray, Edward James, 73, 284.
McNaughton, Andrew George Latta, 99, 284.
McNulty, James Carroll Patrick, 181.
McPhillips, Albert Deburgo, 131.
McRae, Paul, 183, 185.
McWilliam, George Roy, 149, 151.
Meighen, Arthur, v, vi, 49, 51, 52, 53, 55, 57, 63, 64, 70, 77, 78, 79, 84, 93, 284.
Mewburn, Sydney Chilton, 57, 285.
Michaud, Joseph-Enoil, 95, 96, 97, 103, 285.
Mills, David, 7, 41, 285.
Milne, Ross, 175, 179.
Mitchell, Humphrey, 97, 109, 285.
Mitchell, Peter, 3, 285.
Monck, Lord, 2.
Monk, Frederick Debartzch, 51, 285.
Montague, Walter Humphries, 29, 31, 32, 33, 34, 35, 286.
Monteith, Jay Waldo, 123, 286.
Monty, Rodolphe, 67, 286.
Morand, Raymond Ducharme, 79, 81, 286.
Morris, Alexander, 3, 286.
Morris, Edmund Leverett, 133.
Motherwell, William Richard, 69, 83, 286.
Mousseau, Joseph-Alfred, 17, 18, 19, 286.
Mowat, Sir Oliver, 41, 287.
Mulock, Sir William, 42, 43, 287.
Mulock, William Pate, 101, 287.
Munro, John Carr, 147, 149, 151, 159, 160, 169, 170, 203, 287.
Murdock, James, 71, 287.
Murphy, Charles, 43, 71, 73, 288.
Murphy, Thomas Gerow, 89, 288.
Murta, Jack, 201.
Mutch, Leslie Alexander, 107, 119.

Nantel, Wilfrid Bruno, 47, 49, 288.
Nesbitt, Wallace Bickford, 129, 131, 133.
Nicholson, Aideen, 175, 189, 213, 217.
Nicholson, John Robert, 137, 138, 139, 140, 141, 142, 288.
Nielson, Erik H., 195, 288.
Normand, Louis-Philippe, 65, 288.
Nowlan, George Clyde, 121, 125, 126, 289.

O'Connell, Martin Patrick, 159, 171, 172, 187, 289.
O'Connor, John, 3, 4, 17, 18, 19, 20, 289.

O'Hurley, Raymond Joseph Michael, 121, 129, 289.
Oliver, Frank, 39, 41, 289.
Olivier, Jacques, 181.
Olson, Horace Andrew, 153, 203, 290.
Orange, Robert John, 177.
Ostiguy, Marcel, 213.
Otto, Steven, 189.
Ouellet, André, 153, 159, 161, 162, 163, 167, 177, 183, 203, 204, 205, 206, 290.
Ouimet, Joseph Aldéric, 23, 25, 29, 31, 290.

Pacaud, Lucien-Turcotte, 75, 76, 290.
Pallett, John Cameron, 133.
Paproski, Steven Eugene, 197, 198, 291.
Paquet, Eugène, 79, 291.
Parent, Gilbert, 191, 215.
Patenaude, Esioff-Léon, 47, 48, 49, 51, 77, 79, 291.
Paterson, William, 39, 45, 46, 291.
Patterson, James Colebrooke, 23, 25, 31, 32, 33, 291.
Pearkes, George Randolphe, 123, 292.
Pearsall, Jack, 177.
Pearson, Lester Bowles, v, 95, 109, 137, 154, 292.
Pelletier, Sir Charles Alphonse Pantaléon, 7, 292.
Pelletier, Gérard, 147, 153, 163, 164, 169, 170, 292.
Pelletier, Irénée, 175.
Pelletier, Louis-Philippe, 49, 292.
Pennell, Lawrence, 143, 144, 145, 146, 147, 293.
Penner, Keith, 179, 187.
Pepin, Jean-Luc, 137, 139, 140, 143, 145, 146, 151, 155, 156, 157, 158, 159, 160, 165, 166, 207, 293.
Perley, Sir George Halsey, 49, 51, 52, 79, 93, 293.
Perrault, Raymond Joseph, 165, 181, 183, 207, 294.
Peterson, Jim, 215, 217.
Pickersgill, John Whitney, 109, 113, 114, 143, 144, 294.
Pigeon, Louis-Joseph, 131.
Pinard, Roch, 111, 113, 115, 294.
Pinard, Yvon, 185, 205, 294.
Pope, James Colledge, 15, 294.
Pope, John Henry, 1, 13, 14, 17, 295.
Portelance, Arthur, 183.
Poulin, Hugh, 181, 189.
Power, Charles Gavan, 99, 100, 101, 102, 295.
Préfontaine, Joseph Raymond Fournier, 41, 295.
Prior, Edward Gawler, 29, 35, 295.
Prudham, George, 111, 119, 295.
Prud'homme, Marcel, 183, 187.
Pugsley, William, 43, 296.

Railton, Sammuel Victor, 191.
Ralston, James Layton, 85, 95, 96, 99, 296.
Regan, Gerald, 205, 206, 207, 208, 209, 210, 296.

Reid, John Dowsley, 47, 55, 59, 65, 296.
Reid, John M. 173, 174, 185, 296.
Reid, Joseph, 199.
Reid, Thomas, 105, 107, 117.
Rhodes, Edgar Nelson, 89, 90, 297.
Ricard, Théogène, 127, 133, 297.
Richardson, James Armstrong, 159, 160, 165, 166, 167, 169, 170, 297.
Rideout, Margaret, 149, 183.
Rinfret, Fernand, 87, 103, 297.
Rinfret, Gabriel Édouard, 111, 297.
Ritchie, Ronald, 199.
Robb, James Alexander, 69, 70, 73, 74, 83, 85, 298.
Roberts, John, 163, 187, 203, 204, 205, 206, 298.
Robertson, Frederick Greystock, 117.
Robertson, Gideon Decker, 57, 59, 60, 65, 91, 298.
Robertson, Wishart McLea, 105, 115, 298.
Robichaud, Hédard, 137, 155, 298.
Robinson, William Kenneth, 183, 215, 217.
Robitaille, Théodore, 5, 299.
Roche, Douglas James, 199.
Roche, William James, 47, 48, 49, 51, 52, 299.
Rogers, Norman McLeod, 97, 98, 99, 299.
Rogers, Robert, 47, 48, 49, 51, 299.
Rompkey, William, 177, 183, 205, 299.
Rose, Sir John, 1, 300.
Ross, John Jones, 37, 300.
Ross, William, 9, 300.
Rouleau, Guy, 151.
Rowe, William Earl, 93, 300.
Rowell, Newton Wesley, 59, 300.
Roy, Marcel Claude, 181, 189.
Ryckman, Edmond Baird, 79, 91, 300.

Suavé, Arthur, 91, 300.
Sauvé, Jeanne, 153, 155, 156, 163, 164, 301.
Sauvé, Maurice, 139, 140, 157, 301.
Savard, Raymond, 217.
Schellenberger, Stanley Kenneth, 201.
Scott, Sir Richard William, 7, 9, 11, 12, 39, 41, 43, 44, 301.
Sévigny, Albert, 47, 49, 51, 57, 301.
Sévigny, Joseph Pierre Albert, 123, 301.
Sharp, Mitchell William, 137, 138, 143, 144, 155, 156, 161, 162, 302.
Siddon, Thomas, 199.
Sifton, Arthur Lewis, 55, 56, 57, 58, 59, 60, 67, 302.
Sifton, Sir Clifford, 39, 41, 302.
Simmons, Roger, 213, 219.
Sinclair, James, 109, 115, 302.
Sinclair, John Ewen, 73, 302.
Smith, Sir Albert James, 9, 303.
Smith, David, 217.
Smith, Sir Frank, 19, 23, 24, 27, 29, 33, 37, 303.

Smith, Sidney Earle, 121, 303.
Smith, Walter, 185, 189.
Speyer, Christopher, 201.
Spinney, Edgar Keith, 67, 303.
Stanbury, Robert Douglas George, 153, 154, 161, 169, 170, 187, 303.
Starr, Michael, 123, 303.
Stevens, Henry Herbert, 67, 77, 79, 81, 93, 304.
Stevens, Sinclair McKnight, 197, 304.
Stewart, Charles, 69, 71, 83, 84, 85, 304.
Stewart, Hugh Alexander, 91, 304.
Stewart, John Alexander, 65, 305.
Stewart, John Benjamin,147, 151, 185.
Stirling, Grote, 89, 91, 305.
St-Laurent, Louis Stephen, 95, 96, 97, 98, 109, 110, 111, 122, 305.
Stollery, Peter, 213, 219.
St-Pierre, Paul, 177.
Stratas, Diane, 201.
Sulatycky, Allen B., 177, 179.
Sutherland, Donald, 81, 305.
Sutherland, Donald Matheson, 91, 92, 305.
Sutherland, James, 41, 42, 43, 45, 46, 305.

Taillon, Sir Louis-Olivier, 35, 306.
Tarte, Joseph Israël, 43, 306.
Tassé, Yvon-Roma, 133.
Teillet, Roger Joseph, 143, 167, 306.
Tessier, Claude, 217.
Templeman, William, 39, 41, 45, 46, 306.
Thompson, Sir John Sparrow David, ix, 15, 21, 25, 26, 30, 306.
Thorson, Joseph Thorarinn, 101, 306.
Thrasher, Richard Devere, 131.
Tilley, Sir Samuel Leonard, 1, 2, 13, 14, 307.
Tisdale, David, 35, 307.
Tobin, Brian, 215.
Tolmie, Donald Ross, 175.
Tolmie, Simon Fraser, 55, 63, 77, 307.
Tremblay, René, 137, 138, 141, 145, 146, 307.
Trudeau, Pierre Elliott, v, 139, 141, 151, 153, 154, 157, 161, 194, 203, 307.
Trudel, Jacques L., 179, 189.
Tucker, Walter Adam, 107.
Tupper, Sir Charles, ix, 1, 2, 3, 4, 13, 17, 18, 31, 35, 36, 37, 40, 308.
Tupper, Sir Charles Hibbert, ix, 15, 21, 25, 29, 37, 308.
Turner, Charles, 181, 185, 187.
Turner, John Napier, 137, 141, 142, 145, 146, 149, 153, 154, 155, 157, 158, 165, 166, 308.

Vail, William Berrian, 9, 308.
Veniot, Peter John, 85, 309.

Walker, David James, 125, 129, 309.
Walker, James Edgar, 149, 151, 185, 189.

Wallace, Nathaniel Clarke, 27, 33, 309.
Watson, Ian, 185, 191.
Weatherhead, David Bennington, 191, 217.
Weir, Robert, 89, 309.
Weir, William Gilbert, 119.
Whelan, Eugene Francis, 153, 179, 203, 309.
White, Thomas, 13, 15, 309.
White, Sir William Thomas, 47, 55, 309.
Wightman, William, 199.
Wigmore, Rupert Wilson, 63, 64, 310.
Wilmot, Robert Duncan, 19, 310.
Wilson, James Robert, 67, 310.
Wilson, Michael H., 197, 198, 310.
Winters, Robert Henry, 107, 111, 113, 114, 143, 310.
Wise, John, 193, 310.
Wood, Donald, 187.
Wood, John Fisher, 27, 29, 33, 34, 35, 311.

Yanakis, Antonio, 215.
Young, Roger, 181, 189.